11.95

The Hawaiian Monarchy

The Hawaiian Monarchy

By
Norris W. Potter
Lawrence M. Kasdon
Dr. Ann Rayson

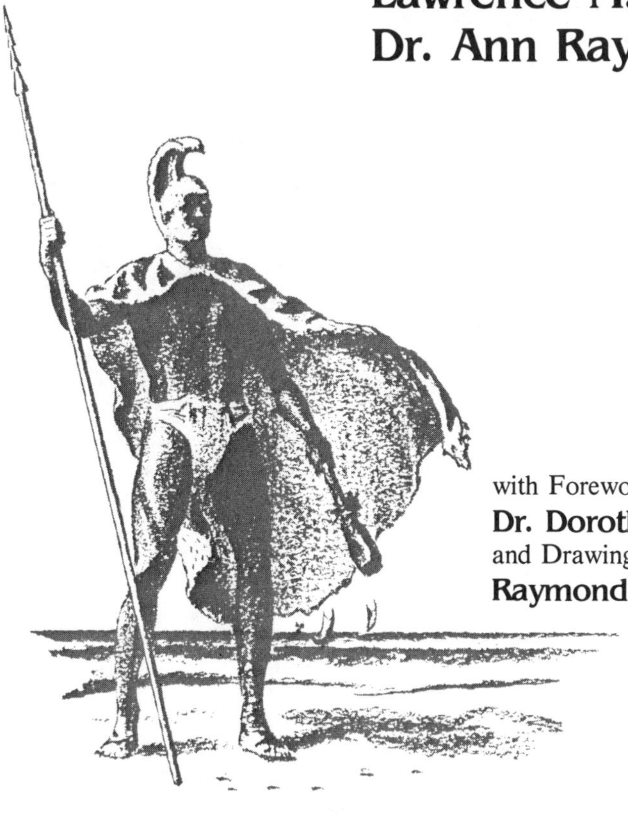

with Foreword by
Dr. Dorothy Hazama
and Drawings by
Raymond E. Lanterman

The Bess Press Inc.
P.O. Box 22388
Honolulu, HI 96822

Iolani Palace, in the foreground, is the only royal palace in the United States. After the Hawaiian monarchy was replaced by the U.S. territorial government, Iolani Palace served as the capitol building, even into statehood. The new state capitol building, in back, was occupied in 1969.

LIBRARY OF CONGRESS CATALOG CARD NUMBER 82-74176

ISBN 0-935848-17-7 HARDBOUND EDITION
ISBN 0-935848-16-9 SOFTCOVER EDITION

MANUFACTURED IN THE UNITED STATES OF AMERICA

Table of Contents

FOREWORD

The lack of appropriate instructional materials about Hawai'i written specifically for Hawai'i's students has been a perennial problem. When Potter and Kasdon's *Hawaii Our Island State* was first published, it attained a highly respected reputation among educators as a well researched and lucid presentation of Hawai'i's history for our students. When the textbook went out of print, teachers requested a reprinting. To meet that need, Bess Press obtained the rights from the authors and republished the text with the addition of a chapter on the twenty years after statehood to bring the textbook up to date.

Now, in the light of the most recent Department of Education guidelines for the seventh grade social studies curriculum throughout the state, Bess Press is publishing *The Hawaiian Monarchy,* which makes available Potter and Kasdon's chapters pertaining to the triumphs and the pressures faced by the monarchs, specifically to meet the needs of the seventh grade teachers and students. In addition, the chapters on geography and geology have been revised and updated.

Most visible and helpful among the several changes in *The Hawaiian Monarchy* is the addition of timelines for the period of the monarchy. Major Hawaiian historical events are indicated on one side with concurrent American and world events on the other side to present a broader perspective on the events in Hawaiian history. A closer scrutiny of the text will reveal that much recent information on the theory of the moving plates of the earth's crust has been added to the chapter on the geological formation of the islands along with clear accompanying diagrams. There is also new information on each island and a full chapter on King Lot, Kamehameha V.

The Appendix in the original textbook was a valuable aspect of that publication. Happily, this portion has been included with the addition of more recent data. The section on "Facts about Hawaii" still provides a ready reference on the rulers of Hawai'i with the dates of

v

their births, deaths, and reigns. The most recent Congressional Districts and population statistics are also included.

The Department of Education's resource guide for the seventh grade social studies curriculum delineates the basic guidelines, suggests resources, and provides a number of instructional activities. *The Hawaiian Monarchy* has been designed to provide the complex chronological content of the monarchy era, which is the major focus of the curriculum.

Dorothy Hazama
Professor of Education
University of Hawaii

PREFACE

This history of the Hawaiian monarchy, its people and its government, was written by educators in the schools of Hawaii. The original book by Norris W. Potter and Lawrence M. Kasdon, *Hawaii: Our Island State,* has been revised and updated by Ann Rayson, Assistant Professor of English at the University of Hawaii, to fulfill the need for a textbook specifically covering the historical period from the discovery of Hawaii by Captain James Cook to the annexation of Hawaii by the United States in 1898.

The authors have kept the needs of school-age readers particularly in mind. However, they have attempted to provide a book that adults and visitors to Hawaii will welcome as a clear, concise description of Hawaiian history and culture under the monarchy as well as a factual account of events that ultimately led to the incorporation of these islands into the American union.

The story has been gathered from the wealth of Hawaiiana available to those who are interested, although many of the essential papers and books have been long out of print and thus are quite difficult to obtain. On the other hand, there has been a renaissance in the publication and availability of materials on Hawaiian history and culture since statehood was obtained in 1959. In this volume footnotes have been held to a minimum, and the principal sources are entered in the bibliography.

Acknowledgments are gratefully made to the following:

To the Bernice P. Bishop Museum, its former director, Dr. Roland W. Force, and librarian, Miss Margaret Titcomb.

To the State of Hawaii Archives and Miss Agnes Conrad.

To the Hawaiian Historical Society and the Hawaiian Mission Children's Society, whose unique resources were always at our disposal.

To the Cooke Library at Punahou School in Honolulu and its former librarian, Miss Frances Kenyon.

To the Honolulu Public Library and the University of Hawaii Library, both of which are important repositories of information about the Pacific, the Polynesians, and the Hawaiian Islands.

To the University of Hawaii Press and its editor, Iris Wiley, for use of *Atlas of Hawaii.*

To the Legislative Reference Bureau and the Library of the Hawaii Sugar Planters' Association.

To Elaine Takenaka and Jane Kinoshita, Social Studies Specialists, State of Hawaii Department of Education.

To Dorothy Hazama, Professor of Education at the University of Hawaii.

To Gordon Bigelow, Professor of General Science at the University of Hawaii, for the greater part of chapter 2.

To Gail Levy, curriculum developer working with the State of Hawaii Department of Education.

The authors of the original book also thanked: Mr. Francis X. Aki, Mr. Riley Allen, Mr. Edwin H. Bryan, Jr., Mrs. Reginald H. Carter, Mr. Brian Casey, Mr. Charles G. Clark, Dr. Samuel H. Elbert, Mr. Joseph Feher, Mr. Leo Fortess, Mrs. Helene Hale, Mrs. Monte Hickok, Mrs. William A. Kanakanui, Mrs. Nora S. Kasdon, Mrs. Victoria L. K. Medeiros, Mrs. Kathleen Mellen, Dr. Norman Meller, Mrs. Fumiyo K. Migimoto, Mrs. Aldythe Morris, Dr. Lawrence Nelson, Mrs. Frank L. Pleadwell, Mrs. Norris Potter, Mrs. Mary Kawena Pukui, Mr. Alvin T. Shim, Mr. Eddie Tam, and Miss Jane Winne.

Publisher's Note—Diacritical Marks

The Bess Press makes every effort to include the glottal *('okina, 'u'ina)* and macron *(kahako)* in all its publications. However, this is not always possible for a variety of reasons. In the case of this book, where the original text did not provide the diacritical markings, we were unable to incorporate them and still provide an affordable text. For clarity and consistency, we have omitted these marks from the new work in this volume.

Hawaii Today

This is the story of Hawaii—once a Polynesian kingdom, next an independent republic, still later an American territory, and now the fiftieth state in our Union.

The Hawaiian Islands were born in violence. They are the peaks of a far-flung range of ancient volcanic mountains, only a few of which rear their heads above the water. Measured from one end of the island chain to the other, Hawaii is by far the longest state in the Union. However, the land area of the state's twenty islands totals only 6435 square miles. Only Delaware, Connecticut, and Rhode Island are smaller.

Hawaii is an unusual state in many ways. It is the only one that cannot be reached by land. It is the only state that contains a palace from which kings once ruled, a semitropical climate with a narrow range of temperature, and a population mainly of Asiatic origin. Finally, its Polynesian heritage and atmosphere give it a character that is different from all the other states.

Before examining its colorful past, let us look at the Hawaiian community as it is today—a community that is our Pacific frontier toward Asia and a cultural bridge between Western civilization and the rapidly developing nations of the Far East.

The People of Hawaii

Hawaii's population is one of the fastest growing in the nation. The 1980 estimate was 965,000 people. Over three quarters of a million persons live on the island of Oahu alone, and most of them make their homes in Honolulu. More than ninety percent of

Hawaii's people are American citizens, for the most part born under the American flag and educated in American schools. It is a young population too, with more than half the inhabitants being under thirty years of age.

Many of the people are of Japanese or Caucasian ancestry. They are followed in order by the part-Hawaiians, Filipinos, Chinese, and Koreans. The number of pure Hawaiians is very small, about 1.1 per cent of the total population. The Islanders have long prided themselves on the remarkable harmony among the racial groups. There is also frequent intermarriage between races.

Education in the Islands

Hawaii's school system is an excellent example of complete racial integration. In 1980-81 there were 202,972 total students in Hawaii's schools. Of these, 165,000 pupils were enrolled in the state's 230 public schools. About 35,000 more attend the 141 private schools, and another 3,000 are enrolled in trade and technical schools.

The Thomas Hale Hamilton Library at the University of Hawaii is one of many modern buildings on the campus.

The public schools of the state are part of a single school system. Unlike Mainland school systems there are no independent local boards of education for county or district units. There are, however, seven elected county advisory councils that advise the state school board. The state school board members are elected by the general populace. The state school board appoints the state superintendent of schools.

College training is provided by the University of Hawaii and several smaller colleges. The university, located in Manoa Valley in Honolulu, has a branch campus in Hilo on the island of Hawaii and a branch in Pearl City, West Oahu College. 50,000 students attend the colleges and universities, including the large community college system, throughout the state. The East-West Center for Cultural and Technical Interchange is located on the main campus. There, foreign and Mainland students take part in a program to promote world peace through education.

Other important cultural institutions in Hawaii are the Bishop Museum for research in Pacific history and Polynesian culture, the Honolulu Symphony Orchestra, an excellent Community Theater, and a small Academy of Arts.

Tourism—the Basis of the Economy

Since World War II the tourist industry has helped greatly to bring prosperity to the Islands. In 1941, before the Japanese attack on Pearl Harbor on December 7, holiday-seekers numbering about 33,000 arrived in Hawaii. By 1980 that number had increased to over 4,000,000 who found their way to Hawaii's beach and mountain resorts not only on Oahu but on all the major islands. It is estimated that the number of annual visitors will soon surpass this mark.

The earliest organized attempt to attract tourists was the forming of a Hawaiian Bureau of Information in 1892. Today the Hawaii Visitors Bureau continues to promote tourist travel to the Islands. From 1970 to 1980 alone, visitors' expenditures in Hawaii rose from $595 million to $3 billion.

There are several reasons for the increase in tourism from the Mainland. A general rise in the level of family incomes together with more leisure time brings travel within the reach of a greater number of Americans. Instead of depending on a 4½-day sea

3

Waikiki Beach, with its many hotels, is a favorite stopping place for tourists. The area consisted of duck farms, coconut groves, fish ponds, and taro patches until transformed by a reclamation project in the 1920s.

voyage, visitors from the West Coast can now choose a 4½-hour flight by plane to Hawaii. Another factor is the Mainland migration toward West Coast states, especially California; over two-fifths of Hawaii's visitors are Californians. By providing better facilities, Hawaii is also attracting convention visitors.

Hawaii's Military-Industrial Role

An important feature of Hawaii's growing economy is the establishment of new manufacturing industries. In recent years a great variety of small plants have been located in or near Honolulu. There are four principal reasons for this new industrial growth.

They are: (1) a growing population with higher living standards, (2) technical research, (3) an increase in Mainland and foreign investments in Hawaii, and (4) tourist spending and heavy Federal defense expenditures.

Returning visitors to Hawaii are amazed at the amount of new building that is going on. As in many communities on the Mainland, new housing developments and shopping centers have moved out into the suburbs. Where in 1895 there were no buildings higher than three stories, now gleaming new office buildings, hotels, and apartment houses mark the skyline. Cranes, bulldozers, and drilling machinery are at work making new throughways, airports, harbors, and public buildings.

The geographical position of the Hawaiian Islands gives them military importance in today's world. More people are employed in national defense in the Islands than in any other industry except tourism. Defense spending thus becomes the second greatest single source of income in the state. In 1937 sugar and pineapples brought

The Space Technology Station at South Point, Hawaii, is operated by the Pacific Missile Range. This station mainly tracks interplanetary probes like Pioneer V, the second U.S. vehicle to orbit around the sun.

Werner Stoy. Camera Hawaii

in more revenue than did the military expenditures. Then, as tension mounted in the Far East, defense spending rose rapidly. It reached a peak after the attack on Pearl Harbor. In the first postwar years spending decreased, only to increase during the Korean conflict and to increase still more during the war in Viet Nam and the continuing "cold war."

The Navy, which obtained the use of Pearl Harbor by a treaty with King Kalakaua in 1887, is the biggest defense spender. New naval facilities are being built to serve the nuclear submarine fleet. The Pacific Missile Range operates a communications center in Oahu, a tracking station on Kauai, and other satellite facilities on the island of Hawaii. The second largest source of military revenue is the Army, which came to Hawaii in 1898. In third place is the Air Force, which has its largest base in the Islands at Hickam Field on Oahu. Hickam Field is the home of the Pacific Air Forces Base Command.

The Soil—Sugar and Pineapple

In the rich volcanic soil, found mostly in valleys and on the slopes of Hawaii's mountain ranges, grow the two crops upon which much of the economy of the Islands is based—sugar cane and pineapples.

Sugar has always been a valuable exportable crop, and sugar cane continues to be the leading crop in the Islands today. Sugar exports have jumped from 8500 tons in 1872 to over 1,000,000 tons in 1982. There are several reasons for this tremendous increase. Irrigation methods have been improved. New types of equipment have been invented. Millions of dollars have been invested for research in fertilizers, plant diseases, insect control, and new varieties of cane.

Today Hawaii's sugar industry pays higher wages and produces more sugar per acre than any other sugar-producing area. The fourteen sugar mills in the Islands produce raw sugar that is shipped to the Hawaiian Sugar Refining Corporation plant in Crockett, California, and to the Gulf and East coasts. About five per cent of the sugar is refined in the Aiea plant near Honolulu for local use.

The delicious pineapples for which Hawaii is famous have been exported from the Islands since 1851. However, it is only in this

6

Pineapples do not grow on trees, as some folks think, but cover acres and acres of Hawaii's ground. The sun-riped fruit is best eaten right from the field.

century that they have become a major product. The value of fresh and canned pineapple in Hawaii was $223 million in 1980. Production exceeded 18 million cases of fruit and juice, and 237,000 cases of concentrated juice.

By 1962 surveys indicated that sugar-milling and pineapple-canning had probably reached their peak. The sugar growers now have increased competition from beet sugar producers on the Mainland. At the same time, new pineapple plantations in Africa, South America, and Asia are cutting into the market once controlled by Hawaii.

Diversified Agriculture

Since World War II there has been a great increase in both truck farming and mixed farming. The large population of Oahu provides a ready market for the products of the truck farmers of that island.

Although the farms are small (averaging fewer than 5 acres each), the year-round warm climate makes it possible to raise a half-dozen or more crops each year on the same land. Diversified agriculture, defined as all crops other than sugar and pineapple, rose from $22 million in 1970 to $91 million in 1980, or approximately 313 per cent. By 1980, Hawaii produced 40 per cent of the fresh market vegetables consumed locally, 23 per cent of the fresh market fruits, 30 per cent of the beef and veal, 24 per cent of the chickens, and 89 per cent of the eggs.

Only about nine per cent of the land of Hawaii is considered good agricultural land. Another ten per cent is fairly fertile. The rest of the usable land is suitable only for ranching, forest reserve, and watershed.

Hawaii's Work Force

The men and women who work in the service industries, on the plantations, in the shops, and in the defense facilities are mostly island born. Wages in most occupations are about the same as those on the Mainland. The number of persons employed varies with the seasons. It is low in January and February and high in summer when the pineapple-canning and tourist industries are in need of extra help.

The movement to organize labor in Hawaii has been growing since the end of World War II. Today about one out of every three laborers belongs to a union. The largest of these are the International Longshoremen's and Warehousemen's Union (ILWU) and the American Federation of Labor—Congress of Industrial Organizations (AFL-CIO).

The "Old" Hawaii

Until now we have been looking at a Hawaii that is much like a Mainland state. It is more developed industrially than some states, more dependent on agriculture than others. However, it faces the same problems in politics, and its economic situation is similar to that of many Mainland states. We have found the same cultural institutions in Hawaii as in the other states. Where, then, is the "Old" Hawaii—the Hawaii of the travel books and tourist posters? It is still there. It is found in quiet Maui valleys where there are

8

taro patches and banana groves, in the simple hospitality of old homes on Kauai, in little settlements along the Kona coast on the Big Island of Hawaii, along the northeast coast of Molokai, on the pineapple plantation of Lanai, in the singing of the Kamehameha School choir, and in sermons given in the musical Hawaiian tongue at Kawaiahao Church.

Pele, the goddess of the volcano, still punishes the sins of men from within the fiery pit of Halemaumau. Children still slide down steep, muddy slopes on green *ti* leaves. Fishermen with throw-nets still search the shallow waters of many an out-of-the-way beach.

Lush shady valleys can still be found. (Hawaii Visitors Bureau)

Despite the bustling, brassy manners of the present, the spirit of olden times still lives in the hearts of those who love these Islands!

Summing Up the Chapter

Hawaii, our fiftieth state, is unusual in its origin, its location, its climate, its people, and its colorful customs. People of many races and nationalities live, study, and work together in peace and harmony. Most of them make their living in three important ways: from the tourist industry, in national defense, and from the soil. Hawaii is moving ahead in industry and in construction of buildings and in means of travel. But despite the "new look" in the Islands, the "Old" Hawaii of the travel books and tourist posters may still be seen in many places.

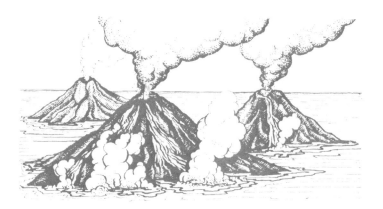

2

Formation of the Island Chain

The Hawaiian Islands consist of many islands, reefs, and shoals strung out in the Pacific Ocean for 1600 miles, about the same distance as that from St. Louis to Seattle. When Hawaii became a state, one or two of the outlying islands were not included in the state boundaries. The boundaries still stretch 1200 miles west of Honolulu to Kure. Since most of the western islands within the state's borders are uninhabited and did not play an important role in the state's history as covered in this book, only the eight main islands—Kauai, Niihau, Oahu, Molokai, Lanai, Kahoolawe, Maui, and Hawaii—are fully discussed in this chapter. These are the islands that are closest to the U.S. Mainland. They extend in a chain for about 400 miles.

Hawaii lies closer to the equator than any other state in the United States. Before the admission of Hawaii as the fiftieth state, Florida was the southernmost state. Hawaii is the only state located in the tropics, that is, between the Tropic of Cancer and the Tropic of Capricorn. It is about as far north of the equator as Hong Kong or Mexico City.

Going north from Hawaii (toward the top of the map) along the 155° line of longitude, we come to the Alaska Peninsula. Following the same line southward from Hawaii, we see that it crosses the equator and passes through the Society Islands. Tahiti, the island from which one group of early settlers in Hawaii probably came, is part of the Society Islands.

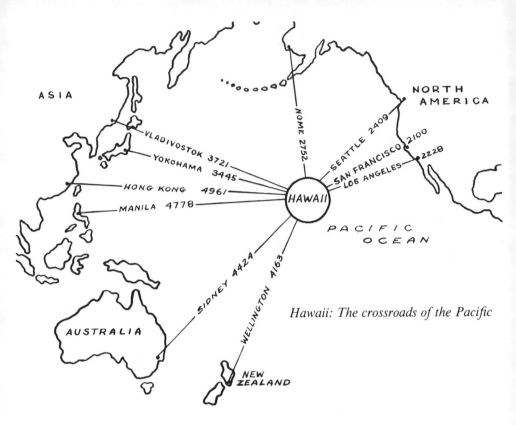

ASIA

NORTH AMERICA

NOME 2752

VLADIVOSTOK 3721
YOKOHAMA 3445
HONG KONG 4961
MANILA 4778

SEATTLE 2409
SAN FRANCISCO 2100
LOS ANGELES 2228

HAWAII

PACIFIC OCEAN

SIDNEY 4424
WELLINGTON 4163

Hawaii: The crossroads of the Pacific

AUSTRALIA

NEW ZEALAND

Distances From Other Places in the Pacific

Another way to think of the location of the Hawaiian Islands is to notice their central position in the Pacific. The distance from Honolulu to San Francisco is about 2100 nautical miles; to Panama, 4700 miles; to Sydney, Australia, 4400 miles; to Manila, 4800 miles; and to Yokohama, 3400 miles. An airplane trip from San Francisco to New York is only 2600 miles. From these facts, we can see that the distances from one major port to another across the Pacific are great. A stop in Hawaii is welcome, especially in the case of a sea voyage.

Formation of the Islands

The Hawaiian Islands are huge volcanic mountains partly submerged in the Pacific Ocean. The tallest, Mauna Kea (13,784 feet above sea level), hardly rivals the world's tallest peak, Mount Everest (29,028 feet above the sea); but when Mauna Kea's height is measured from the floor of the ocean, where its volcanic growth began, it towers more than a thousand feet higher than Mount

An eruption from the slopes of Kilauea in January, 1960 threw out a curtain of fire 2 miles long which destroyed the villages of Kapoho and Koae.

Everest. Because Mount Everest has much steeper slopes, its bulk would fit several times into the space occupied by the low, blister-like form of Mauna Kea.

If the 3-mile-deep northern Pacific Ocean were drained, the Hawaiian Islands would emerge as a gigantic mountain range 2000 miles long and 150 miles wide. Each of the major islands was built by one or a few large volcanoes. These great piles of lava rock grew upward through the ocean by quiet eruptions in which melted rock oozed out in long, tube-shaped fingers, their skin chilled by the water to a glassy crust, but their insides still molten.

At the ends of these fingers, small bulbs of lava about the size of a trash barrel squeezed out and rolled away, flattening from their own weight to a pillow-like shape. A great pile of these pillow lavas is the foundation of every Hawaiian Island.

As the crest of this great undersea mountain built near to sea level, eruptions became violently explosive, because shallow water could not contain the steam released when the hot lava boiled the seawater. Later, when the mountain grew high enough to wall out the sea, lava emerged from the earth by fountaining or by gently streaming from cracks and vents. From these eruptions long, sinuous lava flows wind downslope even today, each adding another strand to the massive mountain, some plunging all the way to the coast and a tempestuous meeting with the sea.

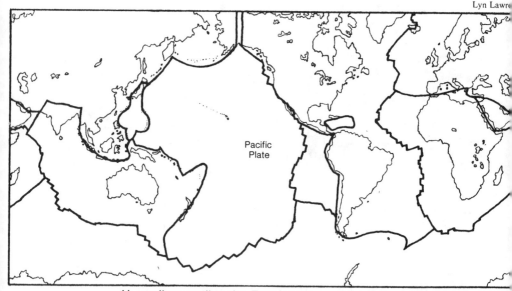

Pacific
Plate

Heavy lines outline the Earth's major crustal plates.

The Earth's Moving Plates

The crust of the Earth is a rocky skin, thinner in relation to the planet's breadth than the skin of an apple is to the whole. The crust is not continuous over all of the Earth. It is broken into more than a dozen rigid plates. Where these plates meet along their edges the major mountain ranges, oceanic deeps, volcanoes, and earthquakes appear.

Along certain plate edges melted rock comes to the surface under the oceans at rift zones thousands of miles long. The waters cool and solidify the magma (molten rock) in these rifts, but more hot liquid surges up from below, opening the cracks wider. In this way, new crust is formed at the surface of the Earth, pushing outward to left and right on the plates all along the spreading zone of the rift. The great rift zone of the north Pacific Ocean is called the East Pacific Rise. It lies just off the western coast of North America, and it is one of the fastest-moving spreading zones on Earth.

If you were an explorer piercing downward through the Earth's crust near Hawaii, you would find the rocks to be increasingly

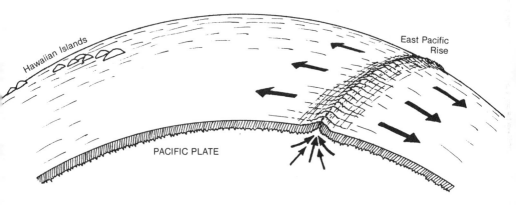

Some of the earth's crustal plates move apart from each other along "spreading zones."

hotter at greater depths. Radioactive minerals throughout the Earth are always heating it. If you descended about 60 miles, the rocks would begin to soften from the intense heat and small pockets of magma would appear.

Rocks at this depth are so hot that they lose strength, forming a tar-like layer, capable of flowing very slowly when pushed. The cooler, more rigid crust above rides along on this hot, softened layer in response to a sideways push from the spreading zone of the

Formation of an Island Chain

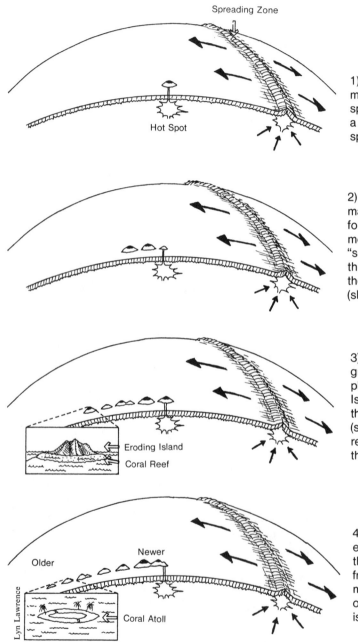

Spreading Zone

Hot Spot

1) Crustal plates move away from the spreading zone over a stationary hot spot.

2) Occasionally, magma builds up to form undersea mountains. If these "seamounts" break the ocean surface, they become islands (shown in black).

Eroding Island

Coral Reef

3) The island chain grows as the crustal plates spread. Islands erode after their building stages (see page 19) and reefs grow around them.

Older
Newer

Lyn Lawrence

Coral Atoll

4) The oldest islands erode and sink into the sea, leaving fringing reefs. These may grow into atolls, or circular coral islands.

East Pacific Rise. The Pacific Plate thus creeps slowly westward beneath the ocean, hauling along its islands, reefs and undersea mountains.

The Hawaiian volcanoes, unlike most others, occur in the middle of a plate. Geologists are puzzled by this. They have tried to explain the chain of Hawaiian Islands by thinking of a hot spot, located now beneath the island of Hawaii, but formerly under each more westerly island in turn. According to this theory, the hot spot stays in place, forcing up magma periodically to build each island as the Pacific plate moves gradually westward. A chain of islands thus trails out from the hot spot with the older islands toward the west. The plate moves only a few inches each year, but this motion has continued for many millions of years.

A steam plume rises where lava flowing from an island volcano reaches the sea. Hawaii Visitors Bureau photo.

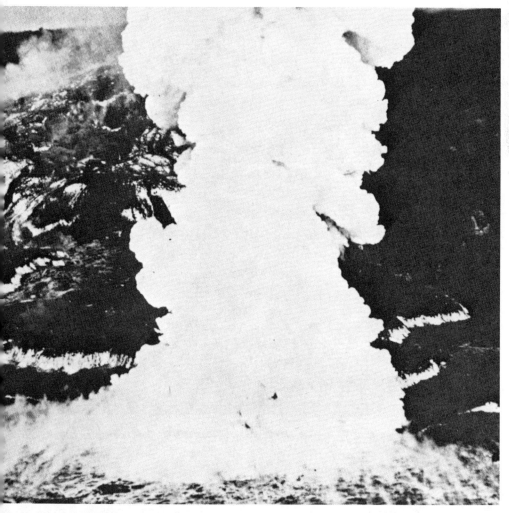

Formation of Undersea Mountains into Islands

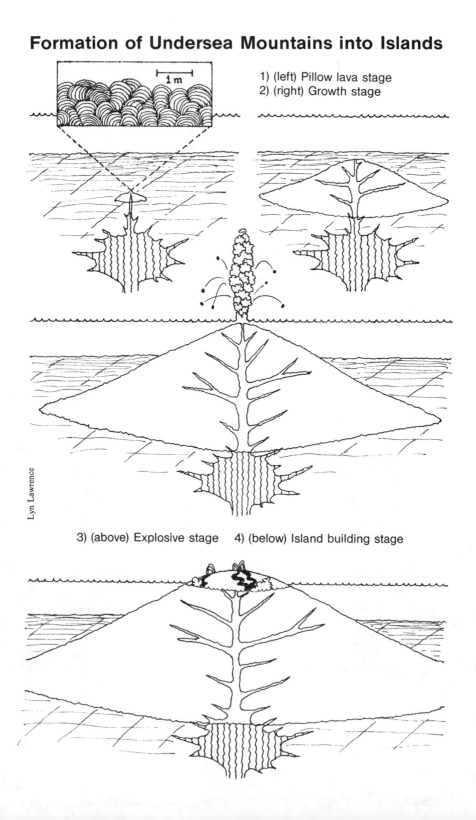

1) (left) Pillow lava stage
2) (right) Growth stage

1 m

3) (above) Explosive stage   4) (below) Island building stage

Lyn Lawrence

The Continuing Stages of Island Growth

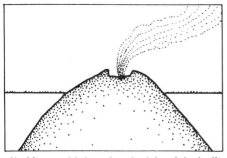

A) After a high volcanic island is built, part of the summit collapses to form a pit-like caldera.

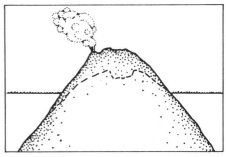

B) Sometimes the caldera is covered by a steep cap of stickier lava. More explosive eruptions top this with smaller cinder cones.

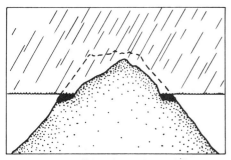

C) Rainwater streams and pounding sea waves wear down the island. Coral reefs (in black) form in shallow coastal waters. Volcanic eruptions have stopped.

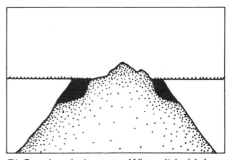

D) Sea level changes. When it is higher. coral reefs deepen and extend inland. The island slowly sinks as the crust bends downward under its weight.

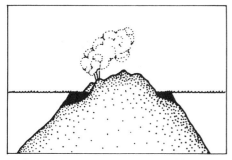

E) Small secondary eruptions build fresh cones on the old worn-down volcanoes. Reefs grow upward as the island sinks. Sea level has fallen lower.

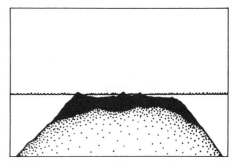

F) Erosion and sinking continue until the volcanic rock is buried under a coral atoll. The reefs finally can't keep pace and the sinking atoll will be a seamount.

Formation of Oahu

Typical in many ways of the formation of all the islands is the making of the island of Oahu. The island, on which Honolulu is located, began as two separate volcanoes—the Waianae Volcano and the Koolau Volcano. After these two volcanoes had risen well above sea level, the Schofield plateau was built between them by lava flowing from Koolau Volcano and banking against the Waianae Mountains. At that time Oahu was 1½ times as large as it is today. The mouths of some streams from that period are now 1800 feet below sea level.

Somewhat later in the island's history some lesser volcanoes appeared. During the time they were active, the sea level was lower

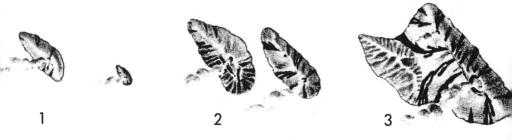

1   2   3

Oahu began as two separate volcanoes (#1), Waianae on the left and Koolau on the right. In the second picture the lava flows, shown in black, continued to build both the Waianae and Koolau volcanoes. In #3 the volcanoes have expanded and joined to form a single island. The volcanoes were deeply

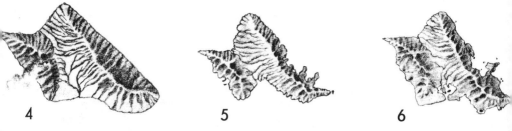

4   5   6

eroded by streams. Smaller secondary volcanoes are shown erupting on the Waianae Volcano in #4. In the fifth view the ocean is higher, covering the mountains nearly 250 feet deeper than at present. The sea then receded; secondary eruptions built Diamond Head, Punchbowl, and the craters from Koko Head to Rabbit Island (#6). Such eruptions may not have ended.

20

than at present. Such craters as Diamond Head and Koko Crater were then inland. Many other well-known landmarks on Oahu, such as Salt Lake, Punchbowl, Hanauma Bay, Rocky Hill (behind Punahou School), Black Point, Rabbit Island, Tantalus, and Round Top, are extinct secondary volcanoes.

The Koolau Volcano, which now comprises more than half of the island of Oahu, probably took about a million years to build. The old lava flows of this volcano that we walk upon today are more than two million years old. The smaller secondary volcanoes of the Honolulu area, such as Diamond Head and Punchbowl, are much younger, and some of them may have formed in a few days or weeks. Volcanoes of the Koko Head area formed during the past 10,000 years.

The Legend of Pele

The Hawaiians have a legend that Pele, goddess of volcanoes, visited each of the islands. Beginning at the northwest end of the island chain, she stopped at each of the main islands in turn. Her present home is in the two active volcanoes on the island of Hawaii—Mauna Loa and Kilauea. In general, geologists agree that the order of Pele's visits as described in the legend was the order in which the islands were formed.

The Reefs of Hawaii

As a tourist walks along the beach at Waikiki, he notices a curious thing. The water at the shoreline, protected by reefs, is often quite calm while the waves break far out to sea. Much of the shoreline of the islands contains reefs, which extend out into the water from ½ mile to 3½ miles. If this tourist were to walk on the reef, he would find it rough and uneven so that he would have a hard time keeping his balance.

Coral reefs are generally built by very small animals called polyps. These polyps live in colonies under just the right conditions of water temperature and salt content. Each new generation attaches its shell to the shells of its ancestors. It is this process of building their homes, one on top of the other, that forms a reef. Other coral-producing marine life, such as algae, make their homes among the shells of the polyps, filling much of the empty space. In time the reef becomes quite solid limestone.

21

Reefs tell a geologist much about conditions when they were formed. Parts of downtown Honolulu and Waikiki rest on old reefs that grew when the ocean stood higher, covering these areas. Drowned reefs hundreds of feet below present sea level show that some of the islands were once much larger than now. Molokai, Lanai, Maui and Kahoolawe joined to form a single large island during a former low stand of the sea.

When a main island-building volcano becomes extinct, the processes of erosion and sinking gradually bring the mountain down to sea level. As sinking continues, the volcanic rock disappears as it is buried under growing coral reefs that cover their volcanic foundation with an ever-thickening layer of limestone. Reef plants and animals build new limestone layers to maintain the islands despite their continued sinking. The resulting coral islands (atolls) often form rings reaching only a few feet above sea level and enclosing shallow lagoons. Later changes in sea level and plate movement of the islands into cooler northerly waters kill the reef organisms. The islands then sink beneath the sea, never to reappear.

A row of flat-topped seamounts, thousands of feet below sea level, extends northwestward from the Hawaiian Islands. These ancient, sunken volcanoes probably stood once as lofty mountains, the Mauna Keas and Haleakalas of their time. Today's Hawaiian Islands will join these ancestral seamounts 25 million years from now in the watery darkness of the ocean floor.

Summing Up the Chapter

Hawaii, in the middle of a moving plate of the Earth's crust, is one of the most isolated island groups in the world. The islands are great piles of lava, built by volcanic eruptions from the ocean floor. They rise to form mountains thousands of feet above sea level. When the eruptions cease, these mountains slowly sink and wear down until only low coral islands remain. Plate movement or changes in sea level eventually kill the coral organisms, and the islands disappear beneath the sea.

3

Geography of the Islands

The islands of Oahu, Molokai, and Maui are made up of two mountain masses carved from their two major volcanic domes,* with low lands between them. The island of Hawaii consists of five volcanic domes. Kauai, Niihau, and Lanai were formed from single domes. Of course, all of these islands are dotted with lesser volcanic cones, such as Diamond Head. The shape of the islands depends in part on the level of the ocean and the length of time the waves have had to work on the land. Rain and winds also play an important part in forming any landscape.

Kauai—The Garden Isle (Menehune Land)

Kauai is the northernmost inhabited island in the state, so we shall begin there and work southeasterly to Hawaii. Kauai, the fourth largest island in the state, has an area of 549 square miles and is circular in shape.

Geologically, Kauai is the oldest of the major Islands of Hawaii and was the first seen by Captain James Cook in 1778. Its rolling hills and wide streams remind visitors of many parts of the Mainland. Kauai's palm-fringed beaches and green valleys provide some of the loveliest scenery in the State. Many movies with South Seas settings have been shot on location on Kauai.

Tourism has developed into the leading industry on Kauai in

*A volcanic dome is a broad and gently sloping volcano.

THE HAWAIIAN ISLANDS

ELEVATION OF CHIEF SUMMITS, SADDLES AND CHANNELS

A large part of the Pacific Ocean surrounding Hawaii has depths from 16,000 to 20,000 feet. Oahu, Molokai, Lanai and Maui stand on a submarine bank with depths less than 2,400 feet, between Maui and Hawaii depths reach 6,000 feet, between Oahu and Kauai, 10,000 feet.

ISLAND	MOUNTAINS	SADDLES AND CHANNELS	SUMMITS	SADDLES	CHANNELS Below Sea Level
	KILAUEA		4,090		
		KILAUEA-MAUNA LOA SADDLE		4,000	
	MAUNA LOA		13,677		
		MAUNA LOA-HUALALAI SADDLE		5,175	
HAWAII		MAUNA LOA-MAUNA KEA SADDLE		6,650	
	HUALALAI		8,271		
	MAUNA KEA		13,796		
		MAUNA KEA-KOHALA SADDLE		2,875	
	KOHALA		5,480		
		ALENUIHAHA CHANNEL, DEPTH (BET. KOHALA & HALEAKALA)			6,810
	HALEAKALA		10,023		
MAUI		ISTHMUS OF MAUI		125	
	PUU KUKUI		5,788		
KAHOOLAWE	LUA MAKIKA		1,477		
		AUAU CHANNEL, DEPTH (WEST MAUI to LANAI)			252
LANAI	LANAIHALE		3,370		
		PAILOLO CHANNEL, DEPTH (WEST MAUI to MOLOKAI)			846
	KAMAKOU		4,970		
MOLOKAI		ISTHMUS OF MOLOKAI		425	
	PUU NANA		1,381		
		KALOHI CHANNEL, DEPTH (MOLOKAI to LANAI)			540
		KAIWI CHANNEL, DEPTH (MOLOKAI to OAHU)			2,202
	KONAHUANUI		3,150		
OAHU		SCHOFIELD SADDLE		950	
	KAALA		4,020		
		KAUAI CHANNEL, DEPTH (OAHU to KAUAI)			10,890
	WAIALEALE		5,148		
KAUAI		KAULAKAHI CHANNEL, DEPTH (KAUAI to NIIHAU)			3,570
	KAWAIKINI		5,243		

Areas and dimensions of the eight chief islands are given in the following table. The island of Hawaii is about one fifth smaller, and the State as a whole is about one-third larger than the State of Connecticut.

WIDTH OF CHANNELS

NAME	LOCATION BETWEEN	MILES
KAUAI CHANNEL	KAUAI and OAHU	72
KAIWI CHANNEL	OAHU and MOLOKAI	26
KALOHI CHANNEL	MOLOKAI and LANAI	9
AUAU CHANNEL	LANAI and MAUI	9
PAILOLO CHANNEL	MOLOKAI and MAUI	9
KEALAIKAHIKI CHANNEL	LANAI and KAHOOLAWE	18
ALALAKEIKI CHANNEL	KAHOOLAWE and MAUI	7
ALENUIHAHA CHANNEL	MAUI and HAWAII	30
KAULAKAHI CHANNEL	KAUAI and NIIHAU	17

TOTAL AREA

ISLAND	Extreme Length Miles	Width Miles	Square Miles	Acres
HAWAII	93	76	4,038	2,573,440
MAUI	48	26	729	465,920
OAHU	44	30	608	380,800
KAUAI	33	25	553	352,640
MOLOKAI	38	10	261	165,760
LANAI	18	13	140	90,240
NIIHAU	18	6	73	46,080
KAHOOLAWE	11	6	45	28,800
MINOR ISLETS			3	1,920
Total		6,450	4,105,600

In the beautiful, scenic Hanalei Valley on the island of Kauai, taro patches and rice paddies thrive at the foot of richly vegetated mountains.

recent years. Diversified agriculture and government are also important.

The island was formed mainly from a single major dome, Mt. Waialeale, which is the highest point on the island. It also receives the heaviest rainfall. Since Kauai is the oldest of the eight islands, it is the most eroded. A smaller volcano formed the Haupu Ridge south of Lihue.

Because of the extensive weathering on Kauai, there are coastal plains and valleys with larger streams and deeper soil deposits than on the other islands. And because nature has been at work there longer, we find deep canyons such as the Waimea Canyon, which reminds us of the Grand Canyon of the Mainland. Another interesting but seldom visited canyon on the northern side of the island is Wainiha Valley. Farther to the west on the northern coast lies the best loved and most celebrated valley on Kauai—Hanalei. Traveling west from Hanalei, we see the spectacular Napali Cliffs.

KAUAI ISLAND

An area of sand dunes on the southwestern side of the island has the unusual name of Barking Sands. When the sand is thoroughly dry and is being blown by the wind, it gives off strange sounds that resemble the barking of a dog.

Kauai has an almost ideal climate with average temperatures near the coast of 71° in February and March, and 79° in August and September. Cooler temperatures in mountain areas such as Kokee offer a pleasant contrast.

Rainfall varies widely depending on location within the County. The summit of Waialeale is the wettest spot in the United States with a recorded rainfall of 451 inches per year. Only 20 miles away at Kekaha, on the southern coast, an average rainfall of 20 inches per year is normal.

Kauai has been eroded into a spectacular scenery of peaks, ridges, canyons, and palis. Kauai has a high wilderness swamp and forest that contain some of the last surviving native plants, insects, and birds. On its coastal lowlands, Kauai has sugar and pineapple plantations, and large mill towns. Here, also, is the increased activity of hotel-resorts and beaches. Residents of Kauai are currently protesting the overdevelopment of their island. Hurricane Iwa, which struck Kauai on November 23, 1982, caused damage to both the reefs and the hotel shoreline that will take years to recover.

Niihau—The Forbidden Island (The Island of Yesteryear)

Niihau, the smallest of the major inhabited islands, is only 73 square miles in area. It is situated 17 miles across the Kaulakahi Channel from Kauai's west side and is part of Kauai county. The island is privately owned by the Robinson family, descendents of

26

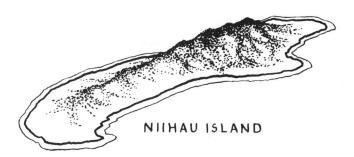

NIIHAU ISLAND

Elizabeth McHutcheson Sinclair, who bought it from King Kame-hameha V in 1864 for $10,000 in gold. The inhabitants of Niihau number fewer than 300 and are mostly pure-blooded Hawaiians who follow many of the old Hawaiian ways.

The island is closed to visitors and there is no plane service. Residents move freely from Niihau to Kauai on a World War II landing craft. There is a village, Puuwai, with a grammar school, but the residents attend high school and college on Kauai or Oahu. Until recently there were no telephones or radios on the island. Communication was carried on with Kauai by means of signal fires or carrier pigeons. The Robinsons prohibit using alcohol and working on Sunday. The residents speak Hawaiian and read their Hawaiian language Bibles by the light of kerosene lamps. During Hurricane Iwa in 1982, the residents of Niihau neither requested nor desired state or federal assistance, although the island was hit directly.

Since the limited water supply does not permit extensive agriculture, the chief occupation of the island is ranching. Sheep, cattle, and horses are raised. Charcoal is made from kiawe trees. The people gather honey and make Niihau shell leis, highly prized off-island. Cut off by the mountains on Kauai, moisture-laden trade winds are almost drained by the time they reach Niihau. Although Niihau is an arid island, at its center is Lake Halulu, at 182 acres the largest natural lake in the Hawaiian Islands.

The Northwestern Hawaiian Islands—The Leeward Islands

The Northwestern Hawaiian Islands extend over nearly 1,200 miles of ocean and are low, tiny islets, reefs, and shoals. They are barren, sparsely vegetated, and battered by winds and waves. Since

27

1909 these islands from Nihoa to Pearl and Hermes Atoll have been preserved as the Hawaiian Islands National Wildlife Refuge, a sanctuary for many species of seabirds and a few surviving kinds of native land birds, for the Hawaiian monk seal, and for the green sea turtle. Fifty people live in the two military stations on French Frigate Shoals and Kure Atoll.

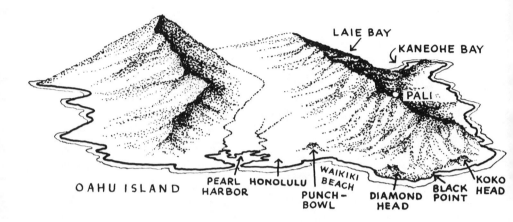

Oahu—The Gathering Place

Oahu, the third largest island in the chain, has an area of 593 square miles. It is shaped somewhat like a diamond.

The highest peak on the island is Mt. Kaala in the Waianae Mountains. These mountains run parallel to the southwest coast of the island, while the Koolau Mountains parallel the northeast coast. Between these two ranges lies the Schofield Plateau, on which is located Schofield Barracks. Honolulu is southwest of the Koolaus, and its two suburbs, Kailua and Kaneohe, are on the other side of this range. Recently, two sets of double-bore tunnels have been built through the Koolaus connecting Honolulu with its two fast-growing suburbs. Along the south shore, Pearl City and Hawaii Kai are linked to downtown Honolulu by a federal interstate freeway.

The Koolau Range is noted for its spectacular cliffs. The most famous of these is the Nuuanu Pali. The Pali (or cliff) was formed by the sinking of the coastline, which allowed ocean waves to wear away the land, and by erosion from the heavy trade wind showers.

Pearl Harbor, one of the most important landmarks on Oahu,

28

This air view of the eastern tip of Oahu includes Koko Head, Koko Crater, and part of the Koolau Range. It shows the rugged terrain of the Islands.

was formed by the sinking of the coast and the drowning of the river valley. Honolulu, the state capital and main commercial harbor of the state, lies 5 miles southwest of Pearl Harbor. World famous Waikiki Beach is about 4 miles down the coast from downtown Honolulu.

Honolulu's climate is close to ideal with very little seasonal variation. For downtown Honolulu, the average annual temperature is 75°; warmest months are August and September, with average temperatures of 79°. Rainfall ranges from 20 inches annually in the lower areas to 185 inches in the mountains.

Oahu has 82% of the state's population and is the social, political, and economic hub of Hawaii. The dense population puts intense pressure on land use. Urban industrial and residential needs must be served; sugar and pineapple plantations and small truck farms must be supported; forest watershed reserves must be protected. Oahu is the center of government, commerce, industry, medical and social services, tourism, the military, entertainment,

29

and the arts. Opportunities for employment, education, and communication are greatest on Oahu. So, too, are the extremes of poverty and affluence, social problems and achievements, environmental upsets and improvements.

Molokai—The Friendly Isle

Thirty miles to the east lies Oahu's nearest neighbor, the moccasin-shaped island of Molokai. It is the fifth in size of the Hawaiian Islands and occupies about 260 square miles.

Most of Molokai was formed by two volcanoes. One is called Mauna Loa, not to be confused with Mauna Loa on Hawaii. Today Mauna Loa is a tableland with its peak, Puu Nana, rising only 1381 feet above sea level, hardly high enough to take moisture from the rain-bearing trade winds. As a result, this end of the island is quite dry.

To the east of Mauna Loa lies a low saddle area. The rest of the island is covered by a large dome into which are gouged deep valleys. This dome makes the eastern half of Molokai quite rugged. The East Molokai dome is now a semicircular ridge reaching almost a mile in height. Because of the geography, pineapple farming and cattle raising are the major industries.

Jutting out from the steep cliffs found in north central Molokai is the Makanalua Peninsula, on which is located the famous leper settlement of Kalaupapa, where Father Damien worked. Kalaupapa, founded in 1866, has recently been declared a national park.

Great reefs surround Molokai, except in the cliff areas. Along the southern coast are fish ponds built by the ancient Hawaiians. Many of these ponds are still used for raising fish.

The Friendly Island has two distinct parts: a wet eastern region of rugged mountains and sea cliffs, and a drier, flatter western region that supports the island's pineapple plantations and most of the ranches and small farms. Plantations, fishing villages, and small tourist resorts are the centers of population. Molokai remains a

KALAUPAPA

KAUNAKAKAI

MOLOKAI ISLAND

Halawa Valley at the eastern end of Molokai.   Hawaii Visitors Bureau Photo

quiet, rural place, but this is already changing with the development of new resorts and townhouses. With the closing of a large pineapple plantation again (Kualapuu) in 1983, residents of Molokai may have to look to the tourist industry and diversified agriculture for future employment.

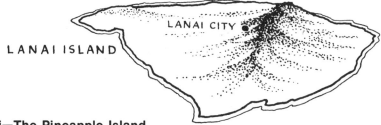

LANAI ISLAND
LANAI CITY

Lanai—The Pineapple Island

The island of Lanai lies south of Molokai and west of Maui. It ranks sixth in size, having an area of 141 square miles. Lanai is shaped like a clam shell. The entire island belongs to the Hawaiian Pineapple Company, and pineapples are grown on most of the good farm land. The population of Lanai numbers 2,119. Lanai City, with its one small hotel, is the only town on the island.

As we have already seen, Lanai was formed from a single volcano that is probably the oldest of any among the major islands. The summit, Lanaihale, is in the east central part of the island and has an elevation of 3370 feet. A series of ridges branch out to the north and northeast. The cliffs of Lanai are on the southwest shore.

There is a large central plateau with a gradual slope toward the sea in the northwest portion of the island. This slope is in the form of terraces. On these terraces, as well as on the central plateau, are found the pineapple plantations.

Kahoolawe—The Target Island

Before Captain Cook arrived, the residents of Kahoolawe (about 200 people) were mostly fishermen who lived near the coast and probably only used the island for a few months of every year. However, archealogists have found a few inland settlements and an adze quarry. The people planted sugar cane and yams, but the soil was too dry for taro. During the 1800s the island was used as a penal colony by the monarchy. After the last prisoner's sentence was ended in 1851, the island was leased for sheep grazing. Then in 1910 it was proclaimed a Territorial Forest Reserve. Efforts to reclaim Kahoolawe went slowly until 1941 when the U.S. Navy began firing practically every type of conventional artillery into the island. By 1953 the Navy was given complete control of the island.

Kahoolawe, 11 miles long and 6 miles wide, is mostly barren and without water. While it once supported a Hawaiian population, then

KAHOOLAWE ISLAND

later cattle and sheep, it is now uninhabited. With the introduction of goats the already sparse plant life was destroyed, and this disruption continues with the military's use of Kahoolawe as a bombing practice site. Because in an island state all land is precious, Kahoolawe may be restored to its original condition to serve future people of Hawaii. In recent years, the Kahoolawe

32

Ohana has been working to stop the bombing of this island as a first step towards its eventual resettlement by the Hawaiian people.

Maui—The Valley Island

Maui is the second largest island in the state with an area of 728 square miles. It is shaped like an hourglass. Together with Lanai, Molokai, and Kahoolawe, it forms a group of islands between Oahu and Hawaii known as Maui County.

The present day island of Maui was formed by two volcanoes, and the two mountainous areas are connected by an isthmus on which is found most of the island's farming. There, too, are the growing commercial and residential areas of Wailuku and Kahului. With Hawaii, Maui shares a pattern of tourist activities centered around the beaches of Kaanapali and Kihei and the historical attraction of Lahaina, the capital of Hawaii during the early monarchy and whaling days, in contrast to the "country" where life

Haleakala, world's largest volcanic crater. Hawaii Visitors Bureau Photo

IAO VALLEY

WAILUKU
LAHAINA
KAHULUI

HALEAKALA CRATER

HAWAII NATIONAL PARK

HALEAKALA

HANA

MAUI ISLAND

is quieter and the population more sparse.

West Maui consists of an 18-mile stretch of rugged mountains. The highest point is Puu Kukui, 5788 feet high. In the beautiful Iao Valley nearby is found the Needle, a rock peak 2000 feet high.

East Maui was formed by the world's largest inactive volcano, Haleakala. Its highest point, Red Hill, is 10,025 feet above sea level. Its last known eruption was in 1750. The crater, or summit, of Haleakala is 7 miles long, 2½ miles wide, and is 21 miles in circumference. Within this crater are meadows, deserts, and cones. One of these cones is taller than the Empire State Building. Most of the summit area of Haleakala is a national park.

Variations in temperature and rainfall depend more on location than season. Normal average temperature in Lahaina in February is 71°, and in August and September, 78°; rainfall averages 15.5 inches. On Maui, Molokai and Lanai, weather ranges from a warm, dry climate in the beach areas to semi-tropical warmth and heavy rainfall on the windward mountain slopes. At the top of Haleakala the temperature occasionally drops below freezing in the winter months and snow covers the summit for short periods.

Hawaii—The Big Island, The Orchid Island

The island of Hawaii is known as the "Big Island," since it is the largest in the chain. Its area of 4038 square miles makes it almost as large as Connecticut. The "Big Island" is almost twice the combined size of all the other islands in the State, measuring 93 by 76 miles.

Hawaii was formed by five volcanic domes—Kohala, Mauna Kea, Mauna Loa, Kilauea, and Hualalai. Kohala erupted long before the others. It formed the northern peninsula of Hawaii. Since the Kohala region is much older than the rest of the island, these

34

mountains are smooth rather than rugged.

The two highest mountains on Hawaii are Mauna Kea (13,784 feet) and Mauna Loa (13,680 feet). Both are covered with snow during the winter months. Mauna Loa and Kilauea are the two active volcanoes in the state. Tourists go to see the smoking pit of Kilauea (called Halemaumau). A volcano observatory stands on the rim of Kilauea's crater where scientists study the volcanic activities of the region.

The eruptions of these volcanoes occur mostly outside of the main cone, especially along the eastern rift. A 1983 lava flow from a Kilauea eruption destroyed three houses and threatened several others. Mauna Loa, Kilauea, and the nearby volcanic wonderland have been formed into Hawaii Volcanoes National Park.

The fifth dome on Hawaii is Hualalai (8251 feet). It can be seen from the well-known resort town of Kailua-Kona. A high barren and dry plateau is enclosed by Hualalai, Mauna Loa, and Mauna Kea. South of Kilauea is the Kau Desert. Hawaii is unusual in possessing such widely different features as deserts, lush tropical forests, and even snow. And even more interesting is the fact that this youngest island in the Hawaiian chain is still being formed.

Principal industries in the County are sugar cane growing and milling, tourism, diversified agriculture and cattle ranching. With the largest singly owned ranch in the United States (the Parker Ranch) and many smaller ranches, Hawaii produces almost three-fifths of the beef and over half of the diversified agricultural crops grown in the state. It also claims the only coffee industry in the

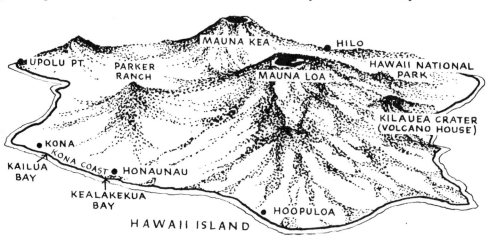

35

Round-up time on the huge Parker Ranch.

United States, the largest orchid growing business in the world, and a rapidly expanding export industry in papayas, macadamia nuts, anthuriums and other tropical flowers and foliage.

There are wide variations in temperature and rainfall on the Big Island, due primarily to the range of elevation and location rather than to seasonal change. Along the coastal regions, the climate is warm and semi-tropical. Average temperature in Hilo ranges from about 71° in February to about 76° in August. In the higher areas, temperatures are lower. The average annual temperature at the 11,000-foot level of Mauna Loa is 44°.

Rainfall varies markedly between regions of the County, ranging from an annual rainfall of 300 inches at the 3,000-foot level northwest of Hilo to six inches near Kawaiahae. The annual average is 134 inches for the city of Hilo and 25 inches for Kailua-Kona.

The Big Island has the greatest feeling of space and distance of any of the islands. It is 123 miles from Hilo to Kailua via Volcano. Most of the population resides in either Hilo or Kailua-Kona, while the rest lives in widely scattered small towns. And so the broad expanses of lava flows, hard-wood forests, pastures, desert and sugar cane dominate the landscape. Tourism and land division for residential growth dominated economic development from 1960-1980, while the sugar industry declined. The pressures of people on the land are less marked on this largest island, but conflicts of interest and problems in planning land use are not.

36

Hawaii's Climate

Although the Hawaiian Islands are located within the tropics, the climate is better described as subtropical. Much of Hawaii's pleasant weather comes from the Bering Sea! Cool waters from that area reach Hawaii, so that the ocean surrounding the islands is 10 degrees lower in temperature than in other Pacific regions lying in the same latitude. Temperatures are mild because the steady northwest trade winds have crossed thousands of miles of cool ocean. In reality there are four factors that influence the climate in Hawaii: (1) the Islands' location within the tropics, (2) their position in the zone of the northeast trade winds, (3) their altitude, and (4) the effect of low pressure fronts that pass generally to the north.

The temperature for the entire state averages 72 degrees. The

On Oahu the annual amount of rainfall varies from 20 inches to 250 inches according to local geographical and climatic conditions.

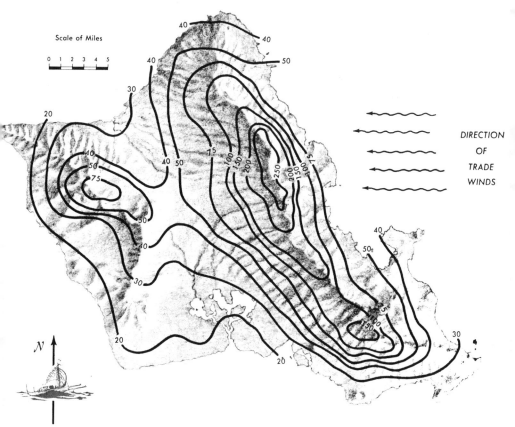

difference between the warmest months, August and September, and the coldest months, January and February is 5 to 8 degrees. The daily temperature range is 10 degrees.

Altitude affects temperature. For every 1000 feet of increase in altitude, there is a drop in temperature of about 3 degrees. Frost rarely occurs below 4000 feet elevation and has never been known in the Islands lower than 2500 feet above sea level. Uncomfortably hot and humid weather occurs occasionally when the trade winds stop blowing and the winds come from the south. This type of weather is called "Kona* weather" because it brings rain to the otherwise dry leeward side of the islands.

The amount of rainfall is closely related to the presence of mountains and the exposure of land to winds from the ocean. Since the trade winds blow across miles of ocean, they reach the islands heavily laden with moisture. As the trades strike the northeastern sides of the islands, they begin to rise because of the mountain peaks. This results in a reduction in temperature and pressure that causes the winds to drop their moisture. Therefore, the northeastern sides of the islands are apt to be the wettest because the prevailing winds are from that direction. As the winds descend the leeward slopes, they become warmer and drier, resulting in an arid or semi-arid climate on the leeward side of the islands. Low islands, such as Kahoolawe and Niihau, the low isthmus of central Maui, and the low ends of other islands, resemble the leeward side of all islands in that they have little rainfall.

Mount Waialele on Kauai has an annual rainfall of about 460 inches, with 624 inches falling in the rainiest year. It is probably the wettest spot on earth. Mana, only 15 miles away, but at sea level and on the leeward side of the island, receives only 10 inches of rain a year.

Because of local conditions, the heads of the valleys on the sheltered or leeward sides of the islands receive a great deal of rain. One of the authors of this book lives near the head of such a valley; across the valley the vegetation is that of a tropical rain forest; but down the valley toward Waikiki, the vegetation changes to the type found in semiarid regions of Southern California.

The huge domes of Mauna Loa and Mauna Kea on the island of Hawaii tower above the trade winds, which are deflected around

*Kona refers to the leeward side of an island.

38

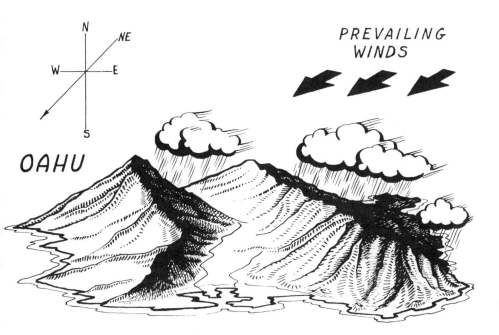

them. The slopes of these domes are large enough for local land and sea breezes to develop. The sea breeze brings rain to the Kona district of Hawaii, creating conditions favorable for growing coffee between the elevations of 1000 and 2500 feet.

Before the coming of Captain Cook the Hawaiians did not live on the dry plains except along the seashore because they did not practice irrigation on a large scale. Now the amount of rainfall is not so serious a problem because modern methods of engineering have made it possible to irrigate many acres of desert land. Much of the semidesert land in such places as the Ewa Plain near Honolulu and the isthmus of Maui has been made highly productive through the use of irrigation. Recently an extensive irrigation project was begun on Molokai so that many more acres on that island can be placed under cultivation. Since most of the islands consist of volcanic rock, much of the rainfall is captured. As a result there is plenty of water in wells for home and agricultural uses.

Plant Life

Because the Hawaiian Islands developed from volcanoes in the middle of the Pacific Ocean, scientists have been trying to learn how plant and animal life made the long trip over the Pacific to Hawaii. A study of parts of the land that have been covered with lava shows us that the first plant life to appear was the ferns. We can guess that the spores, which are very light, were carried to the islands by winds. Or perhaps the spores were in the feathers of birds that were blown off course. Birds may have eaten other seeds. Some seeds may have floated to the islands on ocean currents. The heavy seeds of some plants probably floated on logs and branches. As these plants arrived, they adjusted to the climate and soil conditions of the islands.

FLOWERS AND COLORS

Each of the islands of Hawaii has its own special flower and favorite color. The people of Oahu have adopted the *ilima* flower and their color is yellow. The *lehua* blossom is the flower of the Big Island and red is its color. Maui has the *lokelani* (heavenly rose) and its color is pink.

Kauai has chosen the *mokihana* berry and purple. Molokai favors green and the *kukui*. Lanai, like Oahu, has yellow for its color and the *kaunaoa,* an orange-colored vine. Instead of a flower, the tiny island of Niihau has the *pupu* shell, and white for color. Kahoolawe is represented by the *hinahina,* an air plant, and by the color gray.

The state flower is the red *hibiscus.*

The ancient Hawaiians cultivated certain trees and plants. Among them were the *ilima,* highly prized for making *leis;* the banana, for its fruit and leaves; and sugar cane, which was eaten as a relish after a feast or chewed between meals. The breadfruit tree is believed to have been brought to Hawaii by the earliest Polynesian settlers. It was first planted near their homes, but later it spread to the sheltered valleys and foothills. Yams, sweet potatoes, and dry land taro were cultivated. The Hawaiians showed their greatest skill as farmers by growing taro under water.

Among the present day wild vegetation are many plants that were

40

once introduced into the islands. Examples of such plants that have gone wild are guava, *algaroba, lantana,* and cactus. Of course, large areas have been cleared to produce Hawaii's greatest cash crops, sugar cane and pineapples. Of particular interest to tourists and of increasing economic importance in the Hilo area is the raising of orchids.

Minerals

Hawaii has few minerals because the islands are of recent volcanic origin. Deposits of titanium oxide, a paint pigment, are found on Kauai and Molokai. Bauxite, the ore used in the making of aluminum, is found on Kauai. However, it has not yet proved profitable to develop these deposits of ores for commercial use. Blue lava is used to decorate buildings, but it is not strong enough for use in heavy construction. There are two large cement plants on Oahu. The production of building materials, such as lime, sand, and gravel, accounts for most of the mineral wealth of the state.

Geographic Overview of Hawaii

Some of the interactions between the natural and the cultural in the environment are destructive, while others are protective. For example, the introduction of certain animals, the expansion of farming, and the growth of towns and cities have led to the extinction of several species of native birds. Many plants, birds, and other creatures are now in danger of becoming extinct due to man's impact upon the land. Air pollution from vehicle exhaust gases poses a health problem in urban areas. Fortunately, land zoned for conservation and air pollution controls can offset some negative results of cultural growth.

The natural environments of the Hawaiian Islands provide advantages for human development, but also have limitations. First, the island land area naturally limits city size, farming, recreation, and conservation land. In 1960 there were 6.6 acres of land for every person in Hawaii; in 1970 this had been reduced to 5.2 acres per person. By 1980 four-fifths of the population lived on Oahu, giving that island a density of 1,386 persons per square mile. Secondly, the islands are isolated in the Pacific Ocean. While the islands are separated from more urbanized and aggressive places, Hawaii must, at the same time, import supplies and bear a high cost of living for this isolation. Thirdly, the warm climate is good for soil development and plant growth, but becomes a problem when it speeds up soil erosion or aids air and water pollution. Fourthly, there is a limited water supply and certain areas of the state not considered desert regions occasionally experience droughts.

The islands are lacking in many resources such as oil, coal, and metallic ores. Lumber and water suitable for power generation are scarce. This puts limits on economic activities. However, Hawaii is rich in other resources—the beaches, scenery, and cultural attractions.

Because Hawaii was isolated from most of the world for so many years, there was little competition among plants and animals for survival. Thus, the ecology of the islands was easily disturbed when settlers began to arrive. Introduced plants soon dominated native species in most areas, while foreign insects, birds, and mammals have posed serious threats to the survival of many ecosystems. The human societies that began most of the disturbances have themselves undergone great social and economic change as successive cultures have been introduced to Hawaii. Today the risks of upsetting the islands' ecology are more serious because of the increase in human population and its technology. The margins for human error are smaller on islands than on large land masses. In Hawaii, there is no place else to go but the ocean.

Several factors make the geographic characteristics of Hawaii unique. These include its climate, geology, plant and animal life, the multi-ethnic population, the variety of languages, religions, and arts, and an economy based on tourism, the military, and agriculture.

Summing Up the Chapter

Hawaii, the only state located in the tropics, is a convenient stop-over in the long Pacific crossing. Of volcanic origin, the islands still have active volcanoes. The seven major inhabited islands in order of size are Hawaii, Maui, Oahu, Kauai, Molokai, Lanai, and Niihau. The climate is generally subtropical, and is influenced by the latitude of the islands, their altitude, the northeast trade winds, and passing low pressure areas. All plant and animal life had to be introduced into the islands. Except for building materials, there is little mineral wealth in the state.

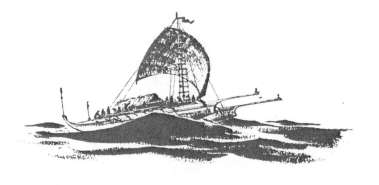

4

Origins and Migrations of the Polynesians

Who are the Hawaiians? How did their ancestors explore the vast Pacific until they found the lovely islands that were to be their permanent home? Much of the story will never be known, but scientists and historians have fitted pieces together until we can see at least the outlines of an amazing saga of the sea.

The setting is the vast island world of Oceania, consisting of more than 10,000 islands, which modern geographers divide into three parts: (1) Melanesia, or the Black Islands, reaching from New Guinea eastward to Fiji; (2) Micronesia, or the Tiny Islands, including the Marianas, Carolines, Marshalls, and Gilberts; (3) Polynesia, or the Many Islands, contained within a triangle anchored by Hawaii, New Zealand, and Easter Island.

Many centuries ago the ancestors of the Polynesian peoples came into this immense area. Scholars believe that these ancient people were of a Caucasian strain. It is thought that they journeyed slowly from South and East Asia, through the islands of Indonesia, and from there to the far-flung islands of the Pacific.

Settlement of Oceania

In the central hall of the Bishop Museum in Honolulu is a mural that shows the main islands in Oceania and the possible routes taken by the daring navigators of long ago. We learn from the printed legend

43

The Hokulea was built by the Polynesian Voyaging Society, a non-profit community group founded in 1973. Launched in 1974, the Hokulea sailed from Hawaii to Tahiti and back in 1976 in a recreation of the first Polynesian migrations to the Hawaiian Islands. Mike Tongg photo courtesy of the Polynesian Voyaging Society.

below the mural that during the last glacial period (15,000 to 20,000 years ago) the ocean level was 150 to 350 feet lower than at present. Many areas now under water were once dry land. Over this land bridge came the ancestors of the native peoples of Australia, New Guinea, and parts of Melanesia. They did not migrate all at once but rather over a period of many centuries. Since the distances between the land masses were short, these people needed only very simple boats for travel and probably were seldom out of sight of land.

Centuries later, other tribal and family groups sailed farther eastward. They settled the rest of Melanesia and the islands of Micronesia and Polynesia. These explorations, which took place many cen-

44

turies before the great voyages of Leif Ericson and Christopher Columbus, make one of the greatest adventure stories of all times.

New Racial Mixtures

These travelers seem to have taken on new physical characteristics as they moved eastward. Many of the native peoples in the southwest Pacific today, including the Melanesians, have dark skin and kinky hair. The Micronesians in the northwest Pacific and the Polynesians, who finally arrived in the central and eastern Pacific, have light brown skin and straight or wavy hair.

Today most people of mixed ancestry in the islands of the Pacific are crosses of native with Caucasian. Some are unions of native and Asiatic. However, more and more represent all three stocks. Small amounts of Negro and other strains can also be seen.

The Discovery of Hawaii

Early in the Christian era, the Polynesians began to move out into the heart of the Pacific. We are not certain what led them to sail ever eastward. Perhaps it was the pressure of other groups moving into their land. Perhaps it was the search for food. Perhaps it was the call of adventure.

Two routes were used by the early seafarers. The southern or Melanesian path starts from the thick cluster of islands in Indonesia, skirts the north coast of New Guinea, passes through the eastern fringe of the Melanesians and goes on to Fiji. Today we believe that this path to central Polynesia was used far less frequently than the more northerly route.

The northern or Micronesian route, starting in Indonesia and the Philippines, leads through Yap, Palau, and the Caroline Islands. Then it divides, one branch leading northeast through the Marshall Islands toward Hawaii, the other going through the Gilbert Islands, the Ellice Islands, and then on to the Samoan area.

By slow stages the islands of western Polynesia were discovered and simple communities founded. Centers of culture were formed in Samoa and the Society Islands in southeastern Polynesia. The stage was now set for further daring expeditions toward New Zealand to the south, Hawaii to the north, and Easter Island to the east—the great "Polynesian Triangle."

45

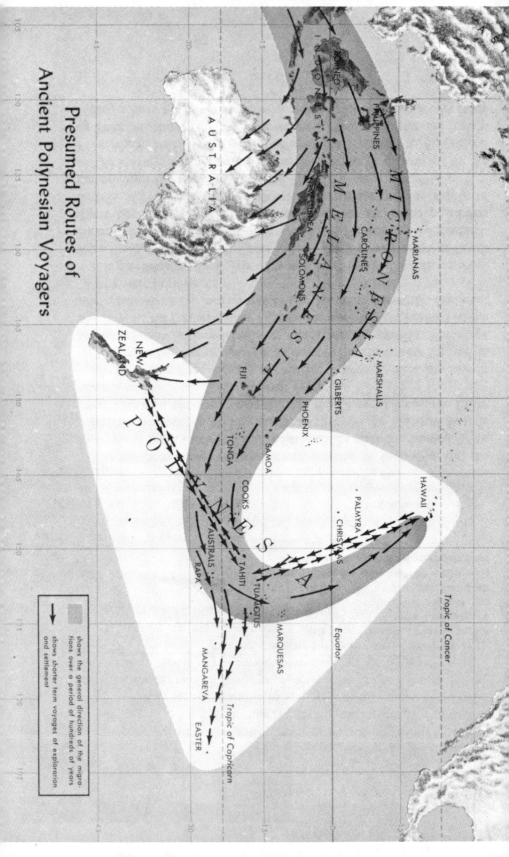

Presumed Routes of
Ancient Polynesian Voyagers

shows the general direction of the migrations over a period of hundreds of years

shows shorter term voyages of exploration and settlement

It is possible that the Polynesians may have reached South America, since the distance between Easter Island and the west coast of South America is less than that between Tahiti and Hawaii or New Zealand. There has been much debate among scientists about the possibility that the Polynesians first came from the Americas, but the weight of the evidence is against this theory.

The Hawaiian Islands were among the last to be discovered by the Polynesians. In the past scholars believed that Hawaii was first settled by Tahitians about 1000 A.D. However, archeologists from the Bishop Museum have now uncovered evidence that the first Hawaiians came from the Marquesas at least 500 years earlier. Because Hawaiian culture is so closely related to Tahitian culture, there is reason to believe that although the first settlers probably came from the Marquesas, the later ones were from Tahiti.

How the Polynesians Crossed the Great Ocean

In what kind of boats did the Polynesians make their amazing journeys? Long before sailors of the Mediterranean and the Atlantic dared to venture far from land, Polynesian canoes were crossing and re-crossing the 2400 miles between Hawaii and Tahiti. From the central Pacific they sailed eastward to discover Rapa-nui (Easter Island), a distance of 2500 miles with no in-between stopping places. Surely they must have been wonderful boat builders and navigators!

For ordinary fishing and travel to nearby islands, the Polynesians used a simple canoe hollowed out of logs with the aid of stone adzes. Usually these canoes were small, although some were more than 50 feet long. A more stable craft was the outrigger canoe, made by attaching a floating *ama,* or outrigger, to a single canoe. The term *ama* means a pole of light wood, fastened to the hull by means of two crosspieces extending outward from the hull. It rests on the surface of the water and helps to keep the canoe from capsizing. Small vessels could now be used for fairly long journeys even in rough water.

For long voyages, two canoes were joined together by wooden crossties or by a platform stretched between them. The large twin canoes had one or two masts set in this platform. Often a deck house thatched with *pandanus* leaves was built on the platform for shelter from the sun and rain.

Kenneth P. Emory, a noted student of Polynesian culture, describes the Tuamotu double canoes as the finest vessels of the Southeast. Un-

47

like the Tahitian and Hawaiian canoes, they were equal-ended and could sail in either direction. The sails, which were also wider than those on the Tahitian vessels, could be lowered and furled. As many as 100 persons might sail on one of these ships.

When the Europeans arrived in Polynesia, they found the natives using the very long Tongan single canoes. These canoes could be as long as 150 feet. A triangular sail was suspended by the middle of one side from the mast, which was fastened to the deck or the front of the canoe. The sail, not the canoe, was reversed when the crew wished to change direction.

By the time the Polynesians had reached the central Pacific, they had become experts in the art of building sailing vessels. As they worked, they asked the blessing of their gods, to whom they dedicated their canoes.

Preparations for the Voyage

When the Polynesians set out on a long voyage to a new home, they planned it very carefully. First they had to inspect their canoes for any weaknesses. Everything had to be in perfect order for the coming battle with the mighty ocean. Then they had to stock the canoe with food and water. Since their new island home might have few natural resources, the voyagers took with them seeds and food plants, pigs, dogs, and fowl.

In his fascinating book, *Vikings of the Sunrise,* Peter H. Buck, a former director of the Bishop Museum, describes how various Polynesian seafarers took care of the problem of food. The sea rations for the voyage were usually cooked. In atoll areas the food supply consisted of ripe *pandanus* fruit grated into a coarse flour, cooked, dried, and packed in cylindrical bundles protected by an outer wrapping of dried *pandanus* leaves. The voyagers starting from volcanic islands had a more elaborate bill of fare—preserved breadfruit carried in fairly large baskets and sweet potatoes that had been cooked and dried. Also on board was dried shell fish, which could be kept indefinitely. Fowls were cooped in the canoes, fed with dried coconut meat, and killed when necessary. Master fishermen caught deep sea fish, including sharks. Food could be cooked over a fireplace laid on a bed of sand on the deck.

Fresh water was carried in coconut water jugs, gourds, or lengths of bamboo. Deep sea fishermen might keep their water cool by trailing their gourds in the sea, but this method was not necessary on the long voyages. Apparently the crews underwent a Spartan training in surviving with a minimum of food and water.

After a group of Polynesians had made the great decision to find a new island home, they hauled their canoe to the water's edge and launched it with proper prayers and gifts to the gods. Then they stocked it carefully with the most essential articles and foodstuffs, since space was very limited. They knew from long experience that the canoe was fast and sturdy, but they also knew the fury of the sea and the many dangers that lay ahead. With favorable winds they could make 8 or 9 knots, but who could predict the storms and currents, and who could tell how many weary leagues they would travel before sighting land?

After waiting patiently for the right season of the year, they decided on the perfect day to set forth. When all the omens were favorable and the gods had been honored, they raised their mat sails, passed through the sheltering reefs, and steered for the far horizon.

The Crossing

They had no compass or log book. They guided themselves by the sun and stars, by the flight of birds, by cloud formations, and by the action of the waves and prevailing winds. It is said that the

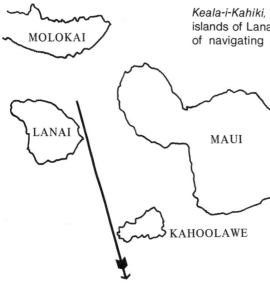

Keala-i-Kahiki, The Road to Tahiti between the islands of Lanai and Kahoolawe, is an example of navigating by landmarks. By aligning the canoe with two or more landmarks, in this case the west and east ends of the two islands, voyagers set upon known courses. The direction and strength of the current was shown by the drift of a canoe away from its alignment. If the voyagers started in the late afternoon, the navigators could take new bearings from the stars before the landmarks were out of sight.

Polynesian navigator could recognize and name 150 or more stars. He kept track of the days by tying knots in a piece of string.

Year after year these daring seamen piloted their double canoes across the waters of the Pacific. Many perished from hunger and thirst. Some lost their lives in storms at sea. But others found their way, and one by one the islands of the Pacific were discovered. Some were barren and not fit for settlement. Others were green and hospitable and could support life. Among the fairest of these were the Hawaiian Islands.

When the ancient Polynesians arrived in the Hawaiian Islands, they brought with them their old ways of doing things and later changed them to suit the conditions of their new home. And then suddenly, for some reason still unknown, the period of the "long voyages" ended. The people who had reached Hawaii lived apart from the rest of the world. In this period of separation they developed certain customs and craft products of their own.

After some centuries the Islands were discovered again, this time by a new race of men, bringing new gods and new ways. Yet in spite of the long years of separation, their language changed very little. When Captain Cook first came to the Islands, he was surprised to discover that he could understand the native tongue and that it was so much like that of the natives whom he had met in Tahiti.

Summing Up the Chapter

The ancestors of the Hawaiians are believed to have been Caucasoids who spread out gradually from Asia by land and water routes until they reached the islands of the central Pacific. As the migrations continued, the people took on new physical characteristics. The Hawaiian Islands were probably first discovered about 450 A.D. by Polynesians who crossed from the Marquesas in outrigger canoes. The second migration arrived from Tahiti about 1000 A.D. Suddenly the long sea voyages ended, and it remained for sailors of a later day to rediscover Hawaii.

5

Lono Returns

History is full of strange coincidences, but none is stranger than Captain Cook's discovery of the Hawaiian Islands. In the first place, he was not looking for the Islands when he discovered them. Secondly, he landed in Hawaii twice at the season of the year when, according to ancient Hawaiian legends, one of their gods would return. The third coincidence was that he and his ships fitted the description given in the native legends. Finally, and of greatest importance, was the fact that the chronometer had just been invented before Cook set sail, so that his navigators could determine the exact longitude of the Islands, thus helping others to find them easily.

The Voyages of Captain Cook

Captain James A. Cook may not have been the first European to visit the Islands. Some historians claim that a Spanish navigator, Juan Gaetano, first discovered the Islands in the mid-1500's. However, it was Cook's discovery that first brought the Islands to the attention of Europe.

During his first two voyages Cook explored the southern part of the globe. He crossed the Antarctic Circle, narrowly missing Antarctica, but shrewdly guessing its existence and thinking it to be of no value. Cook explored New Zealand, the coast of Australia, and some of the Pacific islands. After he completed his first two voyages, many

Pacific islands were accurately charted for the first time with the newly invented chronometer of John Harrison. Cook did his work so carefully that since his day there has been little change in the maps of the islands of the Southwest Pacific.

Before Captain Cook's time, the dreaded disease of scurvy claimed the lives of many members of expeditions. The survivors of the disease would be so weak from it that they could hardly sail their ships. Cook believed that scurvy could be prevented. He insisted that his crew keep their quarters clean, and he secured fresh fruits and vegetables whenever possible. He also carried live animals to be slaughtered as they were needed for food. Most important of all, he included lemon and lime juices in the crew's diet. Sailors who refused to drink the sour juice were flogged with the cat-o'-nine tails, a punishment used commonly by the navies of that period. Scurvy did break out on one of Cook's ships. The cook was brought before the captain and confessed that he had not followed orders about the food he was to serve the crew. As soon as this situation was corrected, the men recovered from scurvy. Thus, it was proved that Cook's theory was correct.

In terms of Hawaiian history, Cook's third voyage is most important. Eight days after the Declaration of Independence was adopted in Philadelphia in 1776, Cook set sail on his third Pacific voyage with two ships, the *Resolution* and the *Discovery*. He sailed around Africa to Tasmania and from there to the Cook Islands and on to Tahiti. At Tahiti, Cook landed the cattle, sheep, and horses which King George III had sent as gifts. Since Cook had visited Tahiti before, he had chosen it as the place to refit his ships before heading northward to explore the northwest coast of North America. Leaving Tahiti, Cook sailed north, taking quite by chance the route followed by the ancient Polynesians who sailed from Tahiti to Hawaii.

The Discovery of the Hawaiian Islands

On January 18, 1778, Cook sighted Oahu first and Kauai not long afterward. He named the islands the Sandwich Islands in honor of the Earl of Sandwich, who was then the First Lord of the Admiralty

Captain Cook, wearing a cape of red *tapa,* is offered a pig at a *luau* in his honor. The feast is held outside the fence surrounding Lono's house.

(a position similar to that of the U.S. Secretary of the Navy). The expedition made its first stop in Hawaii at Waimea, Kauai.

Very soon a thriving trade developed between the English and the Hawaiians. The English needed food, and the natives wanted the iron nails the British offered in exchange. Although the Hawaiians had small bits of iron in their possession before Cook's arrival, this useful metal was hard to obtain and the Islanders recognized its value. Cook was able to get sixty or so pigs, yams, sweet potatoes, cooking bananas, and taro in exchange for nails and some pieces of iron.

When Cook went ashore at Waimea, Kauai, the natives treated him as a chief of the highest rank or as a god. Some historians say that the Kauaians thought he was the god Lono returned. From Kauai Cook sailed to the nearby island of Niihau and obtained yams and salt there. He gave the inhabitants some goats and pigs, as well as melon, pumpkin, and onion seeds. After two weeks, Cook sailed northward to carry out his orders to explore the northwestern part of the North American coastline.

Late in the fall Cook's small squadron turned southward for the purpose of spending the winter in the Hawaiian Islands and exploring them more thoroughly. His second appearance occurred in the Maka-hiki season, which was sacred to the god Lono. After charting the coasts of Maui and Hawaii, Cook anchored at Kealakekua Bay on the Kona coast of the island of Hawaii for the purpose of refitting his ships. Naturally the Hawaiians were quite excited by the sight of Cook's ships as he explored the two islands. The *kahunas* believed that Cook's presence fulfilled the legend of the god Lono. According to ancient myths, the god had sailed away promising to return some day. The Englishmen fitted the description of Lono, and even the sails on their ships were shaped like one of the symbols sacred to Lono. It was only natural, therefore, that when Cook landed the *kahunas* proclaimed him the god Lono in an elaborate religious ceremony.

While the two ships were being repaired, the English engaged in active trading with the Hawaiians. The King, Kalaniopuu, visited Cook aboard the *Resolution* and exchanged gifts with him. During a state visit, the King gave Cook several feather cloaks and a quantity of foodstuff. Cook, in return gave the King a linen shirt and a sword. Later Cook presented the King with a complete tool chest.

Much of the iron traded was in the form of long daggers, made by the ship's blacksmiths on the model of the Hawaiians' wooden *pahoa*. In general, there were no serious quarrels between the English and the Hawaiians, considering that the two groups represented such different cultures. There was nothing to suggest the tragic events to follow.

The Death of Cook

In eighteen days the repairs were completed, and the ships were loaded with supplies. Cook left Kealakekua, intending to return to the Pacific Northwest. However, a few days later he ran into a storm that damaged the *Resolution* and forced him to return to Kealakekua Bay for repairs.

This time Cook was not received so enthusiastically. Supplying food for crews of the two ships had been a severe strain on the resources of the Hawaiians. There was considerable quarreling back and forth, and some English shore parties were stoned. Thievery increased and a large ship's boat was stolen by the Hawaiians and broken up for nails.

Cook had decided that some action to recover the boat was necessary. Because Captain Clerke of the *Discovery* was suffering more than usual from his tuberculosis, Cook took command of the party going ashore. His plan was to lure the King on board ship and to hold him hostage until the boat was returned. Cook almost succeeded, but trouble broke out as he was returning with the King. During the fighting Cook lost his life.

The Hawaiians carried away the bodies of Cook and four sailors who had also been killed in the fight. Cook's body was treated like that of a high chief or a god. As was the custom, the flesh was removed and some of the bones distributed among the high chiefs. Captain Clerke, who became the new commander of the expedition, and most of the Hawaiian leaders favored a peaceful settlement of the dispute. Nevertheless, some fighting did continue until parts of Cook's body were returned. The Hawaiians had shown great courage against the superior weapons of the English, and some of the actions of the English might make some wonder which group was supposed to have been uncivilized.

A monument erected in 1876 at Kealakekua Bay commemorates Captain James Cook's voyages to the Islands. It stands near the spot where he was killed.

Cook was given an appropriate naval funeral. If you visit Keala-kekua Bay today, you will find there a monument to the memory of that distinguished scientist, explorer, and navigator.

Captain George Vancouver

As a result of Cook's voyages, the fur trade developed in the Pacific Northwest at the end of the eighteenth century. Hawaii became a favorite wintering place for fur traders and traders in general. Four years after Cook made his last voyage, ships began to call at the Islands. The famous French explorer, La Perouse, came to the Islands, as did other British and Spanish explorers. Of these early visitors, however, Captain George Vancouver stands out in Hawaiian history.

Vancouver had visited the Islands in 1778 and 1779 as a junior officer under Cook. In 1791 he was sent to the Pacific to receive for England certain lands on the northwest coast of North America from the Spanish and to complete the exploration of the coast which was begun by Cook. His orders also stated that he was to make a survey of the Hawaiian Islands and spend the winter there.

On his first visit to Hawaii he stopped briefly on Kauai and Hawaii. On his second visit he brought cattle and sheep, as well as goats and geese, as gifts to the Hawaiians. Kamehameha realized the importance of conservation and placed a ten-year taboo on the cattle so that they would have a chance to multiply. Vancouver also distributed among the chiefs of the different islands grape vines, orange and almond trees, and various kinds of garden seeds.

While these gifts were important to the Hawaiian people as a help in varying their diet and in supplying traders with beef, Vancouver's attempts to bring peace to the Islands are his most important contributions. There had been considerable warfare among the chiefs before his arrival, and Vancouver was shocked by the destruction from these wars. He used his influence to promote peace among the warring chiefs. Unlike most foreigners visiting the Islands during this period, he refused to supply guns to any of the chiefs in Hawaii. He even tried to serve as peacemaker between Kamehameha and his favorite wife, Kaahumanu!

Not only did Vancouver work for peace within the Islands, but he spent much time with Kamehameha advising him on how to rule his kingdom and how to deal with foreigners. Because of Vancouver's influence, Kamehameha offered to place his kingdom under the protection of Great Britain. He realized that his small island kingdom had little chance to survive among the great nations that were continually taking new territory in the Pacific. The British government did not act upon this offer.

Although Vancouver would not give Kamehameha arms, he did help to strengthen the position of the King in other ways. Vancouver's carpenters helped to build the first European-type vessel in the Hawaiian Islands and promised the King a British man-of-war, which was sent some years later. He also taught the King how to drill his troops. Most important of all, Vancouver gave Kamehameha sound advice about governing his kingdom.

Summing Up the Chapter

Although Captain Cook made three voyages to the Pacific, it was not until the third voyage that he rediscovered the Hawaiian Islands. Because of the conditions surrounding his visit, he was first thought to be the god Lono returned. A thriving trade began between the English and the Hawaiians. Later trouble broke out over the theft of a boat, and Cook was killed in the fighting which followed. Of the other explorers who followed Cook, the English Captain Vancouver played the most important role in Hawaiian history. As adviser to King Kamehameha, he helped to bring peace within the Islands, at the same time strengthening the King's position.

1775 First battle of the American Revolution

1776 Declaration of Independence

1778 Captain Cook lands in Hawaii

1781 General Cornwallis surrenders to Washington at Yorktown, ending the Revolutionary War

1782 Kamehameha I begins his rise to power

1786 Many foreign vessels begin arriving in Hawaii

1789 U.S. Constitution
George Washington becomes first U.S. president
French Revolution begins

1792-94 George Vancouver introduces cattle and sheep to Hawaii

1792 Bill of Rights

1793 Reign of Terror in France
Eli Whitney invents cotton gin

1795 Kamehameha conquers Oahu in Battle of Nuuanu Pali

6

Kamehameha—"The Lonely One"

In the last chapter we saw the entrance of Kamehameha upon the stage of Hawaiian history. Now let us retrace our steps and tell the story of this warrior, whom the Hawaiians rightly look upon as one of the greatest heroes of their race.

The earliest glimpse we get of him is a description by Lieutenant King, one of Captain Cook's officers. The ruling chief of Hawaii had boarded Cook's ship at Kealakekua, and among his attendants was:

> "Maiha-Maiha, whom at first we had some difficulty in rec-
> ollecting, his hair being plastered over with a dirty brown
> paste and powder, which was by no means heightening to
> the most savage face I ever beheld."

From other descriptions of this unusual young chief, we learn that he was powerfully built, agile, courageous and equipped in all ways to lead his people both in peace and in war. The best likenesses of Kamehameha are the portraits painted from life by Louis Choris, a young draftsman who visited Hawaii in 1816 with the expedition of the Russian von Kotzebue.

Today in downtown Honolulu there is a much-photographed statue of Kamehameha. On every eleventh day of June it is draped with flower *leis* in his honor. This public holiday was first proclaimed in

1871 by Kamehameha V "in memory of our Grandfather and Predecessor, Kamehameha I, the founder of the Hawaiian Kingdom." The bronze figure is larger than life-size, and the features are not a true likeness. History records that when the legislature of the kingdom set aside funds for the statue in 1878, King Kalakaua chose the handsomest man in the court as a model. This statue, done by an American sculptor living in Florence, Italy, was lost when the ship bringing it to Hawaii sank. The legislature collected $10,000 insurance and ordered another statue, which now stands near Iolani Palace. The original statue was salvaged, then shipped to Kohala on the island of Hawaii, the birthplace of Kamehameha.

One of the most interesting chapters in Hawaiian history is the one that relates the adventures of the first Kamehameha. It is a story of heroism and sacrifice, of hideous cruelty and oppression, of family rivalries and bloody conflict, of great deeds and low treachery. The chapter ends, however, with the final unity of the Islands and the disappearance of the bitter struggle which had darkened the history of one of the most beautiful spots on earth.

The statue of Kamehameha I that stands in front of the Supreme Court building is an idealized likeness of the king. On every June 11, during ceremonies honoring the monarch, the statue is draped with flower *leis*.

Camera Hawaii

Space does not permit us to trace in detail the rise of Kamehameha and the military campaigns by which he gained control of the Hawaiian Islands. Perhaps we can capture the spirit and flavor of the age by relating a few of its better known stories.

Kamehameha's Early Life

Kamehameha was born at Kohala, on the northern side of the big island of Hawaii. Various dates are given for this event, which probably took place between 1753 and 1760. The parents were the chief Kalanikupuakeoua (Keoua) and the high-born princess Kekuiapoiwa.

Some accounts indicate that Keoua was the accepted father, but that Kahekili, later the grim and warlike king of Maui, was the natural father. Another legend tells that Keoua gave his son to Kahekili, as was frequently the custom among chiefs.

Still another legend claims that the newborn boy was stolen away from his mother by a Kohala chief named Naole. For some mysterious reason Naole was not punished for this abduction but was given the custody of the child for five years. At the end of this time the young chief was taken to the court of the ruling chief of Hawaii, where he received the usual training given to a high-ranking warrior. His tutor in the techniques of warfare was Kekuhaupio, a famous fighter of those early days.

Shortly after the arrival of Captain Cook there occurred an event which was a turning point in the life of Kamehameha. In 1780 Kalaniopuu, perhaps sensing that he had not long to live, called a meeting of high-ranking chiefs. Here he announced that his successor was to be his son Kiwalao, and that Kukailimoku, the ancestral war-god, was to be in the care of his nephew Kamehameha. (This war-god may be seen today in the Bishop Museum.)

A bitter rivalry developed between the two cousins, coming to a head when a rebel chief named Imakakaloa was captured and brought to a *heiau* in the Kau district to be sacrificed to the war-god. As was the savage custom, he was clubbed or stabbed to death; and his body, after certain preliminary rites, was laid upon the altar. Kiwalao, representing the King, was the chief actor in the ceremony; but suddenly Kamehameha stepped forward and conducted the sacrifice himself. It is not known whether he was urged by powerful friends to take this bold step or whether he believed that as custodian of the war-god he should take the central role in the sacrifice. The old King, Kalaniopuu,

61

advised him to retire to his estates for a time and to keep out of court politics. This he did, taking with him his wife Kalola, a group of supporters, and the war-god.

Early in 1782 Kalaniopuu, full of years and with the memory of many glorious battles, died. Two rival groups of chiefs were formed, each looking out for its own interests. On one side were the chiefs of Kona, who had persuaded Kamehameha to join them. On the other side was the young King, Kiwalao, together with his ambitious uncle, Keawemauhili, and his half-brother, Keoua.

The records are not quite clear about the new boundaries that were drawn. Evidently they were not pleasing to Kamehameha and his allies. Within a few months the two sides were at war. The climax of the struggle took place at Mokuohai in the summer of 1782, where the forces of Kamehameha were victorious and Kiwalao was killed. The surviving chiefs seized the areas that they believed they could hold. Keoua took Kau and part of Puna; his uncle took Hilo and adjoining areas in Puna and Hamakua; and Kamehameha took Kona, his own Kohala, and the northern section of Hamakua.

For the next decade the history of Hawaii is one of civil war. We shall not relate the details of the bloody struggles among the chiefs of Hawaii, which are available elsewhere. The long struggle finally ended with the victory of Kamehameha over Keoua, Keawemauhili, and Kahekili, and with the unification of the Islands. Following this period of strife came a time of great change resulting from the arrival of a stream of Caucasian settlers.

The "Law of the Splintered Paddle"

Out of this civil war period there came a number of stories which the Hawaiians like to tell. Abraham Fornander in his classic history of Hawaii tells this tale:

"A short time after his debarkation at Laupahoehoe, Kamehameha started one day with his own war canoe and its crew alone, without making his object known to his counsellors, and unaccompanied by any of them. Steering for the Puna coast, he ran in upon the reef at a place called Papai in Keaau. A number of fishermen with their wives and children were out fishing on the reef, and, as they were about returning ashore, Kamehameha rushed upon them with the object

62

of slaying or capturing as many as he could, they being the subjects of Keawemauhili. The greater number of these people saved themselves by flight, but two men were hemmed off and they engaged in fight with Kamehameha. During the scuffle Kamehameha's foot slipped into a crevice of the coral reef, and, while thus entangled, he was struck some severe blows on the head with the fisherman's paddle. Luckily for Kamehameha the fisherman was encumbered with a child on his back, and ignorant of the real name and character of his antagonist. Extricating himself with a violent effort, Kamehameha reached his canoe and returned to Laupahoehoe."[1]

Many years later Kamehameha commemorated his narrow escape from death, which was a result of his own cruel attack on peaceable and unoffending people, by a strict law punishing robbery and murder with death. To that law, which has been called the first Bill of Rights in Hawaiian history, he gave the name of *Mamalahoe,* the "splintered paddle." This edict, issued in 1797, is remembered today by awards given on behalf of the state of Hawaii and the Honolulu Chamber of Commerce to distinguished persons who have benefited Hawaii. The award of the "Order of the Splintered Paddle" is a silk-screened *tapa* scroll. The first to receive the award was President Dwight Eisenhower on May 3, 1956.

The Death of Keoua

Another tale tells of the misfortunes of Keoua. This energetic and warlike chief, after an indecisive battle with the forces of Kamehameha, had retreated through Hilo enroute to his home in Kau. On this return march a great disaster struck part of his army. The great volcano of Kilauea erupted suddenly during the night, terrifying Keoua's forces camped nearby. The men tried to appease the goddess of the volcano by rolling stones into the crater. But more eruptions came on the second and third nights. On the third day, Keoua ordered his army to set forth in three different companies. The lead company had not gone far when a new explosion sent vast clouds of hot cinders into the air. A few men were burned or suffocated to death by falling cinders.

[1] Abraham Fornander, *An Account of the Polynesian Race* (London: Trubner & Co., 1878-1885), Vol. II, p. 318.

Kamehameha I probably looked very much like he does in this engraving. It is taken from a drawing of the King made by Louis Choris in 1816.

The rear group, which was not seriously harmed, pressed forward to escape the danger. They were horrified to see that the bulk of the deadly ashes had apparently fallen upon their comrades in the middle group. Not one of the whole party, including women and children, had survived. Seeing this, the men of the rear group hurried on and overtook the company in advance at their camping place.

In the following year, 1791, Keoua was approached in Kau by two principal advisers of Kamehameha, who urged him to meet their leader at a large new *heiau* built in honor of Kamehameha's war-god at Puukohola, Kawaihae. Here, they said, peaceful relations would be restored between the two famous warriors and the disastrous civil war ended.

Although he was suspicious, Keoua agreed to the meeting and gathered some of his followers in a fleet of canoes for the journey to Kawaihae. When the canoes approached the shore, he noted that a crowd of armed warriors and chiefs surrounded Kamehameha, who stood on the beach. As he was in the act of leaving his canoe, Keoua was killed by a spear in the hands of Keeaumoku, one of Kamehameha's loyal lieutenants. All of Keoua's immediate company were cruelly butchered. Finally, as the second detachment of Keoua's escort approached, Kamehameha put a stop to the slaughter. The body of Keoua was carried to the *heiau* and sacrificed to the war-god.

Although some early historians have suggested that Kamehameha was not directly responsible for this murder, it remains as a dark shadow on the reputation of the great King. It was carried out in his presence by his most trusted advisers. Nor did Kamehameha ever publicly disapprove of the act or punish those who were responsible.

The most charitable comment we can make is that the King was merely following the rough code of his day. Perhaps he could not safely resist the will of his powerful lieutenants, or perhaps he realized that there must be an end to the bitter rivalries that were wasting the land. In any event, the island of Hawaii was now firmly in his hands, and he could proceed with his plans to extend his control to the other islands.

Kamehameha accomplished this feat not only because of his own qualities of leadership but also because of his shrewdness in making use of the weapons and skills of foreigners who joined his forces. The most important of these were John Young, the English boatswain on the American ship *Eleanora,* commanded by Captain Simon Metcalfe, and Isaac Davis, a sailor on the tiny schooner *Fair American,* commanded by Metcalfe's son. After a series of colorful adventures these two men came under the protection of Kamehameha, served him loyally, and were rewarded with wives and valuable property in a manner suitable to Hawaiian *ali'i.*

Civil War in the Islands

The chief obstacle in Kamehameha's path of conquest was the wily Kahekili, who had won control of the islands of Maui, Lanai, Molokai, and Oahu. Through his brother Kaeo, Kahekili also held Kauai in his grasp.

Suddenly, as though to demonstrate that the gods looked with favor upon Kamehameha, came the news of the death of Kahekili at Waikiki, Oahu. His dominions were to be divided between his brother Kaeo, and his son Kalanikupule, the former being on Maui and the latter on Oahu.

Then, as though to further the intentions of the gods, these two kinsmen fell to quarreling. The first skirmish between Kaeo and the warriors of Kalanikupule took place at Waimanalo on Oahu in the summer of 1794. It was brought to an end by the arrival of Kalanikupule, and peace was restored. Shortly thereafter, Kaeo learned of a plot against him organized by his own followers. In order to put down this mutinous spirit, he outlined a plan to turn upon Kalanikupule and plunder his domain.

So in November of 1794, Kaeo started overland from Waianae through the Ewa district to Aiea, which is near Pearl Harbor. At first Kaeo was successful. The tide of battle was turned when three trading vessels, two English schooners under the general command of Captain William Brown, and one American sloop under Captain John Kendrick, entered Pearl Harbor. The hard-pressed Kalanikupule sought the aid of Brown, who furnished guns and boats manned by a small group of volunteer sailors. The main action took place on December 12. Kaeo's forces broke in panic and retreated in the face of fire from the boats. Kaeo and a few followers fought bravely to the last but were finally killed.

Apparently Captain Brown, overjoyed by the success of his gunners, ordered a salute fired from the *Jackal.* Fornander reports what followed:

"A wad from one of the guns entered the cabin of the *Lady Washington* and killed Captain Kendrick, who was at dinner at the time. Captain Kendrick was buried ashore, and the natives looked upon the funeral ceremony as one of sorcery to procure the death of Captain Brown. The son of Captain Kendrick requested Kalanikupule to take good care of his father's grave; but that very night the grave was opened and robbed by the natives, as alleged, for the purpose of obtaining the winding-sheet. Shortly afterwards the *Lady Washington* left for China."[2]

Now Kalanikupule and his chiefs conceived a treacherous plan. They would seize the two English ships, the *Jackal* and the *Prince Lee Boo,* kill the captains, and use these great foreign ships to lead an assault on Kamehameha himself.

While the ships' boats, returning with a load of salt, were grounded by low water on the reef at Keehi, Kalanikupule's company attacked

2 Ibid., p. 266.

Using clubs, knives, and guns, the forces of Kamehameha defeated the army of the Chief of Oahu at Nuuanu. The warriors fought to the very edge of the *pali,* where many met their death by being pushed over the precipice.

the remaining crews of the two ships, killed the captains, and forced the crewmen who were left to make ready for sea. As the expedition was about to start, however, the English crews regained control of the ships, killed or drove off the natives and raced for Hawaii. Here they provisioned their ships, left word for Kamehameha about the startling events on Oahu, and continued on their way to China.

The Battle of Nuuanu

Kamehameha knew that the time had now come to try to take control of all the islands. Swiftly he gathered a great fleet of canoes, thousands of warriors, and—significantly—a group of foreign artillerymen headed by Isaac Davis and John Young. The time was February, 1795.

The first destination for his armada was Maui, which he laid waste so that no opposition could arise from the rear. Next he secured Molokai. Then came the great assault on Oahu. The long line of canoes landed on the shore extending from the present Waialae golf course down to Waikiki. Here Kamehameha grouped his forces for the attack on

67

Kalanikupule, who had taken positions in the Nuuanu valley. Adding strength to the army of Oahu were the famous chief Kaiana, his brother Nahiolea, and their immediate friends and followers, all of whom had deserted Kamehameha after the voyage from Hawaii had begun.

The battle of Nuuanu, which took place in April of 1795, is for newcomers to Hawaii perhaps the most fascinating story in Hawaii's history. The beautiful valley, which once resounded with the shouts of warriors, is now a favorite spot enjoyed by visitors to our country's fiftieth state. The outcome of the battle, according to Fornander, was as follows:

"At Puiwa the hostile forces met, and for awhile the victory was hotly contested; but the superiority of Kamehameha's artillery, the number of his guns, and the better practice of his soldiers, soon turned the day in his favor, and the defeat of the Oahu forces became an accelerated rout and a promiscuous slaughter. Of those who were not killed, some escaped up the sides of the mountains that enclose the valley on either side, while a large number were driven over the pali of Nuuanu, a precipice of several hundred feet in height, and perished miserably. Kaiana and his brother Nahiolea were killed early in the battle. Koalaukani, the brother of Kalanikupule, escaped to Kauai. Kalanikupule was hotly pursued, but he escaped in the jungle, and for several months led an errant and precarious life in the mountain-range that separates Koolaupoko from Ewa, until finally he was captured in the upper portion of Waipio, killed, brought to Kamehameha, and sacrificed to the war-god Kukailimoku."[3]

The battle of Nuuanu was a turning point in Hawaiian history, but it did not lead immediately to the firm unification of the Islands. Revolts broke out from time to time and had to be put down, and the island of Kauai still remained independent. However, it was only a question of time until Kamehameha would become the single great ruler of the whole island chain.

Although the bitter wars among the chiefs had now come to an end, there was a new influence at work in the Islands that would change

[3] Ibid., p. 348.

greatly the character of Hawaiian life and manners. Increasingly during the civil wars, *haoles* (foreigners) of various nationalities had visited or taken residence in the Islands, bringing with them their virtues and their vices. In the next chapter we shall describe the effects of this alien culture during the remaining years of Kamehameha's reign.

Summing Up the Chapter

Kamehameha I, probably the most colorful of Hawaii's rulers, was born at Kohala some time between 1753 and 1760. Having been given custody of the war-god by King Kalaniopuu, Kamehameha became a bitter rival of the King's son, Kiwalao, for the control of Hawaii. In the wars which followed Kamehameha's forces were victorious. The victory on the Big Island was followed by victories over Keoua, Keawemauhili, Kahekili, and Kalanikupule and the final unification of the chain of islands under the leadership of Kamehameha. Kamehameha combined his own skill and qualities of leadership with the help of weapons and men furnished by the foreigners who were coming to the Islands in greater numbers. They too were to change the character of the people of the Hawaiian Islands.

1795 The Battle of Nuuanu (Kamehameha becomes ruler of all islands except Kauai)

1796 Kamehameha's invasion of Kauai fails due to storm

1796 John Adams elected 2nd U.S. president

1800 Washington, D.C. becomes new U.S. capital

1801 Thomas Jefferson inaugurated 3rd president

1803 Horses introduced by American Captains Shaler & Cleveland

1803 Louisiana Purchase

1804 Lewis & Clark expedition Napoleon becomes Emperor of France

1805 Sandlewood trade begins

1808 Henry Opukahaia leaves Kealakekua Bay for Connecticut

1810 Kaumualii cedes Kauai and Niihau to Kamehameha

1812 James Madison elected 4th U.S. president

War of 1812 with England

1813 First pineapple planting by Don Francisco de Paula Marin

1815-16 Russians try to seize Kauai; erect fort at Waimea

1815 Napoleon defeated at Waterloo; Louis XVIII becomes king of France

1817 James Monroe inaugurated 5th U.S. president

1819 Kamehameha I dies

1819 Panic of 1819

7

The Old Order Changes

After the battle of Nuuanu, Kamehameha's great task was to unite and improve his enlarged domain. He based his government largely on the old Hawaiian land system, rewarding his principal chiefs with grants of land and collecting taxes in the traditional way.

Despite the advice of a friendly Englishman, Captain William Broughton of the ship *Providence,* the King determined to conquer Kauai. In 1796 he gathered his fleet at Waianae and set forth. In mid-channel a great storm arose, sank many of his canoes, and forced him to give up the attempt. Several months later, a revolt broke out in Hawaii. It was led by Namakeha, the brother of Kaiana. Kamehameha quickly smashed this revolt, captured Namakeha and offered him as a sacrifice at a *heiau* in Hilo.

This was the last important military action of the conqueror. Now he was free to take on his new role as administrator. Some of the more restless chiefs he kept near his court; others, whom he trusted completely, he installed as governors of the various islands. The able John Young became governor of the Big Island, and the faithful Keeaumoku took the reins on Maui. At court Kamehameha depended greatly on the powerful Kona chiefs and their sons and on Kalanimoku, "the iron cable of Hawaii," whose ability led admiring English sailors to name him after their own prime minister, William Pitt. They called Kalanimoku "Billy Pitt."

Pu'uhonua-o-Honaunau or Place of Refuge: *Ki'i*s (or *Tiki*s) shown here are at the Place of Refuge, a revered site of Hawaiians, located at the southern end of Kealakekua Bay on the Island of Hawaii. Many students of Polynesian culture visit the area to study the heiau which once held the remains of Hawaiian kings. Hawaii Visitors Bureau photo.

The King strictly enforced the *kapu* system, believing that it was an aid in strengthening his control. Perhaps, as one historian suggests, he was right in holding to this system, barbarous as it was. Until the Hawaiians had become accustomed to the new law of the Gospel, it was better for them to follow the old harsh law rather than to have no moral law at all.

One of Kamehameha's first projects was to rebuild his war-torn land and to revive the simple agriculture of the day. He set his people to work terracing hills, banking up taro patches, digging long irrigation ditches, and building fish ponds. In these public works the King himself took an active part. Archibald Campbell, in his first-hand description of Hawaii about 1810, mentions seeing Kamehameha deep in the mud of a taro patch:

"... This mode of culture is particularly laborious, and in all the operations those engaged are almost constantly up to the middle in mud. Notwithstanding this, I have often seen the king working hard in a taro patch. I know not whether this was done with a view of setting an example of industry to his subjects. Such exertion could scarcely be thought necessary amongst these islanders who are certainly the most industrious people I ever saw."[1]

The Naha Stone is a huge boulder on the grounds of the public library in Hilo. According to legend, moving it was a test for chiefs who aspired to be king. Kamehameha, so it is related, accomplished the feat.

[1] Archibald Campbell, *A Voyage Around the World,* 4th American ed. (Roxbury, Mass.: Allen Watts, 1825), p. 162.

The Fur Trade

During Kamehameha's reign, trade with foreigners increased greatly. When Captain Cook's journals were published in 1784, the world learned of the wealth of China as well as that of the Pacific Northwest, which included what we know as Washington, Oregon, and British Columbia. British traders exploited the fur resources, using the furs to pay for tea and other goods purchased in China.

Up to 1791 nearly all of the ships arriving in Hawaii were those of British fur traders. The first person to engage in the fur trade was probably Captain James Hanna, who was sent to the northwest coast in 1785 by "some gentlemen of China." In the spring of 1786 two British vessels, commanded by captains Nathaniel Portlock and George Dixon, remained in the Islands some twenty days and traded nails and other articles of little value in exchange for water.

Soon after gaining independence, Americans began to engage in the Pacific fur trade. The earliest voyage to obtain furs to be sold in China was undertaken by captains Kendrick and Gray. In August, 1789, Captain Gray stopped at the island of Hawaii, where he purchased "five Punchions of Pork and . . . one hundred & fifty live hogs." Following the return of Captain Gray to Boston in 1790, American interest in the Pacific trade grew rapidly. Ten years later the Americans controlled the lion's share of the fur trade between the northwest coast and Canton.

There were two reasons for the increase in American trade with the Hawaiian Islands: the fur trade on the northwest coast of North America and the expansion of American commerce after the Revolutionary War. After the war the Americans were cut off from their normal markets in the British Empire and had little silver or goods to trade. They were anxious to obtain the tea, cotton cloth, and silk of China, but they needed to find goods that would interest the merchants at Canton in return. The Chinese were willing to pay well for furs, and this led the Americans to take part in the fur trade in competition with traders of several nations. Fortunately for the Americans, their European rivals became involved in the Napoleonic Wars and offered very little competition for a quarter of a century.

Soon after the fur trade began, ships began to stop at the Hawaiian Islands for "refreshments." The Islands became a popular stopping place for vessels in the fur trade for many reasons. First, provisions in the quantities needed for ships were not available along the West

Coast. Second, the men on the West Coast did not make good sailors, whereas the Hawaiians were excellent seamen. Third, scurvy plagued the early fur-trading ships, and fresh fruits and vegetables were necessary in the diet. Fourth, the Islands offered a convenient place to refit and repair ships. Fifth, after 1805, few ships were able to complete their trading in one summer because of the increasing scarcity of furs and sea otter skins. Sailors were more anxious to sign on a ship for the longer journeys if they knew the ship would winter in the Sandwich Islands.

In the early 1800's most of the vessels carrying furs that stopped in the Islands were American. Not only did the early traders obtain food, water, and firewood, but also salt for curing hides. In the early days of the fur trade the common people were eager to exchange their provisions for a few scraps of iron and nails. Before the Islands were united, the chiefs obtained arms and ammunition in exchange for their provisions. After the unification, cloth became the most important item of exchange. The natives quickly developed a reputation for skill in bargaining and steadily raised their prices. The Russian world-traveler, Lisianski, wrote that a small pig cost him an iron ax; for a suckling pig, he traded a piece of printed linen, three yards in length but cut in half. A hundred pounds of sweet potatoes could be purchased with three yards of linen, while a small knife was the price of a fowl.

Originally, the ships traveled around Cape Horn and into the Pacific, going either directly to the Islands or first to the Northwest. After a while the traders learned of high profits to be earned by carrying on smuggling operations with the Spanish settlements in California and Mexico. At times, they carried on a small but profitable trade in supplying the Russian outposts in Alaska and Kamchatka, taking furs in exchange. By 1812 they added sandalwood from the Hawaiian and Marquesas Islands to their cargoes of furs. After the Spanish colonies achieved their independence, the Yankee traders engaged in trade with all of Spain's former colonies on the Pacific coast.

The Sandalwood Trade

Just how Hawaiian sandalwood came to the attention of traders is not certain. Probably some sticks of sandalwood were included in a load of firewood furnished to an American vessel. It has been reported that sea captains, as early as 1790, sent men from their crews to search for sandalwood. So far as is known, only small amounts of sandalwood were exported for a number of years, but by 1805 it had become an important export item. The peak of the trade was reached in 1818, by which time it had become almost an American monopoly.

Sandalwood has been highly prized through the ages and in the Bible is referred to as the *almug* tree that Hiram brought back, together with the gold of Ophir and precious stones. In the Buddhist religion the incense used in their rituals is made from sandalwood. Because of its fragrance, sandalwood was used in making fans, small boxes, and other bric-a-brac. The small twigs and shavings were highly prized as an ingredient in salves, as sandalwood was thought to possess rare medical qualities.

Realizing its value, Kamehameha declared the sandalwood trade a royal monopoly. Whatever trading the chiefs did was in the name of the King. The King entered into the bargaining personally and became quite skillful at it. If he were unsure of a trade, he would not complete it until he had consulted one of his trusted advisers, such as John Young.

Travelers to the Islands reported that whole villages were deserted while the people were in the mountains cutting sandalwood. The Hawaiians owned few horses; therefore, the sandalwood was carried many miles by hard working natives. This enforced labor weakened the natives physically and left them without enough time to cultivate their fields. When the King learned of this condition, he ordered the chiefs and commoners not to spend all of their time cutting sandalwood. The King is reported to have placed a *kapu* on the young, small trees in order to conserve this natural resource.

Kamehameha was interested in building up a fleet of vessels, both for trade and for military purposes. In 1817 he added to his fleet by buying the ship *Columbia* and paying for it in sandalwood "twice the 'full' of the ship." Before his death, he had bought no less than six ships. Two months before his death, Kamehameha bought sixteen kegs of rum, a box of tea, and eight thousand dollars worth of guns and ammunition, paying for these supplies with sandalwood.

Toward the end of his reign, Kamehameha attempted to enter into the overseas sandalwood trade by outfitting a ship and sending it

76

Men, women, and children worked long hours gathering sandalwood and carrying the heavy loads of wood from the hills to the beach.

loaded with sandalwood to Canton. The sandalwood could not be sold at a profit and port charges added to the expense of the voyage. From this experience, Kamehameha learned that other nations were accustomed to charge visiting vessels for harbor, pilot, and port fees. He decided to adopt this practice for Honolulu harbor.

> Sandalwood was measured in *piculs*. A *picul* equals 133⅓ pounds. The price of sandalwood in China fluctuated, but ranged between $8.00 and $10.00 a picul. In 1821, the United States Agent for Commerce in the Hawaiian Kingdom noted that the sandalwood trade was worth $300,000 to Hawaii.

Although sandalwood was valued at from eight to ten dollars a *picul,* it was usually bartered for goods. In the early years of the trade, simple items such as bits of metal scraps and nails could be offered. By the 1820's, however, the Hawaiians began to desire different types of goods. They wanted such items as blankets, cotton, silks, turpentine, hardwood, muskets and powder, spirits, and rice. A few years later, goods manufactured in England were added to the list.

With the death of Kamehameha, all royal controls on the sandalwood trade, which had become the main source of the Islands' prosperity, were ended. Liholiho, who succeeded his father as Kamehameha II, allowed favorite chiefs to engage in the trade. The following years saw competing traders trying to persuade chiefs to sell sandalwood for goods for which they had little need. Many chiefs could not resist the urge to buy almost anything the traders offered.

The Yankee traders, too, were so anxious to sell their wares that they extended a great deal of credit to the chiefs. Since they could not always deliver the sandalwood immediately, the chiefs signed promissory notes to pay a certain number of piculs of the wood. Often the notes could not be collected. Also, if the traders pressed too hard for their payment, the chiefs would only buy less goods. The chiefs were also reluctant to pay when they found, for example, that ships purchased as sound vessels turned out to be rotten. Then, too, the supply of sandalwood became more scarce each year.

By 1829 the American traders were becoming impatient at the mounting debt and requested assistance from their government in collecting it. The United States sent warships to the Kingdom of Hawaii to investigate. The debt of the chiefs, which was determined to be 15,000 piculs of sandalwood, was finally paid in 1843.

Results of the Fur and Sandalwood Trade

The fur and sandalwood trade resulted in great changes in the lives of the Hawaiian people. Before the arrival of Captain Cook, the Hawaiians produced nearly everything they needed and only as much as they could use. The fur and sandalwood trade resulted in the introduction of new goods from Europe, the United States, and China. The Hawaiian economy was now one of trade and gain.

At first only the king and chiefs benefited very much from this trade. Even under the royal monopoly, the chiefs were allowed to keep four-tenths of the sandalwood they collected for private trading. As we have seen, the royal monopoly ended with the death of Kamehameha I.

Typical of the imported *haole* goods were American cottons, woolens, copper sheathing, nails, English saddles, Russian canvas, Guayaquil cocoa, flour, soap, rice, hemp, French wines, Manila cordage, Chinese cotton cloth ("Blue Nankings"), turpentine, crockery and glass, harness, iron pots and pans, papers, quills, and ink. Very little money was used up to 1825, most of the imports being bartered for provisions or sandalwood.

A list of goods received by King Kamehameha
in exchange for a shipload of sandalwood.

3 paintings on paper
1 box of Chinese wood
3 dozen ordinary cotton stockings
2 crystal lamps
1 bundle of metal pipes
6 boxes
1 bundle of blue stones and white
    for a gaming table
1000 large beads
10 boxes of silk handkerchiefs
6 shiny hats for soldiers
12 black straw hats
50 silk hats
6 reels of thread
50 Chinese cutlasses
3 pieces of flowered flannel
6 fishing rods
100 Chinese mats
135 lbs. large glass beads
1 iron hearth
1 saddle
3 pieces flowered satin
3 boxes of sweets
1 large cloak [2]

New foodstuffs were added to the native diet. By 1825 cabbage, potatoes, corn, limes, and pineapple appeared in the market of Honolulu. By this time ducks, turkeys, European varieties of chickens, pigs, and dogs were also introduced. In 1824 Captain Meek brought mango trees to Hawaii.

Another result of the fur and sandalwood trade was the settlement of foreigners in the Islands. Some worked for the kings and chiefs, performing such tasks as helping to build sloops and schooners for

[2] Letter of the British Consul, Richard Charlton, to the Hon. George Channing, June 1825. (Archives of Hawaii.)

interisland trade, transporting provisions, and gathering sandalwood. Other foreigners were businessmen, ranchers, or missionaries; but the majority of the foreign residents were drifters and stranded or runaway sailors.

The coming of foreigners was disastrous to native health. The common diseases of foreigners, such as measles, influenza, and common colds, to which the Hawaiians had no natural immunity, were fatal to large numbers. Also, excessive drinking, introduced by the foreigners, weakened the health of the natives. There was a constant struggle after the arrival of the missionaries between those who influenced the native habits and the missionaries who tried to protect the Hawaiians from the foreigners' vices.

The Cession of Kauai

Although storm and disease had broken up his first two attempts to conquer Kauai, Kamehameha did not give up his plans. In 1810 Kaumualii, the ruler of Kauai, realized that his army could not long resist the military force that was building up on Oahu and that it would be better to surrender. Through a friendly American trader named Captain Nathan Winship, he arranged to meet Kamehameha. Taking passage on Winship's vessel, he journeyed to Oahu. Kamehameha received him generously and honorably. In return for the surrender of the island, he was allowed to remain as its governor as long as he lived, after which it would go to the Kamehameha line.

An interesting sidelight to these events was a plot on the part of certain of Kamehameha's chiefs to poison the stubborn King of Kauai, who had held out against their lord for so many years. The *haole* chief, Isaac Davis, learned of the plot and persuaded Captain Winship to take Kaumualii back to Kauai on short notice. The grim sequel to this incident was that the chiefs, angry at Davis' interference, succeeded in causing his death by poison. Thus passed from the scene one of Kamehameha's most devoted servants.

The Russians Come to Hawaii

During the last years of Kamehameha's reign, foreign ships, mostly British and American, were familiar sights along the Honolulu waterfront. In 1804, and again in 1809, vessels flying the Russian flag made brief visits to the Islands.

Some years earlier, the Russian government had given a monopoly of the fur trade in the north Pacific to the Russian American Company. In 1812 the Russians founded a settlement at Fort Ross, on the California coast north of San Francisco. To supply this settlement, the governor of the Russian company, Alexander Baranoff, sent a ship to Hawaii in 1814 to pick up a cargo. After loading, the ship set sail in January of 1815 but was wrecked on the shore at Waimea, Kauai.

Baranoff then commissioned a German doctor named Georg Scheffer as agent to recover the cargo and possibly set up a permanent trading post in the Islands. Scheffer, who must have been a rather heavy-handed conspirator, paid his respects to Kamehameha on the Big Island and then proceeded to Kauai on a ship which Baranoff had sent to him. Here he wormed his way into Kaumualii's confidence, and in the spring of 1816 started trading operations. Apparently he also succeeded in involving Kaumualii in a treasonable agreement to make the island a protectorate of the Russian czar.

Scheffer then returned to Honolulu. With a force from three Russian vessels anchored in the harbor he built a blockhouse, mounted guns and hoisted the Russian flag. This daring action was reported to

Russian fur traders, in an attempt to establish their influence in the islands, built a fort at the foot of what is now the Fort Street Mall. Aloha Tower stands on the site of the fort, which was torn down in the 1860s.

Kamehameha, who sent word to his chiefs on Oahu to oppose the invaders. Faced with superior force, the Russians retired to Kauai. Kamehameha promptly ordered John Young to build a strong fort which included the Russian blockhouse. Young mounted sixty guns on it and placed others on the slopes of Punchbowl Hill overlooking the little town. Fort Street in today's downtown Honolulu takes its name from this incident.

By this time the American traders had convinced Kaumualii that this Russian influence was dangerous. When orders came from Kamehameha to expel Scheffer, Kaumualii agreed to follow them. Scheffer left suddenly for Canton and finally reached St. Petersburg.

Thus Baranoff's scheme ended in failure. He had not acted under orders of the Russian government, for when the imperial navy ship *Rurick* visited the Islands late in 1816, its commanding officer, Lieutenant Otto von Kotzebue, showed his approval of Kamehameha's action in expelling Scheffer and stated that his government had only the friendliest feeling for Hawaii.

The Last Days of Kamehameha

In 1811 Kamehameha set forth on a tour of his kingdom on his schooner *Keoua,* with Hawaii as his first port of call. Enroute to the Big Island, however, the *Keoua* sprang a leak and had to return to Honolulu. From here Captain Winship gave the King passage on his ship to Kealakekua Bay, where Kamehameha stayed for a short time. He then visited Maui and Molokai, where he organized the system of collecting taxes and inspired his subjects to improve their farming methods. In this period of his life he was made happy when Queen Keopuolani bore him another son. This was Kauikeaouli, who was later to succeed Liholiho, with the title of Kamehameha III.

During the last seven years of his life, Kamehameha spent most of his time in the beautiful settlement at Kailua on the Kona coast of the Big Island. Here he died on May 8, 1819.

Although by uniting the Islands and bringing them peace, he prepared the way for civilization and Christianity, he had no knowledge of Christian doctrine or contact with Christian missionaries. Had he lived one more year, he would have met the first company of missionaries from New England. We can only guess how he would have received them. It is not likely that he would have welcomed their efforts to destroy the old ways. To the very last he held firmly to the

82

old *kapus* and the worship of the Hawaiian gods. As late as 1818 he ordered the execution of three men for minor violations of the *kapus*. Yet, when the priests surrounding the dying King proposed that human sacrifices be made to speed his recovery, he forbade it.

The funeral rites were conducted according to the ancient customs already described. The most important part of the ceremony was the disposal of the dead King's bones. This act was called *hunakele,* which means "to hide in secret." The friend chosen to ensure that Kamehameha's remains would never be touched was chief Hoapili, according to one account, or Hoolulu, according to another. To this day no one knows where the bones were deposited. There is a story that years later Kamehameha III, on a visit to Kailua, persuaded Hoolulu to show him the spot. They began their journey to the hills together, but when Hoolulu saw that they were being followed, he turned back. It is just as well. Today, "only the stars of the heavens know the resting place of Kamehameha."

Summing Up the Chapter

When Kamehameha's attempt to conquer Kauai, the last of the major islands, failed, he devoted himself to organizing and ruling the rest of his island kingdom. He used the *kapu* system to strengthen his authority. The first traders to come to the Islands were the British. They were soon followed by the Americans. The Islands were used as a place to refit and repair ships, to stock provisions, and to stop over during the winter months. Soon the Hawaiians too entered into trade, exchanging provisions and sandalwood for iron, nails, tools, and cloth. As the demand for sandalwood grew, they began to import useful and luxury articles from all over the world. Until the death of Kamehameha I, the sandalwood trade was a royal monopoly. The trade and the coming of foreigners greatly influenced the lives, health, and habits of the Islanders. Kauai finally came under Kamehameha's rule when the king of that island surrendered it in 1810. A plot against Kamehameha by the governor of a Russian trading company was put down. When Kamehameha I died in 1819, he had succeeded in uniting the Hawaiian Islands and bringing them peace and progress, thus unknowingly preparing the way for the introduction of Christianity..

1815-16 Russians try to seize Kauai; erect fort at Waimea

1815 Napoleon defeated at Waterloo

1819 Kamehameha I dies
End of the Kapu system; abolished by Kamehameha II

1820 Arrival of the first missionaries from New England

1820 Missouri Compromise

1821 First Christian Church dedicated

1822 First printed material in the Hawaiian language

1822 Mexico and Brazil become independent

1823 Monroe Doctrine

1824 Kaumualii, king of Kauai, dies
Kamehameha II & Queen Kamamalu arrive in London
Death of Liholiho & Kamamalu

1825 Queen Kaahumanu rules for minor Kauikeaouli as *kuhina nui* until 1832

1825 John Quincy Adams is inaugurated 6th U.S. president

Whaling takes the place of sandlewood trading

8

The Christian Pioneers

According to the will of Kamehameha, his son Liholiho became the new King, Kamehameha II. The war-god was placed in the care of his nephew, the powerful Kekuaokalani. On the whole Liholiho was a reckless and intemperate man with few of the statesmanlike qualities of his father. Knowing this, Kamehameha had appointed his favorite wife, Kaahumanu, as *kuhina nui,* a new office much like that of a prime minister. The proud queen was now in a position to exercise as much power as Liholiho.

The End of the Kapu System

For some years there had been a slow weakening of belief in the *kapu* system. Even the high priest, Hewahewa, came to agree with Kaahumanu and the queen-mother, Keopuolani, that the cruel old gods should be toppled, the *heiaus* burned, and the *kapus* abolished.

At this point events began to move rapidly. On the morning of Kamehameha's death, the chiefs present advised Kaahumanu to do away with the *kapus,* but she decided that it was too soon to act. About two weeks later Liholiho was crowned at a great ceremony in Kailua. At the end of the ceremony, Kaahumanu proposed that the *kapus* be overthrown. The young King, who had been carefully trained in the old religion, refused to give his consent. Shortly thereafter, however, Keopuolani and her younger son, Kauikeaouli, deliberately ate together in violation of the *kapu*. The King did not object to this but could not yet bring himself to break the rule.

Now another event of religious importance occurred. In August, 1819, the French ship *Uranie,* commanded by Captain Louis de Freycinet, dropped anchor at Kailua. Kuakini, the governor, received Freycinet hospitably. The Frenchman pleased his hosts by declaring that he would help Liholiho maintain law and order in his restless kingdom. Thereupon Kalanimoku, the King's adviser, asked to be baptized in the foreigner's religion. Freycinet was delighted and ordered the ship's chaplain to perform the ceremony on the deck of the *Uranie.* A few weeks later, when the *Uranie* had reached Oahu, the governor of that island, Boki, who was the younger brother of Kalanimoku, also asked to receive the sacrament of baptism. It is highly improbable that the two chiefs had much understanding of the ceremony, but quite clearly the old ways were changing!

Now the two queens, Kaahumanu and Keopuolani, renewed their pressure on Liholiho. After giving the matter much thought, he journeyed with his court to Kailua, where he found that a great feast had been prepared. Liholiho sat down with a large mixed company and

Queen Elizabeth Kaahumanu, (1772-1832) favorite wife of Kamehameha the Great, appointed by him to be the *kuhina nui* to King Kamehameha II.

openly feasted with members of both sexes.

When the people saw that no great punishment followed his act, they rejoiced that the *kapus* were ended. Quickly the news spread throughout the islands. Everywhere the idols and *heiaus* were burned, with the high priest himself leading the destruction. This was in November of 1819.

The *kapus* did not die easily, however. Doubtless some Hawaiians kept their idols, and some chiefs were fearful and horrified because of the sacrilege. Among these was the brave young chief Kekuaokalani. In December he went to Kaawaloa, where a crowd of priests, chiefs and commoners rallied to his support and offered him the crown if it could be taken from Liholiho.

Kaahumanu, Kalanimoku, and the royal party were at Kailua. They were worried by this revolt and decided to try to settle it peaceably, if possible, or by force, if necessary. Luckily they were well supplied with arms, having bought a shipment of muskets and ammunition from an American trader some months before. Efforts to avoid fighting failed. As in so many sad cases before this time, brave Hawaiians, including Kekuaokalani and his wife, died in useless battle. All of those who survived were finally pardoned by Liholiho.

Soon after this battle the King sent one of his chiefs to put down a revolt of the people of Hamakua. The revolt was quickly ended, and the ancient gods of the Hawaiians were no more. But little did the Hawaiians know that even as they fought this last battle, the servants of a new God, the God of the Christians, were sailing around Cape Horn on their way to the "Sandwich Islands."

The Story of Opukahaia

One of the most touching stories in Hawaiian history is that of a lad named Opukahaia. In 1808 this sixteen-year-old boy swam out to an American ship anchored in Kealakekua Bay and begged the master, Captain Brintnall of New Haven, Connecticut, to take him to America. He had been orphaned in one of the tribal wars. Terrified by this experience, he had resolved to seek a new home in a foreign land.

Although Brintnall already had one Hawaiian cabin boy, he agreed to take Opukahaia (also known as Obookiah) with him on his return trip to New York, by way of China. Pleased by Opukahaia's progress in learning English, Brintnall installed the boy in his home in New

Henry Opukaha'ia

Haven. It is recorded that Opukahaia was found one evening on the campus of Yale College weeping. On being asked why he wept, he replied that "nobody gave him learning."

Several of the students undertook to teach him, and a Yale professor took him into his home. Here he learned the basic beliefs of Christianity and was received into the faith. His earnest desire to carry the Gospel to his native Hawaii interested the American Board of Commissioners for Foreign Missions, a Boston interdenominational group made up chiefly of Congregationalists and Presbyterians. The Board decided to found a missionary school at Cornwall, Connecticut, for the "education of heathen youth." Opukahaia and several other Hawaiian youths then in New England entered this school.

Opukahaia never achieved his dream of returning to Hawaii. In February of 1818 he contracted typhus fever and died. He is buried in West Cornwall, and it is said that even today fresh flowers are often found on the tablet over his grave.

The Board, although they had lost a promising missionary, held to their great project of saving the souls of the Sandwich Islanders. On a tablet at Napoopoo, near the rock from which Opukahaia leaped into the sea, is this inscription:

"In memory of Henry Opukahaia. Born in Kau, 1792. Resided in Napoopoo 1797-1808. Lived in New England until his death in Cornwall, Conn., in 1818. His zeal for Christ and love for his people inspired the first American Board Mission to Hawaii in 1820."

The Arrival of the Missionaries

In October of 1819 the Board organized the first company of missionaries to the Hawaiian Islands. On the twenty-third of October they sailed from Boston in the 240-ton brig *Thaddeus* on a painful and exhausting 160-day voyage around Cape Horn. By mid-century, eleven other companies were to follow them and each would make its own special contribution. The trials and labors of the first company, however, are of greatest interest to us today.[1]

The seventeen members were led by two ordained ministers, the Reverend Hiram Bingham and the Reverend Asa Thurston. There were two teachers, Samuel Whitney and Samuel Ruggles; a physician, Dr. Thomas Holman; a farmer, Daniel Chamberlain; and a printer, Elisha Loomis. With these seven men were their wives, who were expected to aid in the great work of teaching. Three young Hawaiians were on the company's roster—William Kanui, John Honolii, and Thomas Hopu. Also among the passengers were the five Chamberlain children and George Kaumualii, a son of the King of Kauai, who had been placed in the care of a sea captain at the age of six and taken to Boston to receive an education.

The missionaries, who differed in talents and temperaments, had been given a difficult assignment. They were instructed to set their mark high; to cover the islands with fruitful fields, dwellings, schools, and churches; to learn the language of the people; to teach them to read the Bible. Above all, the missionaries were to lead the Hawaiians away from their superstitions and worship of idols.

---

[1] The members of the twelve companies, together with the missionaries who arrived individually, are listed in alphabetical order in Bradford Smith's *Yankees in Paradise*.

89

This copy of a drawing in "From a Narrative of the U.S. Exploring Expedition During the Years 1838-1842" by Charles Wilkes, USN shows a missionary preaching under the shade of a *kukui* tree.

On March 30, 1820, the *Thaddeus* anchored at Kawaihae on the Big Island. Messengers were sent ashore to find out what had been happening. They returned with the news that Kamehameha was dead and that Liholiho had abolished the *kapus*. The missionaries interpreted this report as proof that God had blessed their plans, and they sang the hymn, "Wake, isles of the South! Your redemption is near . . ."

Learning that the King and chiefs were at Kailua, Captain Blanchard sailed there. After being received by Prime Minister Kalanimoku, Bingham and Thurston called on Kuakini, the governor, and John Young, the King's *haole* adviser. They then gained an audience with Liholiho, presented gifts, and asked for permission to stay in the Islands.

For several days the King withheld his decision while he talked with his chiefs. On April 6 Bingham invited him and his queens to dine on the *Thaddeus,* an experience which the royal party enjoyed thoroughly. The next day some of the ladies in the missionary party went ashore with the men. The Hawaiians had often seen *haole* men and their children by native women, but the sight of *haole* women was new to them. Samuel Kamakau describes the excitement as the party came ashore and walked along the beach:

". . . the people came in crowds, men, women, and children, and exclaimed over the pretty faces of the white women, their deepset eyes, their bonnets that jutted forward, their long necks which won for them the name 'Long neck' (*'A'ioeoe*). Crowds gathered, and one and another exclaimed, 'How white the women are!' . . . 'What long necks! but pleasing to look at!' 'What pinched-in bodies! What tight clothing above and wide below.' "[2]

On the next day Bingham again pressed the King for a decision. "Let us proceed to Honolulu," he said. "It is not wise for all of us to remain here in Kailua. Some of us should proceed to Oahu, where our work can bear great fruit and where we can be self-supporting."

John Young and the dowager queen supported the missionaries in their request for permission to stay. Among their opponents were some of the chiefs and a scheming *haole* drinking companion of the King, a Frenchman named Jean B. Rives, who had somehow gained a strong influence over Liholiho. It is probable that the shrewd Rives foresaw that the presence of the determined men of God would loosen his hold on the young, pleasure-loving King. He argued that the missionaries were dangerous, that they would try to seize the government, and that in any case their religion was not true Christianity. Later on in Honolulu, other foreigners, traders, and whalers, would try to arouse the chiefs by charging that when the missionaries dug cellars under their houses they intended to store powder there in preparation for an armed uprising.

Finally the King made his decision. "You may go to Honolulu, where quarters will be provided. But the doctor and one of the ministers must remain here. You shall not send for more missionaries, and you may stay here only one year."

[2] Samuel M. Kamakau, *Ruling Chiefs of Hawaii* (Honolulu: Kamehameha School Press, 1961), p. 247.

Encouraged by this decision, the missionaries made their plans. The first necessity was to determine which missionary should remain at Kailua. In good old town-meeting style, the question was decided by voting, and Thurston was chosen. On April 12 the trunks and boxes of the Holmans and the Thurstons were brought ashore, as well as the baggage of the two Hawaiian youths, William Kanui and Thomas Hopu, who were to stay. With typical Yankee vigor, the new arrivals began to set up housekeeping. An entry in Lucy Thurston's simple journal describes their first evening in their new home:

"At evening twilight we sundered ourselves from close family ties, from the dear old brig, and from civilization. We went ashore and entered, as our home, an abode of the most uncouth and humble character. It was a thatched hut, with one room, having two windows made simply by cutting away the thatch leaving the bare poles. On the ground for the feet was first a layer of grass, then of mats. Here we found our effects from the *Thaddeus;* but no arrangement of them could be made till the house was thoroughly cleaned.

"On the boxes and trunks, as they were scattered about the room, we formed a circle. We listened to a portion of scripture, sang a hymn, and knelt in prayer. The simple natural fact speaks for itself. It was the first family altar ever reared on this group of islands to the worship of Jehovah."

About a week later the remainder of the party landed at Honolulu. Here they were courteously received by Governor Boki and by a number of Caucasian residents, who gave them temporary shelter until houses could be built for them. Toward the end of April, the *Thaddeus* sailed for Kauai, bearing Whitney and Ruggles, who, with their wives, were to establish the first mission station on that island. Also on board was George Kaumualii, eagerly looking forward to a reunion with his royal father.

In August Kalanimoku requested that a teacher be sent to Hawaii. Elisha Loomis, whose wife the month before had given birth to the first *haole* child born in the Islands, was chosen to go. On his way he stopped at Maui to confer with the Holmans, who had moved to Lahaina without waiting for permission from the Mission. Shortly

Early missionaries watch the construction of one of the first Christian churches. Stones from an old *heiau* were used for the foundation. Thatched with *pandanus* leaves, the finished building was 30 feet wide and 60 feet long.

thereafter the Holmans were recalled to Oahu. Since the doctor's relations with Hiram Bingham had become strained, they moved on to Kauai. Now only Bingham and Chamberlain were left in Honolulu. Before the end of the year, however, Loomis and the Thurstons were able to join them. The King was making plans to reside in Honolulu, and it seemed best for the missionaries to concentrate their energies in the vicinity of the court.

The story of their labors is an inspiring one, but space is lacking to tell it in detail.[3] When their first year of probation had ended, they succeeded in persuading the King, who had moved to Honolulu by this time, to allow them to stay permanently. The work of building houses, conducting religious services, and establishing schools went on at a rapid pace. In August, 1821, they dedicated the first Christian church, which was located where Kawaiahao Church, "the Westminster Abbey of Hawaii," now stands.

[3] For further details see *The Hawaiian Kingdom, 1778-1854,* by the distinguished historian of Hawaii, Ralph S. Kuykendall, and *Yankees in Paradise,* a sparkling narrative by Bradford Smith.

93

Summing Up the Chapter

Largely through the influence of two of the wives of Kamehameha I, the new King Liholiho soon abolished the *kapu* system. Unfortunately the system did not die peacefully. The American Board of Commissioners for Foreign Missions, located in New England, became interested through the efforts of a Hawaiian boy, Opukahaia, in sending missionaries to the "Sandwich Islands." The first missionaries arrived in 1820 and after a time were given limited permission to stay in the Islands. Little by little, they won the favor of the King and many of the chiefs. Their services became so important that they were given permission to stay permanently.

We can summarize the work of the missionaries by saying that they helped to fill a moral and spiritual vacuum that resulted from the breakdown of the ancient pagan faith. They helped to undo some of the evils brought into the Islands by earlier groups of Europeans and Americans. In many ways the missionaries were too narrow and rigid in their ideas, but by their zeal they won the confidence of kings and chiefs and left an indelible mark on Hawaiian history.

9

In the Days of Liholiho

All through the Hawaiian Islands in 1819 the people felt the spirit of change. Old customs and old beliefs were being challenged as the *haole* tide rolled across the Pacific. With the *kapus* gone, a new religion was trying earnestly to meet the spiritual needs of the Hawaiian people. The short reign of Liholiho as Kamehameha II was a confused and uncertain period. During his reign, and even more so in the reign of Kamehameha III, a technically advanced foreign civilization was moving in on the simple and defenseless Hawaiian way of life.

Decline in Population and Health

When Kamehameha I was alive, he controlled the sandalwood trade and tried to conserve the supply of trees. Liholiho, by opening the sale of sandalwood to his chiefs, caused the common people to be driven almost beyond endurance to cut and transport the valuable wood for the chiefs. In the United States, the Panic of 1819 had cut off the money supply needed for trading in China, so the merchants began to flood the open Hawaiian market with all sorts of goods that might tempt the chiefs. In order to pay for these new luxuries, the chiefs forced their people into the hills in search of sandalwood. The health of the people was often ruined and their farms were left untended. This decreased the food supply and caused much suffering.

95

Another blow to native health was the introduction of foreigners' diseases. The high death rate in the reigns of Kamehameha II and III is described vividly by Kamakau:

"Then too the foreign ships which arrived at Oahu during Kamehameha's occupation of that island brought in many diseases, especially the severe pestilence of 1804 when so many chiefs and commoners perished . . . In 1831 the school teachers began to take the census. Although it was not complete, they reported a little under 200,000. It is therefore evident that the population declined after the arrival of the missionaries even though all wars ceased, and robbery and murder were wiped out. . . . In 1826 thousands died, especially in the country districts, of an epidemic of 'coughs, congested lungs, and sore throat.' . . . In February, 1839, a ship arrived from Valparaiso whose Captain, Henry Peck, had died at sea. This ship brought a pestilence from which many died, Kinau among others. In September, 1848, an American warship brought the disease known as measles to Hilo, Hawaii. It spread and carried away about a third of the population . . . Again in March and April of 1853 smallpox was discovered by Dr. Potter at Kahakaaulana, and it broke out in Honolulu the following May. It was first seen in the house of Kaaione in Kakaako. Its first victim was a woman with a tattooed face (makapaele), and the disease raged on Oahu but did not extend to the other islands . . . Leprosy is another disease brought to this country and still prevalent. From all these diseases the native population of these islands has suffered decrease."[1]

Kamakau, who died in 1876, was able to learn at first hand about the disastrous effects of the foreigners' civilization. He also points to certain harmful Hawaiian customs which existed both before and after the arrival of the foreigners. One was infanticide, or the deliberate killing of unwanted babies. Another was the inhuman slaughter of women and children during the wars and feuds of the chiefs. Heavy drinking was another harmful habit which the Hawaiians learned from the traders and whalers who poured into the Islands. By 1822 at least

[1] Kamakau, op. cit., Chap. XIX.

King Kamehameha II, (1797-1824) Liholiho, son of Kamehameha The Great and Keopuolani, the daughter of Kiwalao. Liholiho reigned from 1819 - 1824.

two distilleries had been set up, and the Hawaiians learned to make liquor from fermented sugar cane juice, sweet potatoes, or *ti* root.

The Death of Kaumualii

One of the most attractive figures in Hawaiian history is Kaumualii, King of Kauai. He was a handsome man, light in complexion, rather slightly built, with an erect carriage. He "was gentle in temper, spoke English well, was kind and simple in his ways." Kamehameha, we recall, had allowed him to remain as King of Kauai at the time of its surrender.

In July, 1821, Liholiho determined to test the loyalty of Kaumualii. He set sail for Kauai in a small, overloaded boat, accompanied by Boki, governor of Oahu, and a few members of the royal court. On Kauai he was welcomed by the people with the firing of guns and ringing of bells. Kaumualii "stepped down from his place as ruler to act as steward for the King, preparing his food and attending to his wants in every way."

Seeing that he had no choice, Kaumualii placed his lands, his armed forces, and his vessels at the disposal of Liholiho. In a generous gesture the King stated that Kaumualii might stay in peaceful possession of the island as a tributary ruler. A few weeks later, however, after Liholiho had thoroughly tested Kauai hospitality and was about to leave for Oahu, he persuaded Kaumualii to board his ship under false pretenses and took him as an unwilling prisoner to Honolulu.

Here the dowager queen, Kaahumanu, in the informal manner of those days, took the attractive Kaumualii as her husband. He lived with the *kuhina nui* until his death in 1824. His body was taken to Lahaina, Maui, for burial as he had requested. His lands on Kauai were redivided, and a high-ranking chief named Kaikioewa was sent to govern the island. Thus ended the independent kingdom of Kauai.

Liholiho's Journey to London

In May, 1823, William Richards and Charles Stewart, two newly arrived clergymen, were ordered by the mission to set up a station on Maui. Keopuolani, the King's mother and the highest-ranking chiefess in the Islands, had by this time become impressed by the work of the missionaries. She left with the newcomers.

In August a new church was ready for dedication. Liholiho, Hiram Bingham, and all the great chiefs were present for the ceremony. Soon afterwards Keopuolani fell ill. There seemed to be no hope of recovery, despite the efforts of Dr. Abraham Blatchely, a recently arrived physician. In September, after being baptized in the Christian faith, the queen mother died.

After her burial, Liholiho spoke to his chiefs at Lahaina of a project that he had been considering for some time—a visit to England. Passage could be obtained in the British whaler *L'Aigle,* Captain Valentine Starbuck commanding. Although not all of his councilors favored the expedition, arrangements were finally made, and the King and his party sailed from Honolulu late in November, 1823.

"Chiefs, hear me," said Liholiho. "I shall sail to a foreign land and if I do not return, my younger brother Kauikeaouli shall be your king." Since the prince was only nine years old, Queen Kaahumanu was named as regent, in supreme authority, and Kalanimoku continued as prime minister.

Why did Liholiho wish to take this voyage? Historians do not agree on the reasons. Probably the King wished to satisfy his curiosity about the foreigners' world. Also he may have wished to declare again Hawaii's friendship for England as once expressed by his father and to ask the help of George IV in the event of an enemy attack. Among

King Kamehameha II; Queen Kamamalu; Liliha, the wife of Governor Boki; and Governor Boki, watch a play at the Drury Lane theater during their trip to London in 1824. Their attendants stand in the background.

those accompanying Liholiho on the voyage were his favorite wife, Kamamalu; Governor Boki of Oahu and his wife, Liliha; James Young Kaneloa, a son of John Young, who served as interpreter; and the ever-present Rives.

L'Aigle arrived at Portsmouth in May, and the royal couple and their party were given quarters at the fashionable Caledonian Hotel. Later they were entertained by Foreign Secretary George Canning and other London notables, and plans were made to introduce them to King George. The Hawaiians were delighted with the great city and aroused much comment wherever they went.

On May 31 they had seats in the royal box at Covent Garden Theater for a performance of "Pizarro." It is said that the young queen was greatly affected by the play and wept at some of the scenes. Several days later they witnessed Mr. Macready in "Rob Roy" at Drury Lane, and at another time watched a balloon ascent at White Conduit Gardens.

The Death of Liholiho and Kamamalu

Late in June it was announced that the Hawaiian monarchs would be introduced to King George. Before this could happen, however, the couple were stricken with the measles. The others in the party fell ill too but managed to recover. Kamamalu, weakened by inflammation of the lungs, passed away on the eighth of July. An attending physician, who issued an official statement of the death, spoke of the King's firmness of mind in the face of his great sorrow. But the effects of his illness and the shock of his loss were too much for Liholiho to bear, and within a week he too was dead.

Many years later a Honolulu merchant, Theophilus H. Davies, at the request of the then Princess Liliuokalani, inquired into the circumstances of the death. His letter to the princess, dated July 26, 1889, tells a pathetic story:

"On Saturday, July 7th, the remains lay in State in a large apartment on the ground floor of the hotel, the central part of the room was divided from the rest by a frame-work 14 feet square, open on three sides, the floor being covered with small feather cloaks. Around the frame-work were placed very large cloaks, and a number of capes and helmets. The large royal cloak was at the head of the coffin.

100

"On Sunday, July 18th, at 5 o'clock, a hearse and six horses conveyed the coffin to St. Martin's Church, and it was deposited beside the coffin of the Queen.

"On Sept. 1st, at one in the morning, it was reported that three men attempted to break into the church to steal the King's body, for which it was said 200 pounds had been offered, but every avenue to the church was strictly guarded and the men made off. On Tuesday night, 7th, at 10 o'clock, two hearses, followed by two mourning coaches with the suite, conveyed the remains from St. Martin's Church to the London Dock, where they were embarked on board the Frigate 'Blonde' for conveyance to Honolulu.

"On the following Saturday, Sept. 12th, King George IV received the suite at Windsor Castle, and on Wednesday, Sept. 30th, the 'Blonde,' sailed for Honolulu."[2]

The ship was commanded by George Anson, Lord Byron, a cousin of the great poet. News of the King's death had been brought to Honolulu two months before the *Blonde* arrived, and memorial services had been held in the Christian churches. After stopping at Lahaina, the ship proceeded to Honolulu, where, on May 11, 1825, the bodies were brought ashore. Impressive funeral services were held, attended by a company of marines from the *Blonde* and by Richard Charlton, a sea captain familiar with the Pacific area, who had been appointed as British consul for Hawaii.

A significant aftermath of the King's death and burial was the growing importance of the missionaries and the Congregational Church. By the end of the year the church, even though opposed by the foreign traders, had succeeded in enrolling most of the important Hawaiian chiefs, including Kaahumanu, Kalanimoku ("Billy Pitt"), and several of the wives of the first two Kamehamehas. Indeed, there was a new spirit in the land!

Summing Up the Chapter

Hawaii's population and health declined under the influence of the unlimited sandalwood trade, the introduction of the foreigners' dis-

---

[2] Copy of letter presented by Mr. Davies to the Hawaiian Historical Society.

eases, and the habit of heavy drinking. The last King of Kauai, Kaumualii, was taken as an unwilling prisoner to Oahu, where he ended his days as the husband of Kaahumanu. In 1823-24 Liholiho and his favorite wife, together with a few of his loyal supporters, paid a visit to London. What began as a triumph ended in tragedy when the royal couple contracted measles and died within a few days of each other.

10

Whalers and Traders

In the spring of 1825 the young Kauikeaouli became the new king of Hawaii. The real ruler, however, was the regent Kaahumanu, who was ably assisted by Kalanimoku. She tried to deal with the disorder that arose as more and more *haoles* found their way to the Islands. One of her first tasks was to enforce order in the two chief whaling ports of Honolulu and Lahaina.

Whaling now took the place of the sandalwood trade as the chief source of income. After 1819 most of the whaling ships were American on their way to the new rich sperm whale grounds off the coast of Japan. They usually arrived in the Islands in March or April and left for Japan in May. Then in September they would return to Hawaii to have their vessels overhauled.

The number of whalers anchored in Hawaiian ports increased rapidly. In 1830 there were 157 arrivals, and by 1844 the number had tripled.

The Effect of Whaling on the Hawaiian Economy

The whaling trade was a dangerous and uncertain one, depending upon luck and upon the changing prices for sperm oil. But there was no doubt that it had a great effect on the life of the Islands.

As one whaler after another anchored at Honolulu and Lahaina during the spring and fall seasons, activity in the ports increased. The

1825 Queen Kaahumanu rules for minor Kauikeaouli as *kuhina nui* until 1832

Whaling takes the place of sandlewood trading

1826 C. Brewer & Co. founded

1825 John Quincy Adams inaugurated 6th U.S. president

1829 Andrew Jackson inaugurated 7th U.S. president

1830 First covered wagons cross Missouri River to Rocky Mountains
July Revolution in France

1831 Lahainaluna School built

1831 Nat Turner's Revolt

1832 Kaahumanu dies, Kinau succeeds as *Kuhina nui*

1833 Kauikeaouli ascends throne as Kamehameha III

1835 First successful sugar plantation started on Kauai

1836 First issue of *Sandwich Island Gazette*
Hilo Boarding School opened

1836 Siege of the Alamo

1837 Panic of 1837

1839 Introduction of the Declaration of Rights
Chief's Children's School opened

1839 Martin Van Buren becomes 8th U.S. president
Opium War

1840 First constitution is proclaimed

Beginning of 20 year boom period of Hawaiian whaling

King Kamehameha III, (1814-1854) Kauikeaouli, son of King Kamehameha the Great and Queen Keopuolani. Kauikeaouli reigned from 1825 - 1854.

ships needed new provisions. Blacksmiths and carpenters were kept busy repairing the damage and wear on hulls and deck gear after long months at sea. And like sailors everywhere, the crews swarmed ashore seeking amusement.

The visiting seamen had a bad influence on the native social order, not only because of the diseases they spread but because their behavior set a poor example for the Hawaiians. From the reports of British and American consular agents and the journals of missionaries, we know that the seamen often reacted violently when attempts were made to enforce law and order where they were concerned. Sailors who knowingly spread contagious disease ashore were punished. There were fines for carrying dangerous weapons, breaking the Sabbath, drunkenness, fighting, and other unlawful forms of conduct. Desertions, either because of the hard life aboard ship or because of the charms of Hawaiian weather and people, were very common.

Many a wild tale can be told about the deeds of sailors who roamed around the seaports of Oahu and Maui. "There is no God west of the Horn!" they exclaimed, and their actions showed that they believed this. One of the best-known stories tells of the sailors' riot in Honolulu

From 1840 to 1860 many ships stopped at the port of Lahaina on Maui. Lawbreaking sailors from the ships were imprisoned in this old jail.

in 1852. A rowdy sailor named Burns was seized by the constables and locked with some of his mates in a cell in the fort. Here he went berserk and created such a disturbance that the constable hit him on the head with a club in order to quiet him. Unfortunately he hit the sailor too hard, and Burns died a few hours afterwards.

The next day a group of sailors appeared at the fort, demanding that the constable be punished. When their demand was refused, they waited until after Burns' funeral the next day. Then they poured into the streets, armed with knives and clubs. Descending upon the police station, they put the police to flight, wrecked the furniture, and finally set fire to the station. Fanned by the wind, the flames spread to two nearby buildings and destroyed them. For a short time there was danger that the fire would spread to the oil-laden whaleships anchored in a solid mass in the harbor. All that day and evening the mob terrorized the town.

The next day, because of the danger to the fleet, the ships' officers joined with police and civilians to put down the riot. Under Governor Kekuanaoa's orders, the natives, with the backing of armed police, succeeded in clearing the streets and the great riot ended.

Aside from its evil effects, the whaling trade brought other developments to the Islands. For one thing, the production of cattle and salt increased. The cattle that Vancouver had brought to the Islands had multiplied into large herds in the mountains and inland plains. Ambitious *haoles* bought or leased from the king and the chiefs the right to shoot them. The meat was salted and sold in great quantities to the ship owners. In the 1830's a man from Massachusetts, John Parker, started one of the world's great cattle-raising centers, the Parker Ranch on the Big Island. At first the salt was gathered in small amounts in tidal pools, but later it was dug from the bottom of Moanalua (Salt) Lake near Honolulu and ground in a mill powered by the wind.

Agricultural production was also encouraged. The Irish potato was introduced by 1830 and grown in great quantities in the Kula district of Maui. Also in demand were coffee, pumpkins, cabbages, breadfruit, taro, bananas, arrowroot, melons, pineapples, and firewood.

Another side-effect was the increasing use of young native Hawaiians as crewmen on the whalers. Thus they became better acquainted with the ways of foreigners and with foreign ports. The enlistment of Hawaiians was caused partly by the frequent desertions

107

Aboard the whalers the sliced blubber is boiled in the tryworks (kettles set in a brick furnace) to extract the oil from it.

of seamen, especially in slack seasons. So many natives were being enlisted from the Islands that a law passed in 1859 provided that no native could be shipped without permission of the governor of an island under penalty of a $500 fine.

The whaling trade increased the importance of seaport cities. As whales became scarcer and more difficult to catch, vessels were forced to make longer voyages away from home and had to depend upon Hawaii for refitting and provisioning. All of this brought profit to island merchants.

The Decline of Whaling

The boom period of Hawaiian whaling lasted from 1840 to 1860. By 1840 new fishing grounds in the Kodiak area (near Alaska) were being exploited, and in 1848 the grounds in the Arctic Ocean north of Bering Strait were discovered. Although there was a slack period at the time of the California gold rush, prices of sperm oil, whale oil, and bone remained high until the Civil War.

The war had a disastrous effect. The whaling fleet was seriously damaged by privateers like the *Alabama* and the *Shenandoah,* which reportedly sank about fifty ships. As the war went on, competition from petroleum caused whale oil prices to drop. Perhaps the most important reason for the decay of the industry was that while the cost of the voyages was increasing, the herds of whales were on the decrease.

The whaling industry suffered a final destructive blow in 1871. Thirty-three out of forty whaleships that had entered the Arctic Ocean in the spring of that year were caught in the ice and destroyed. Only one of the seven Hawaiian whalers sailing under the Hawaiian flag escaped. On October 28, 1871, the *Pacific Commercial Advertiser* carried a vivid and detailed account of the disaster. In addition to the loss of the cargoes, there was a huge loss to Honolulu merchants and ship chandlers who had expected to provision and equip the original forty ships.

During the 1860's, as the number of whaling vessels decreased, business slackened in the Hawaiian Islands. Efforts to find new sources of income led to experiments in increasing the production of silk, cotton, rice, sugar, and coffee. Only the last two continued as important items in the local economy.

The Growth of Trading

Throughout the long reign of Kamehameha III (1825-1854) Hawaii steadily grew more important as a center for transpacific commerce. In the early part of this period trading vessels sailed between the Latin American countries on the Pacific coast and trading ports in Asia and the East Indies, stopping in Hawaii to refuel and take on supplies. As time went on a lively trade also developed with the Russians in Alaska and Kamchatka and with the Spanish settlements in California.

This general Pacific trade, in addition to the business in fur, sandalwood, and whale products, led to the growth of a stable business community in Hawaii. By 1830 Honolulu was no longer a straggling little village. It was large enough to support a dozen merchants with their clerks; a score of liquor dealers and innkeepers; and a half-hundred cooks, carpenters, blacksmiths, tailors, sail-makers, calkers, herdsmen, and farmers. Ten years later, in 1840, Honolulu had a population of about 7000; and the settlements of Lahaina in Maui,

Hilo in Hawaii, and Waimea in Kauai were large enough to be called towns. At least four Hawaiian merchants had branch dealers in the smaller community of San Francisco on the Mainland!

A BIT OF HARBOR HISTORY

The existence of Honolulu Harbor was known to white mariners such as Portlock, Dixon, and Vancouver but was thought to be navigable only by light boats and canoes. According to several old accounts the first ship to negotiate the entrance was the British schooner *Jackal,* Captain Brown commanding. This happened late in 1794, a few months before the battle of Nuuanu.

Eventually the harbor became a bustling, noisy port of call and a winter haven for sailing ships in the Pacific trade.

To provide for berthing ships, a wharf was constructed in 1825 by hauling an old sunken hulk to the foot of Nuuanu Street. It is related that in those early days ships entered the harbor under full sail. Lines were then thrown to Hawaiians who towed the ship in. The tow path was along Richards Street, then the only straight street in the waterfront area. Oxen and later a steam tug were used for towing. As the years went on, the frontage between Fort and Alakea Streets was filled in to provide additional wharfage.

The increase in trade between the Islands and England and the United States made it necessary for these countries to appoint consuls to represent their countrymen in Honolulu. John C. Jones, Jr., the first United States consul, and Richard Charlton, the British consul for the Sandwich Islands, were both disagreeable, headstrong men and, therefore, poor choices for the positions.

Unsolved problems, such as the payment of debts and the conduct of seamen, caused President John Quincy Adams and his Secretary of the Navy, S. L. Southard, to send a man-of-war to Honolulu in 1826. The commander, Captain Thomas ap Catesby Jones, was instructed to promote friendly relations with the native rulers and to arrange for the protection of American nationals and trade. In his stay of less than three months, Captain Jones proved to be a skillful sailor-diplomat. He helped to settle the long-standing feud between the

110

missionaries and the majority of other foreigners in Honolulu. He was able to arrange for a debt settlement satisfactory to the native chiefs and their *haole* creditors. Finally he proposed the "articles of arrangement" devoted to the protection of American commerce. These articles were signed by the regents and by Jones in December, 1826. They required the Hawaiian government to suppress deserters, to offer "most favored nation" treatment in regard to tariffs and tonnage dues, and to help in the salvage of wrecked vessels.

Although the United States Senate never officially accepted this treaty, it served as a working agreement for more than a decade. Altogether, the efforts of Captain Jones served in some degree to increase American influence in a kingdom where the British had been the most influential foreigners since the days of Kamehameha I.

Effects of the Death of Kaahumanu

In June of 1832 the strong-willed Kaahumanu was stricken with a fatal illness. Even the best efforts of Dr. Judd failed to cure her. She died at her home in Manoa Valley in Honolulu. Not only native chiefs and commoners, but the missionaries whom she had sturdily supported, mourned her death. Kinau, a wife of Liholiho, inherited her lands and offices. In July she assumed the office of *kuhina nui* with the title of Kaahumanu II. She also served as governor of Oahu and as regent until the King became of age.

In March, 1833, Kauikeaouli announced that he was now of age and would take charge of the kingdom. He ascended the throne and was crowned Kamehameha III. Kinau remained second in command. At this stage of his life the King was an irresponsible, pleasure-loving young man. Kinau lacked the strength and political skill of Kaahumanu I. Thus for several years the kingdom suffered from lack of good leadership.

As he grew older Kamehameha III became a stronger ruler and earned the respect and love of his people. The last two decades of his reign were to see the change from a strong Polynesian monarchy into a modern constitutional monarchy in which *haole* advisers and lawmakers were to play a leading part. Land reform, the spread of education, the ambitions of foreign nations, the growth of a great plantation system—all of these developments in the reign of Kamehameha III will be described in later chapters.

In the years following the death of Kaahumanu, the traders and promoters, chiefly American and British, began to build a stable business community. The prominent institution of C. Brewer and Company in present-day Hawaii started in connection with trade in sandalwood in 1826. A branch of Hudson's Bay Company came to Honolulu in 1834; and another British firm, which today operates under the name of Theo. H. Davies & Company, started in 1845 as Starkey, Janion & Company. In 1849 a German, Captain H. Hackfeld, started a firm that developed into American Factors, Ltd., another giant in Hawaii of today.

The first permanent bank to do business in Hawaii was that of Bishop & Company (now known as the First National), which opened in 1858 as a partnership of Charles R. Bishop and W. A. Aldrich.

COMMERCIAL ADS IN 1840

Sam and Mow
Bakers from Canton
    Good people all—walk in and buy
    Of Sam and Mow, good cake and pie;
    Bread hard or soft, for land or sea,
    "Celestial made"; come buy of we.

For sale
The good schooner Clarion, 33 tons burthen, well found in tackle and apparel; good seaboat and fair sailor. Apply to Peirce and Brewer.

Henry Paty & Co.
Have for sale on the most reasonable terms, for cash, approved credit or barter, a great variety of merchandise, including: Medicines: Extract Sarsaparilla—Extract Buche—Epsom Salts—Calcined Magnesia—Opodeldoc—Oil—Essences—Cephalic and Maccaboy Snuff—Stoughton's Elixir.

E. Espenser
Has just received per Barque Forager, direct from London, the following articles, which he is now retailing at the most reasonable prices:—Fowling-pieces. Muskets. Fine sporting Gunpowder. Manila hats. Manila cigars. Ginghams. Hair and Tooth Brushes. Bridles. Halters. Stirrups and Leathers. Girths, etc., etc.

From *The Polynesian,* 1840

Another great enterprise, which still carries on business today under the name of Alexander and Baldwin, Ltd., began about 1870 as an informal partnership between Samuel T. Alexander and Henry P. Baldwin. This business began not as a store but as a plantation development on the island of Maui. The work of the two young partners and their success in constructing the famous Hamakua Ditch for the irrigation of their sugar lands is told in Chapter 19.

Not all of the shipping and trading was carried on by foreigners. The King and chiefs owned and operated a number of small brigs and schooners manned partly by native Hawaiians. These ships plied between the islands, and several made trips to the Russian settlements in North America, to Manila, and to Hong Kong. The most active native trader was Governor Boki of Oahu. This ambitious chief engaged in trade partly for his own gain and partly to obtain funds to pay off debts of government chiefs during the reign of Liholiho. By the time Kamehameha III came to the throne, these debts, owed mostly to American traders, were a heavy burden for the little kingdom.

In 1827 Boki bought the cargo of an English trading ship and opened a retail store in Honolulu in a two-story building given to him by Kaahumanu. Part of the building he converted into a hotel, which he named "The Blonde" after the English frigate that had brought him home from England several years earlier. He also entered into several overseas trading ventures, none of which seems to have been very successful.

Late in 1829 a report reached Honolulu that excited Boki. He learned that sandalwood could be gathered easily on the island of Eromanga in the New Hebrides. Heavily in debt and in disfavor with the regent Kaahumanu, Boki decided to leave Hawaii and seek his fortune elsewhere. He fitted out two of the King's brigs, the *Kamehameha* and the *Becket*. Loading them with from four to five hundred of his followers and friends, he sailed to the southern islands.

From the very beginning it was a mismanaged and disastrous venture. The two brigs met at an island near Fiji, whereupon Boki, who was aboard the *Kamehameha*, decided to press on ahead of the *Becket*. At the last moment he took on board a large number of natives to help in cutting the sandalwood he hoped to find. The vessel was never seen or heard of again. Was there a mutiny? an explosion? a violent storm? Nobody knows, and the fate of the colorful Boki will remain forever a mystery.

The *Becket* reached Eromanga and stayed there about five weeks. No sandalwood was cut since the natives were hostile and many of the crew died of disease. The survivors began the long journey back to Hawaii. It was a ghastly voyage, as starvation, disease, and brutality cut down the seamen one by one. When the forlorn ship reached Honolulu on August 3, 1830, there were only twenty men on board, including eight foreigners who had joined the ill-fated expedition.

Both commercial and agricultural activity during the reigns of the first three Kamehamehas was largely a matter of experimenting. It was still not clear what industry or product would be the basis of the country's future growth and prosperity. Events were conspiring, however, to make one crop outstanding. It needed plenty of arable, irrigated land, technical know-how, a stable market, a supply of labor and capital, and a favorable political situation. This crop was sugar. It deserves a chapter by itself.

Summing Up the Chapter

When Kamehameha III began his reign, whaling had replaced the sandalwood trade as the chief source of income. It provided work and business for Hawaiian merchants and natives, but the visits of the seamen also brought sickness and disorders to the native population. Whaling began to decline in the 1860's. The King and some of the native chiefs, as well as foreigners, engaged in trading and shipping activities. Governor Boki of Oahu lost his life while on an expedition to the South Pacific in search of a new source of sandalwood. Some of the problems between the United States and Hawaii resulting from trade were solved during the visit of the American Captain Jones, who represented President Adams. Kinau succeeded Kaahumanu as regent until Kauikeaouli became of age and ruled as Kamehameha III. Although he began his rule as a weak, irresponsible leader, the new King later gained the respect of his followers. Many present-day Hawaiian businesses began during the period of the early and middle 1800's.

11

Teachers and Preachers

Long before the missionaries gave them a written language and a foreign curriculum, the Hawaiians had an educational system of their own. It was based not upon books but upon practical needs. Its purpose was to teach vocational skills and the arts of navigation and warfare, to pass on the legends and history of the race, and to preserve religious and social customs.

Since they were held in great honor, it was necessary that the *ali'i* be well trained. The *maka'ainana,* or commoners, had to learn the ordinary skills that they would need in everyday life. These were taught to them by the *kahunas*—the expert canoe builders, medicine men, genealogists, navigators, farmers, housebuilders, and priests.

Although we know little about educational methods in old Hawaii, it seems likely that some sort of group teaching existed. Much of the training, of course, was carried on in the home. Others learned by watching craftsmen and professional *kahunas* at work. In any case the missionaries found an intelligent, eager and adaptable people who were ready to learn.

The Task of the Missionaries

For the Protestant missionaries, there was only one road to salvation: communion with God through the Holy Scriptures. Their first task, therefore, was to teach the natives to read. This meant that a

Beginning of 20 year boom
period of Hawaiian whaling

1841 Oahu College (Punahou)
was founded

1841 First covered wagon
arrives in Oregon

1842 Kawaiahao Church is
completed

1843 Paulet episode

1843 George Brown appointed
first U.S. diplomatic representative to Hawaii

1844 First telegraph message
sent by Samuel Morse

1845 Theo. H. Davies & Co.
started

1846 War declared on Mexico

1847 Liberia established as
first independent black republic
of Africa

1848 The Great Mahele begins
Parker Ranch started

1848 Gold discovered in
California
Mexican War ends

1849 H. Hackfeld and
Company (Amfac Inc.) started

1850 Compromise of 1850
Millard Fillmore becomes the
13th U.S. president

1852 First Chinese arrive to
work on the plantations

New constitution

1853 Smallpox epidemic

1853 Gadsden Purchase
Admiral Perry goes to Japan
Franklin Pierce inaugurated
14th U.S. president

1854 Death of Kamehameha III
Alexander Liholiho is proclaimed Kamehameha IV

written Hawaiian language must be invented, a printing press provided, and a school system started. This was surely a tremendous undertaking, but the missionaries accomplished it.

The work of the missionaries in developing education in Hawaii can be divided into three periods. The first period, lasting from 1820 to 1831, was one of experimentation. The Hawaiian language was written down, with the result that textbooks could be printed and native adults could learn simple reading and writing. During the second period, which lasted from 1831 to 1840, children rather than adults were the chief concern of the educators. Teachers were trained, and schools were started. The last period extended from 1840 to 1863. During those years, the missionaries gradually gave up their control of education, and the government started a number of public schools.

Some of the *haoles* living in the Islands were opposed to education for the natives. Even before 1820 a *haole* sailor named Archibald Campbell, who attempted to teach a chief to read, was opposed by Isaac Davis. "They will soon know more than ourselves," complained Davis. Some of the traders accused the missionaries of using religion in order to win control of the Islands for themselves.

Despite all obstacles the missionaries plunged ahead. The first school was at Kailua, Hawaii, and was taught by the Thurstons, Dr. Holman, and Thomas Hopu. King Liholiho, his two queens, and his brother Kauikeaouli, then about five years old, were among the students. Mr. Loomis went to Kawaihae and taught Kalanimoku and a few of his followers. At Honolulu Hiram Bingham and his wife held the first quarterly "examination," which was observed with great interest by several sea captains and other foreign visitors. Mr. Ruggles and Mr. Whitney journeyed to Waimea, Kauai, where King Kaumualii helped them to start a school in which he was the first student enrolled. So enthusiastic were the King and Queen that they studied their Bible while bathing in the Waimea River!

This was a good beginning, especially when we remember the many other duties of the missionaries. Whereas other foreigners who had lived among the natives for years had done nothing about educating them, the missionaries within four months of their arrival had established four schools.

The missionaries soon realized that they could not wait for the Hawaiians to learn English. If the Word of God was to reach people, it must be taught in the Hawaiian tongue. The work of translation

117

FIRST HAWAIIAN PRINTING
JANUARY 7, 1822
IN A GRASS HOUSE NEAR THIS
SITE HIGH CHIEF KEEAUMOKU
PULLED THE FIRST SHEET
IN THE PRESENCE OF ELISHA
LOOMIS, PRINTER, THE REVEREND
HIRAM BINGHAM, AND JAMES
HUNNEWELL, MISSION BENEFACTOR.

This tablet commemorates the printing on January 7, 1822 of the first material in the Hawaiian language. The sheet was printed on a small hand press located in a mission house on King Street in Honolulu (the present location of the Mission Houses Museum).

began, but it was not until the arrival of the Reverend William Ellis in 1822 that real progress was made. Ellis stopped in the Islands on his way to the Marquesas. Having had years of preaching experience in the Society Islands, he knew the language of Tahiti, which is closely related to Hawaiian. He was soon able to speak in Hawaiian, and this skill was of great help to the missionaries in writing down the native language.

An alphabet (*pi'apa*) of twelve letters was selected, and the work of translation went on. On January 7, 1822, the first publication in the Hawaiian tongue came off the small press owned by the missionaries. Chief Keeaumoku made the first copy, to the great delight of the Hawaiians. The material was a little printed page, which later went into an eight-page pamphlet containing the alphabet, a spelling exercise, and a few simple sentences and verses.

The history of the little mission press is an interesting one. As the mission expanded during the 1820's and 1830's, printed matter from the press poured forth in astonishing volume——primers, hymn books, government proclamations, and job printing for traders. In

1838 it produced the *Hawaiian Spectator,* the first quarterly review in the Pacific Ocean area. A second press was built in 1834 at Lahainaluna Seminary; and from it was issued the first Hawaiian newspaper, *Ka Lama Hawaii.* With the coming of printing, learning to read became a fascinating challenge, especially to the chiefs. Within a few years they became enthusiastic about teaching the *palapala* (printing of any kind, but especially the Scriptures) to the common people.

Early Missionary Schools

The early missionary schools were, of course, very simple, both in equipment and in subjects taught. Classes were called together not by a bell but by blowing on a conch shell. There were no desks or chairs, and pupils sat on blocks of dried bricks covered with mats. In one of her colorful sketches of Hawaiian life from 1828 to 1861, Laura Fish Judd described the grand annual exhibition of all the schools on Oahu, held at the church on April 28, 1828:

". . . Adults compose these schools, as the children are not yet tamed. The people come from each district in procession, headed by the principal man of the land (konohiki), all dressed in one uniform color of native cloth. One district would be clad in red, another in bright yellow, another in pure white, another in black or brown. The dress was one simple garment, the 'kihei' for men, and the 'pau' for women.

"It is astonishing how so many have learned to read with so few books. They teach each other, making use of banana leaves, smooth stones, and the wet sand on the sea beach, as tablets. Some read equally well with the book upside down or sidewise, as four or five of them learn from the same book with one teacher, crowding around him as closely as possible.

"The aged are fond of committing to memory, and repeating in concert . . . Their power of memory is wonderful, acquired, as I suppose, by the habit of committing and reciting traditions, and the genealogies of their kings and priests.

"As yet, only portions of the Bible are translated and printed. These are demanded in sheets still wet from the press. Kaahumanu admires those chapters in Paul's epistles,

119

where he greets his disciples by name; she says, 'Paul had a great many friends.'
"The children are considered bright, but too wild to be brought into the schools. We intend, however, to try them very soon."[1]

As the number of schools increased, the task of education at the mission centers became too heavy for the missionaries and their wives to handle by themselves. As soon as pupils learned to read, they were sent out to teach others. After 1824, the *ali'i* also assisted in education. The regent Kaahumanu issued a proclamation of the first general laws of Hawaii in June of that year in which she declared that all Hawaiians must learn the *palapala*. Keopuolani, the queen mother, and her husband Hoapili, governor of Maui, furthered the work on that island. Another worker on Maui was David Malo, who later became the first superintendent of schools in the Islands.

The American Board cooperated by sending out more missionaries to help in establishing new schools. The missionary system reached its peak in 1832 when about forty per cent of the people of Hawaii were enrolled in 900 schools throughout the Islands. Attendance dropped after that year for a number of reasons. The schools were poorly constructed, there were few qualified teachers, there was a shortage of printed materials, and the people were confused by the change from the old way of life to a strange new one.

What was needed was a complete reorganization of the whole educational system with special attention to the teaching of children, to obtaining qualified teachers, and to constructing permanent school buildings. This was the task which faced the missionaries in the decade of the 1830's.

Independent Schools

At the general meeting of the mission in June, 1831, the members gave serious thought to the matter of proper training of teachers and preachers for service in the Islands. To carry out this plan Lahainaluna (upper Lahaina) on the island of Maui was chosen as the location of a high school or seminary. The site was chosen by William Richards and Lorrin Andrews, the latter having been assigned to

[1] *Honolulu: Sketches of Life in the Hawaiian Islands,* reprinted from the *Honolulu Star-Bulletin,* 1928.

The earliest missionaries to Hawaii were New Englanders. Here some of their wives dress Hawaiian women in more "proper" attire—the loose, floor-length *muumuu.* The *muumuu* replaced a short skirt called the *pa'u.*

head the school. On September 5, 1831, the school, built on a 1000-acre grant from Governor Hoapili, received its first students.

Historically, Lahainaluna is one of the most interesting schools in Hawaii. After classes in printing had been held for about a year, the little press turned out a newspaper, *Ka Lama Hawaii,* which has been called the first newspaper west of the Rocky Mountains. The Reverend Sheldon Dibble, who was one of the original teachers of the school, in 1843 produced, with the aid of his students, the first published history of the Hawaiian Islands. He also helped to organize the first Hawaiian Historical Society, which was later strongly supported by Kamehameha III.

As the years went on, this high school (which changed its official name to the Mission Seminary in 1837) played a worthy part in religious education. Gradually control passed from the hands of the missionaries to the government until it is now part of the public school system of Hawaii. It can be proud of its long record of producing teachers and pioneering in vocational education.

In Hilo a school similar to that at Lahainaluna was opened by another early missionary, David Lyman. With the support of the Reverend Titus Coan, Lorrin Andrews, and others, he was able to convince the mission board of the need for a boys' boarding school at Hilo. On a 40-acre grant of land given by the chiefs, Mr. Lyman built Hilo Boarding School, which then consisted of two native grass huts. There were only eight boys in the first class, which opened in 1836. The next year Abner Wilcox arrived as assistant teacher and remained for a few years. The school was soon so successful that a board of trustees was chosen to guide it, and a few years later it received a charter from the government.

The wives of the Hilo missionaries were of much help to their husbands in the work of the school. For example, Mrs. Titus Coan opened a boarding school for girls in 1838. The Hawaiians cut timber and put up a simple building, which took care of twenty girls from seven to ten years of age.

It was supported by the neighbors, who brought in weekly supplies of taro, potatoes, bananas, and fish.

"Little gifts of money were sometimes made by strangers who came to Hilo, by officers of whaleships and men-of-war; or a piece of print or brown cotton was given, and thus the real wants of the school were supplied. Mrs. Coan toiled faithfully from day to day, in spite of pressing cares, teaching her charges the rudiments of necessary book knowledge, and of singing, sewing, washing and ironing, gardening, and other things. Most of the girls became members of the Hilo church, and we had hopes that all were the children of God . . . The school was sustained about eight years . . . As domestic cares increased and her strength was weakening the faithful teacher at length felt compelled to give up her charge."[2]

Throughout its history the Hilo Boarding School continued to give vocational training and to produce Hawaiian leaders. Lyman remained with the school until poor health forced him to retire in 1874.

[2] Titus Coan, *Life in Hawaii* (New York: D. F. Anson, 1882), p. 163.

Punahou School, which occupies about 80 acres of land surrounding the lily-covered spring from which it takes its name, is one of the most colorful schools in the nation. It includes classes from kindergarten through the twelfth grade. By 1962 it was the largest independent college preparatory school west of the Rockies. The names of its teachers and graduates are outstanding in the history of Hawaii.

The school was founded to provide education for the children of the missionaries. Previously the children were sent around Cape Horn to their homeland for their schooling. This long separation of parents and children was sad indeed! Because they were too busy with other duties to train their own children, the missionaries had only two choices: to continue sending the children across the seas or to found a school in Hawaii. They chose the latter course.

In 1829 Kaahumanu, wishing to give Mr. Bingham some land for the use of the mission, spoke to Hoapili, governor of Maui. The old chief suggested the Punahou land, which he had given to his daughter Liliha. Liliha, the wife of Governor Boki of Oahu, was not anxious to give up the lands, but Boki consented. In order to watch over this princely gift to the Binghams and the mission, Kaahumanu ordered two thatched houses, one for her and one for the Binghams, to be built near the spring. Later Mrs. Bingham set out the first night-blooming cereus plants on the outer walls of the grounds. Today they are often photographed by flower lovers.

At first it was intended that a school for Hawaiians should be built on the land, but there was not enough money. In 1839 this need was met when the Chiefs' Children's School was opened in town. It was a boarding school run by Mr. and Mrs. Amos S. Cooke. In 1841 a sum of money was set aside for the building of Punahou School. The scholarly Daniel Dole, a new arrival in the Islands, agreed to take charge of this new, experimental boarding school. The rest of the staff consisted of Mrs. Dole and Miss Marcia Smith. Mr. Dole was the father of Sanford Dole, later to become president of the Republic of Hawaii and first governor of the Islands as an American territory.

Special Schools

St. Louis College, the oldest Catholic school in Hawaii, was organized under Bishop Maigret in 1880. In 1883 it was turned over to

The Kamehameha Schools, established in 1887 to provide education for children of Hawaiian ancestry, strive to keep alive the customs of old Hawaii.

the Brothers of Mary. Other Catholic schools are St. Joseph's in Hilo, St. Anthony's on Maui, and the schools under the Maryknoll order. All are part of an impressive system of education by which the church has supplemented public instruction in Hawaii.

The Kamehameha Schools, founded in 1887, were started with funds provided by Princess Pauahi, a descendant of Kamehameha the Great. She married Charles R. Bishop in 1850. Since they had no children, they decided to use the estate for the special benefit of boys and girls of Hawaiian blood. After Mrs. Bishop's death in 1884, the estate was under the control of a board of trustees of which her husband was a member.

Three years later, in 1887, the board carried out Mrs. Bishop's wishes and opened the boys' division of the school. The Reverend William B. Oleson, principal of Hilo Boarding School, left there to become first principal of the new school. The girls' school opened in 1894 with twenty-seven girls enrolled. Miss Ida M. Pope from Kawaiahao Seminary in Honolulu was the first principal of the girls' division.

124

Another special school, Iolani, was established by the Anglicans under Bishop Willis in 1872. An older Anglican school, St. Alban's College in Honolulu, became a part of Iolani about 1887. At first only Hawaiians attended Iolani, but later young people of other races were accepted. The famous Chinese patriot, Sun Yat-sen, was a student at Iolani. The Anglicans also established St. Andrew's Priory for girls. In 1902 it was taken over by the reorganized Episcopal Church in America.

This is only part of the story of the private school movement in Hawaii. Many other schools were founded or influenced by the missionaries. Some passed from the scene. Others were combined or reorganized under new names. All of them were helpful in preparing the way for public secondary education, in furnishing vocational training, and in training the leaders of Hawaii.

Public Education and the Constitution of 1840

Rapidly changing political conditions in the early years of the reign of Kamehameha III showed the need for a more highly organized educational system. The missionaries were forced to admit that they could not meet the need alone.

The first landmark in the development of public schools was the Constitution of 1840. This document was largely the work of William Richards, a Lahaina missionary. The first minister for public instruction was, quite fittingly, William Richards. His short term was ended by death in 1847. He was replaced by Richard Armstrong, another missionary. Armstrong was so successful in his thirteen years as minister that he has been called "the father of American education in Hawaii." Only a few of his accomplishments can be given here. He improved the training of teachers, inspected schools, held examinations, and worked to secure public lands for schools. In addition, he tried to settle religious differences between Catholic and Protestant missionaries and served as the King's agent in chartering private and select schools. Armstrong died in 1860 from injuries received when he was thrown from a horse.

The Common Schools

Under the able leadership of Richard Armstrong, Hawaii developed a strong program of public education for the common people. Laws

125

were passed supplying money to the common schools in the form of labor taxes. The education act of 1850 set aside one-twentieth of all government land for the support of education. The labor tax was changed to a school tax of two dollars in cash or three dollars in kind. All taxable males had to pay this except school teachers, inspectors and school trustees, aged and infirm people, missionaries and two of their servants, constables, soldiers, and certain others. In 1855 another act placed the control of public education in the hands of a board of education with Armstrong as its president. During this period local school boards existed, but they were not to remain as a permanent feature of the Hawaiian school system.

At first the common schools were grass huts without floors or equipment. The teachers had to provide most of the materials used for teaching. Instruction was in Hawaiian as were the textbooks, which were printed at Lahainaluna. Under Armstrong's leadership better textbooks were supplied, the quality of teaching was improved, and more adequate schoolhouses were built. The pupils were taught reading, writing, ciphering, geography, singing, and, above all, becoming God-fearing citizens. Armstrong felt that the schools should develop the habit of industry among the common people. He believed that a part of each school day should be devoted to labor with the hands, particularly in school gardens.

Toward the end of Armstrong's career, a number of important changes took place in public education. The laws of 1859 specified curriculum content and required the teaching of reading, writing, arithmetic, and other similar elementary subjects. All taxable males now had to pay a school tax of two dollars. Separate schools to teach English to Hawaiians were established. Lahainaluna was incorporated into the public school system and the Oahu Charity School was turned over to the Honolulu district superintendent. Established for the education of Caucasian-Hawaiian children, the Oahu Charity School was one of the earliest schools set up in Hawaii. Both Pohukaina School and McKinley High School stem from the Oahu Charity School. The Chiefs' Children's School, or Royal School, was made a normal and preparatory school. By 1860 the common schools had assumed much of the responsibility for the education of the common people. In 1863, three years after Armstrong's death, the American Board of Missions withdrew from education activities in Hawaii.

Hawaii's First Newspapers

The growth of newspapers is also a part of the growth of education in any community. This chapter, then, should close with a brief look at Hawaii's early journalists and the brave little papers which they presented to a bustling Polynesian town more than a century ago.

The first English-language newspaper was the *Sandwich Island Gazette and Journal of Commerce.* It was edited and published by twenty-two year old Stephen D. Mackintosh.

The first issue of the *Sandwich Island Gazette* came off the press on July 30, 1836. It was a four-page Saturday weekly printed on Chinese wrapping paper. The subscription cost six dollars a year, which could be paid in cash or in goods. To fill space Mackintosh had to depend on months-old world newspapers, local shipping notices, and contributions from his readers. Like most editors, he fought

A printing press like this one may have been used to print some of the early newspapers and books in Hawaii. Fifty books had been printed by 1840.

for special causes and for community improvements. His favorite cause was raising money for the Oahu Charity School, founded and supported by traders for all children not in the American Mission schools.

By the end of 1838 Mackintosh was heavily in debt. He returned to the United States, leaving the paper in the hands of a group of subscribers. The last issue appeared in July, 1839. Mackintosh himself died two years later.

Another noteworthy paper was the *Polynesian,* a four-column, four-page weekly which first appeared in June, 1840. Its editor was a young Bostonian named James Jackson Jarves. It was a better paper than the *Gazette,* but it was dropped after eighteen months because of lack of support. In 1844 it reappeared as a government newspaper, perhaps to counterbalance the opinions in S. C. Damon's *The Friend,* which was sometimes critical of royal policies. Jarves once more was the editor until his departure from the Islands in 1848. Jarves is remembered also as the author of *History of the Hawaiian or Sandwich Islands.* A series of editors managed the *Polynesian* until it was finally discontinued in 1864.

During the 1840's a number of papers appeared briefly on the scene. Among them were the *Cascade, Monitor, Fountain,* and the *Honolulu Times,* the last edited by the able Henry L. Sheldon. We do not have many records of their contents.

The oldest paper in Hawaii with an unbroken record down to the present is the *Advertiser.* The first copy came off the press on July 2, 1856, under the editorship of Henry M. Whitney. He named his paper the *Pacific Commercial Advertiser,* a weekly with three pages in English and one in Hawaiian. (Mr. Whitney also started an Hawaiian paper, *Ka Nupepa Kuokoa* or *The Independent.*) The *Advertiser* had various owners, including Claus Spreckels, the "sugar king." His editor was Walter Murray Gibson, who later became prime minister under King Kalakaua. In 1882 the *Advertiser* became a daily.

The first daily paper in Hawaii was the *Daily Hawaiian Herald,* started in 1866. The first daily to live on to the present was the *Evening Bulletin,* which later was joined with the *Hawaiian Star* to form today's *Star-Bulletin.* The *Bulletin* appeared on April 24, 1882. One week later the *Advertiser* came out as a daily. Recently the two newspapers combined their advertising and printing facilities.

128

Summing Up the Chapter

Before the coming of the *haoles,* the Hawaiians had a simple educational system suited to their needs. Because they thought that men must read the Christian Bible to be saved, the early missionaries wrote down the Hawaiian language and taught the natives to read. The printing press helped them to spread learning more quickly. The first school was at Kailua, Hawaii. Other missionary schools were established all through the Islands. Some of those schools still exist. When the need arose for a more highly organized school system, the government stepped in. Hawaii was one of the pioneers in having a state department of instruction. In 1840, the new constitution aided the development of public schools. One of the first ministers for public instruction in the King's cabinet was Richard Armstrong, Hawaii's "father of education." Under Armstrong, public schools, set up to provide educational facilities for the common people, greatly expanded. The first English-language newspaper appeared in 1836. The important newspapers in Hawaii today are the *Advertiser* and the *Star-Bulletin.*

12

Foreign Entanglements

Now let us retrace our steps and follow another thread of Hawaiian history. In this chapter we shall look at the fortunes of the kingdom in its dealings with other countries during the reign of Kamehameha III. As trade grew and as more and more foreigners began to make their homes in Hawaii, problems involving other nations began to arise.

As we have seen, Hawaii's first knowledge of the outside world came with the visits of English explorers. Later, other Englishmen— Vancouver, Davis, Young, Beckley, and others—became friends and advisers to Kamehameha I. Indeed, both Kamehameha I and II looked upon the English King as the protector of the Islands.

In 1815-1816 came the Russian adventurers, whose attempts to seize the island of Kauai we have described in an earlier chapter. In 1820, the year that the American missionaries arrived, John Coffin Jones became the first American commercial agent. He was the first official representative of a foreign country. As we have seen, the British sent Richard Charlton as their consular agent. His arrival was soon followed in 1826 by the appearance of Captain Thomas Jones, in the United States sloop-of-war *Peacock,* who negotiated Hawaii's first treaty with a foreign power—the United States.

The French Catholic Mission

A new foreign influence appeared on the scene when a small French missionary group led by Father Alexis Bachelot arrived from Bordeaux in July, 1827. They came to Hawaii on board *La Comète*, which was under the command of Captain Plassard. The day after the party landed, Bachelot called on Don Francisco de Paula Marín, a long-time resident who had served Kamehameha I in various ways. Marín was unable to offer help but referred them to the American agent. Jones received them courteously and invited them to stay for dinner in order to meet Governor Boki. At this meeting it became apparent that Boki favored the Catholic mission. He may have hoped to win their support against the regent Kaahumanu, who was an ally of the Protestants.

Although they had no permission to remain, the priests went ahead boldly with their plans to establish a mission. One of the lay brothers rented for eight dollars a month an enclosure containing three grass huts. One of the huts served as a chapel, and here the priests celebrated their first Mass. For the next two weeks they remained quietly in their new quarters, busy with their devotions and the study of the Hawaiian language. Soon Kaahumanu openly showed her opposition to the missionaries. She summoned them to appear before her. They guessed that she would order them to leave the Islands, so they did not answer her call. Next she ordered Captain Plassard to take them on his ship. When he refused to do so, she sent for Governor Boki, intending to have them put on board by force. However, *La Comète* sailed two hours before the governor arrived, and so the priests were left behind.

After the departure of the vessel, a French lawyer who acted as the local leader of his countrymen obtained from the King the cession of a parcel of land. Here a chapel was erected in 1828. The French mission proceeded with its work under the uneasy watch of the American Protestants. The next year the Catholics lost the support of Boki, who died while on an expedition to the South Pacific in search of sandalwood. Then there began a dark period of persecution of Catholic converts and a campaign to expel their priests.

In April, 1831, Fathers Bachelot and Short were ordered to appear at the fort before an assembly of chiefs presided over by Kaahumanu. Here they were given a document ordering them to leave the Islands. Although Bachelot tried to defend their labors, the priests were forced

Sacred Hearts Church at Wailua on the island of Maui is one of the oldest Roman Catholic churches in the islands.

some months later to board the brig *Waverley*. They sailed to California, where they were warmly received by monks of the Franciscan order. The Catholic lay brothers remained with the mission in Honolulu.

Although this is an unpleasant episode in Hawaiian history, it can be explained in part. The American Mission did not want to share a field where they had set up virtually an Established Church. As for the chiefs, it would have been strange if they had been able to understand the idea of religious toleration. They had been brought up to believe that worshipping the gods of a rival chief was treason. Also, they associated the Catholic converts with the policies of Boki and Liliha, who openly opposed the King. To the older chiefs, the Catholics were a danger to the state.

But the religious issue was not settled at this point. The year 1836 brought new squabbles involving foreign governments and their representatives. By this time Kaahumanu had passed from the scene, and the young King had taken personal control, with Kinau as *kuhina nui*. The time seemed ripe for a new effort by the Catholics.

Return of the Catholic Mission

In September, 1836, Father Arsenius Walsh, a British subject, arrived in the Islands. Kinau promptly ordered him to be ready to leave on the British man-of-war *Acteon,* which was expected at any moment. At this embarrassing moment the French corvette *La Bonite,* under the command of Captain A. N. Vaillant, sailed into Honolulu harbor. A few hours later Father Walsh called on the captain, told him the story of Bachelot and Short, and asked protection for himself. Vaillant was happy to oblige. At a dinner party on board for the King and Kinau, Vaillant reminded the Hawaiians of the power of France. The King then promised that in the future the nationals of France would receive just treatment. Captain Vaillant also persuaded the King to allow Father Walsh to remain in Hawaii as long as he preached only to European Catholics and not to natives.

Just as *La Bonite* departed on October 24, the *Acteon,* under Lord Edward Russell, anchored in the harbor. During his three-week stay, the English captain also was able to make a treaty that guaranteed trading and residence rights to his countrymen.

Then, on the following April 17, another ship arrived to stir up the government. This was the *Clementine,* a brigantine owned by a Frenchman named Jules Dudoit and flying British colors. On board were sixteen horses being shipped from California—and Fathers Bachelot and Short! Evidently the priests believed that times had changed enough for them to go on with their missionary efforts. Father Short was recognized as he came ashore, even though he was somewhat disguised by a long beard and a wide-brimmed hat. He was followed by a curious crowd as he headed for the French mission. Father Bachelot soon joined him there.

The next few weeks saw a series of bewildering events. Governor Kekuanaoa, with the approval of Kinau and the King, ordered the priests to leave on the ship. Kinau arrived in Honolulu on April 30 to enforce the order. Once it was unloaded, the captain of the *Clementine* turned it over to the owner, Mr. Dudoit. On May 10 Dudoit chartered the ship to an American trader, who immediately began to load his cargo. Who now was responsible for giving passage to the priests? The British captain no longer was in charge, Dudoit opposed Kinau's order, and the American had other business.

On May 20 the exiles were forced on board by Kekuanaoa's officials. Immediately the furious Dudoit ordered his crew ashore, hauled down the British ensign, and delivered it to the British consul, Charlton. The consul promptly burned it in the street as a sign of protest against the Hawaiian government.

The controversy simmered until July 7. Then the British sloop-of-war *Sulphur,* commanded by Captain Edward Belcher, arrived at Honolulu. It was followed three days later by the French frigate *Venus* under Captain du Petit Thouars. The two captains called on Kinau. After a stormy interview, they left, announcing that the *Clementine* would be prevented from sailing. Then a party of marines from the *Sulphur* boarded the ship, rescued the priests and escorted them to the mission.

On July 20 the King arrived from Lahaina. After a long talk with the two captains, he agreed to allow Bachelot and Short to remain but not to preach until a ship arrived that would give them suitable transportation.

In October Father Short sailed for Valparaiso on the ship *Peru.* In November two more priests arrived on the *Europa,* Fathers L. D. Maigret and C. J. Murphy. Kinau demanded a $10,000 bond of the captain to guarantee that he would not land the priests without a permit. Father Murphy managed to get ashore after the British consul told Kinau he was not an ordained priest. Maigret was kept on board. Eventually Maigret and Bachelot sailed for Micronesia on board a schooner bought by the mission. Father Bachelot died at sea while enroute and was buried in one of the Caroline Islands.

In December of this exciting year of "Big Stick" diplomacy, the King and chiefs issued severe rulings forbidding the teaching of Catholicism or the landing of priests except in cases of necessity. The persecution of Catholic natives began once more.

Kinau died in April, 1839, and the King appointed Kekauluohi, one of Liholiho's wives, to take her place. Now there was a better climate for religious toleration. The King, influenced by Richards, issued an order on June 17 providing for freedom of religion in the Islands.

Danger from France

The danger from France was not yet ended, however. The French ministry in this period was following a strong colonial policy in the Pacific, especially in the Marquesas and Society Islands. On July 9, 1839, Captain Laplace of the frigate *Artemise* dropped anchor in

Honolulu harbor. His orders were to protect the rights of French nationals and of the Catholic religion, by force if necessary. Without making any real investigation and paying no attention to the King's new policy of toleration, he accused the chiefs of being misled by treacherous advisers. He then made a series of high-handed demands.

To enforce these demands, he kept the King's secretary on board the frigate as hostage. He also declared a state of blockade and prepared to attack. In notes to the British and American consuls, he offered protection on board the ship to their countrymen. He did not include the American missionaries, who, he charged, were "the true authors of the insults offered to France," and were to be thought of as part of the native population.

The helpless Hawaiian government was forced to yield. The *kuhina nui* and Governor Kekuanaoa boarded the frigate with the desired treaty, signed on behalf of the King, and a $20,000 guarantee that the treaty would be kept. Two days later, when the King had arrived from Maui, Laplace added more demands. No Frenchman was to be tried for any crime except by a jury of foreign residents chosen by the French consul. French wine and brandy were to be admitted with a duty of not more than five per cent. Having been successful in this outrageous mission, Laplace sailed on July 20.

There were to be later demands by arrogant French officials; but they were met in one way or another, and France gained no permanent foothold. However the threat to Hawaiian independence remained. This time it was to come from another quarter—Great Britain.

The Paulet Episode

In an earlier chapter we mentioned the bill of rights and the Constitution of 1840 that Kamehameha III granted to his people. Such matters as property rights of foreigners, rights on entry, and treaty-making had to be made clear if the kingdom were to meet threats from abroad.

Before the constitution could be put into workable order, however, the kingdom was shaken by new difficulties. The danger from France had lessened for the time being, but now British actions were causing uneasiness. Many foreign residents felt that annexation was in the air. This seems to have been the hope of the British consul, Richard Charlton.

The activities of Charlton were a prelude to the Paulet episode, a story that has so many elements of melodrama that it would furnish good material for a movie. Briefly, this is what happened:

The American firm of Ladd & Company signed a contract with the government in November, 1841, whereby they would receive leases of valuable land for sugar cultivation. The project was to be a joint stock affair, with subscriptions open to the King and to foreign capitalists. In order to attract this foreign capital, it seemed wise to obtain guarantees of Hawaiian independence from England, France, and the United States. Peter A. Brinsmade, a member of the firm, carried letters from Kamehameha III to the heads of these governments asking for such a guarantee. He went first to Washington to present his case to Secretary of State Daniel Webster.

Back in Honolulu William Richards and the chiefs consulted with Sir George Simpson, governor in North America of the great Hudson's Bay Company. He gave them friendly advice about the problem. "Brinsmade is not armed with enough authority," he said. "You should send a formal commission with full powers to negotiate. I am on my way to London by way of Alaska and Siberia, and, if you wish, I shall serve as a member of the commission."

His offer was accepted. Other members of the commission were Richards and Timothy Haalilio, an able young Hawaiian who was secretary and confidant of the King. To take Richards' place as adviser to the government came the medical missionary, Dr. G. P. Judd, who was to play a principal role in Hawaiian politics for the next decade.

The Richards-Haalilio delegation sailed quietly in July, 1842. As soon as Consul Charlton learned about this, he packed his bags and sailed for London. He was at that time engaged in a dispute over land and wanted to defend his interests in London. He also hoped to defeat the move to recognize Hawaiian independence. Before leaving, he appointed Alexander Simpson, a cousin of Sir George Simpson, as acting consul. Simpson, unlike his cousin, openly favored annexation, and his ungentlemanly conduct resulted in his being declared unacceptable by the King.

Richards and Haalilio reached Washington early in December and were courteously received by Daniel Webster. They were also able to lay their case before President John Tyler and his cabinet. They presented the case for Hawaii so well that Webster gave them an official

King Kamehameha III (far right) confers with his privy council during the difficult period of the Paulet episode. At the left, William Richards and Dr. Gerrit P. Judd are seated across the table from Robert C. Wyllie.

letter stating the view of the United States that the government of the Sandwich Islands ought to be respected.

Overjoyed at winning this first important battle, the envoys sailed in February, 1843, to join Sir George Simpson in London. The British Foreign Secretary, Lord Aberdeen, was of the opinion that Great Britain should not become too powerful in the Islands. But as the envoys spoke with him, little did they know of the startling events taking place in Hawaii at that moment.

On a stopover at Mazatlán, Mexico, Consul Charlton complained about his treatment to Lord George Paulet, commander of the British frigate *Carysfort*. Alexander Simpson had also written that British property rights were being violated. Admiral Richard Thomas, commander of British naval forces in the Pacific, decided to send the *Carysfort* to Hawaii to investigate.

Upon arriving, Paulet withheld the usual salutes and sent an abrupt note to Kekuanaoa demanding a private interview with the King. The King refused, saying that any private business could be discussed with Dr. Judd. Paulet refused to deal with Judd, charging that he was the one behind the anti-British feeling. On February 17 he presented six demands, one of which was that Charlton's lands should be re-

137

turned to him. The others dealt with the rights of Englishmen in the Islands. The King was given until four o'clock the following afternoon to meet the demands.

The King had no choice but to meet with Paulet and Simpson. At two later interviews, other insulting demands were laid before the King. Dr. Judd advised him not to resist but to turn over the Islands to the British government temporarily in the hope that favorable news would come from the envoys in faraway London.

On February 25 the King issued a short and touching announcement to his chiefs and his people:

> "Where are you, chief, people and commons from my ancestor, and people from foreign lands!
> "Hear ye! I make known to you that I am in perplexity by reason of difficulties into which I have been brought without cause; therefore, I have given away the life of our land, hear ye! But, my rule over you, my people, and your privileges will continue, for I have hope that the life of the land will be restored when my conduct shall be justified."[1]

The document was signed by Kamehameha III and Kekauluohi. Dr. Judd as "translator for the government" declared it to be a faithful translation.

The British occupation now proceeded rapidly. Their flag went up and the Hawaiian flag came down. A commission, of which Dr. Judd was a member, was to run the government. Judd had no real power, however, and he soon resigned in disgust. All Hawaiian flags were destroyed. Government ships were put under British registry. Money was taken from the treasury to maintain a small army of natives called the Queen's Regiment. Various laws of the kingdom were changed at the will of the British commander. The King retired to Lahaina, while the people remained in a state of confusion.

Results of the Paulet Episode

Today it seems strange that a naval commander could act in such a fashion. We must remember that communication was slow in those days and naval officers had more authority in international relations

[1] Sheldon Dibble, *A History of the Hawaiian Islands* (Honolulu: Thos. G. Thrum, 1919), p. 393.

than they do today. Besides, Paulet did not know about the attitude Lord Aberdeen had taken about Hawaiian affairs.

Paulet was eager to send an account of his doings to the British Foreign Office. As his messenger, he sent the ill-mannered Alexander Simpson on board one of the government schooners he had seized.

The King and Judd knew that they must get their story of what had happened to Washington and London as soon as possible. They also knew that Paulet would try to stop this if he knew about it. It happened that the seized ship was under charter to Ladd & Company, which had reserved the right to embark their commercial agent on her.

Now the affair took on the air of a conspiracy. Why not send the government's dispatches by the Ladd agent, James Marshall? Secretly he was given formal papers addressed to the Queen of England and other documents prepared by Dr. Judd. In order to maintain secrecy, Judd did his work in the royal tomb, using the coffin of Kaahumanu as a desk. The King's signature was needed, so a canoe was sent to Maui for him. Slipping into Waikiki at night, he signed the papers and headed back to Maui.

Simpson and Marshall, who disliked each other intensely, set sail together in March. They parted at Vera Cruz, Mexico. Simpson raced for London and Marshall for Washington. After telling his exciting story in Washington, Marshall joined Richards and Haalilio in London. There they prepared a reply to the accusations of Simpson and Charlton against the Hawaiian government.

Back in Honolulu, the British commission continued its harsh methods. In order to prevent possible seizure of public records, Judd carried them all to the royal tomb. In July the United States frigate *Constellation* arrived from China. Her skipper, Commodore Kearney, made a heated protest against Paulet's actions.

Help for the hard-pressed Hawaiian government arrived on July 26. The British flagship *Dublin*, flying the pennant of Rear Admiral Richard Thomas, arrived from Valparaiso, Chile. The news quickly spread along the waterfront that he had come to restore the independence of the Islands. It was reported that he had interviewed the King in the most courteous manner, and that a fine flag-raising ceremony would be held on July 31.

The memorable day dawned bright and clear. The entire population of Honolulu poured into a flat area east of town where pavilions and a flagstaff had been put up. A company of marines in dress uniform came ashore from the British man-of-war and made a colorful formation awaiting the coming of the admiral and the King. At length they arrived, the King on horseback and the admiral riding in the King's carriage. A twenty-gun salute roared from the marines' field battery. The Hawaiian flag was raised, and a royal salute from the guns of the ships in port was answered by the guns at the fort and around the crest of Punchbowl. The joyous Hawaiians later named the site of the ceremony "Thomas Square" in honor of the admiral. It is located on the present Beretania Street across from the Honolulu Academy of Arts.

After some hours of feasting and pageantry, the people gathered at Kawaiahao Church—that church which has been the scene of so many of Hawaii's historical events. Here the faithful Hawaiian, John

Kawaiahao Church, in which many historic events have taken place, has been rebuilt several times since fire destroyed the original building in 1824.

Ii, gave a speech, and the King told his subjects that independence had been restored. He used the words which are familiar to most of Hawaii's schoolchildren today: *Ua mau ke ea o ka aina i ka pono* ("The life of the land is preserved by righteousness"). This became the motto of the State of Hawaii.

For the next ten days the community celebrated. Admiral Thomas took quarters ashore and helped to restore order. Judd, with his usual zeal and efficiency, recovered the state papers from the royal tomb and set to work improving government machinery. Meanwhile, far across the sea, the King's commission was rejoicing because the British and French had signed a joint declaration which recognized the independence of the Sandwich Islands.

The United States showed that it recognized Hawaii's growing importance by appointing a diplomatic representative rather than a consul. Commissioner George Brown presented his credentials to the King in October. He was a poor choice, as was the next commissioner, Anthony Ten Eyck, who made himself so unpleasant that the government refused to deal with him. Later commissioners showed better judgment and more courtesy.

In February, 1844, a new British consul general, General William Miller, came to Honolulu to replace Charlton. He brought with him a treaty, which contained several objectionable articles. However, the King signed it in the hope that better arrangements might be made later. The French continued to act under the terms of the unsatisfactory treaty presented by Laplace. The United States would make no formal treaty but declared once more that Hawaii should be looked upon as an independent nation.

Reforms in Government

The Constitution of 1840 marked the change from an absolute to a constitutional monarchy. Based upon a simple bill of rights, which the King had granted the year before, it was probably as advanced as the times would permit.

Like the American Constitution, it provided for a separation of powers. The executive power was in the hands of the king, the *kuhina nui,* and four governors. Laws were to be made by a two-house legislature. One branch, the House of Nobles, was to be made up of the king, the chiefs, and the *kuhina nui.* The other, the House of Representatives, would contain representatives chosen by the people. The judicial branch consisted of the king, the *kuhina nui,* and four judges chosen by the House of Representatives. Later laws set up five departments, each headed by a minister in the king's cabinet.

Now that the ship of state was fairly launched, it became necessary to modernize the framework of government and improve upon the Constitution of 1840. The king must rule over foreign elements in the Islands as well as over the native Hawaiians. Dr. Judd, now the first secretary of state, began to gather around him men whom he thought qualified to start the kingdom on its new course.

First came John Ricord, an adventurous young American lawyer. For three years he held the post of attorney general. At the end of that time he left the Islands because of accusations against him back in the United States. Nevertheless he did perform a great service for Hawaii's legal system and worked out a plan to modernize Hawaii's government.

Another valuable recruit was Robert C. Wyllie, a cheerful Scotsman who had come over with General Miller. Wyllie was named minister of foreign affairs. William Richards, as we have already noted, became minister of public instruction after his return from Europe. Serving as prime minister and minister of the interior was the handsome John Young (Keoni Ana). He was the son of the old John Young who had been a close adviser to Kamehameha I. The fifth member was Judd himself, who took the post of minister of finance.

Lorrin Andrews from Maui was judge of cases involving foreigners. A newly arrived lawyer, William Lee, was widely respected for his calm good judgment. His eleven years of service were to be of great value to the kingdom. When the Organic Act of 1848 created a three-man superior court, Lee was appointed chief justice, with Andrews and John Ii as associate justices.

As mid-century drew nearer, it seemed that the missionaries had won a leading place in the Hawaiian community. The foreign merchants and some of the leading Hawaiians charged them with an over-fondness for money and power. Even the American Board at home criticized them for their political activities and their failure to train Hawaiians to take office. Catholics complained that their schools were not being treated fairly. The arrival of George Q. Cannon and a Mormon mission in 1850 brought new complications. Dr. Judd was the target of many attacks, including some from the American commissioner and the British consul general.

New Troubles with France

New troubles with France arose in the spring of 1849. Patrick Dillon, the French consul, claimed some mistreatment of French residents. His conduct was so offensive that the government asked that he be returned to France. In August Admiral Legoarant de Tromelin arrived with two men-of-war. He backed up Dillon and made a series of harsh demands on the Hawaiian government. These demands were met by a calm refusal.

French forces then landed and committed acts of vandalism. They occupied government buildings, dismantled the fort, seized the King's yacht, and destroyed furniture and ornaments in the governor's house. When the Hawaiians watched their actions with curiosity rather than fear, the bewildered French set sail once more with Dillon on board.

Worried by the outrages of de Tromelin, the King and his council decided to send a special commission to France. Dr. Judd was assigned this duty. He was also to escort the two young princes, Alexander Liholiho, who was heir to the throne, and his brother, Lot Kamehameha. A large crowd cheered them as they began their journey on September 11. They received cordial greetings in San Francisco and New York. In London their old friend Admiral Thomas entertained them. Everywhere on their travels in Europe the two princes met with the greatest courtesy and interest. In Paris Judd was unable to persuade a stubborn ministry of foreign affairs to sign a new treaty, but the princes enjoyed their stay in the French capital.

They were not so pleased with their experiences in the United States. In a handwritten journal which is now preserved in the Hawaiian Historical Society library, Prince Alexander Liholiho made an angry entry. His journal, with a little editing, describes an incident in New York on June 5, 1850, as follows:

". . . while at the station waiting for the baggage to be checked, Mr. Judd told me to get in and secure seats. While I was sitting looking out of the window, a man came to me and told me to get out of the carriage rather unceremoniously, saying that I was in the wrong carriage. I immediately

143

asked him what he meant, he continued his request, finally he came around by the door, and I went out to meet him just as he was coming in. Somebody whispered a word into his ears. By this time I came up to him and asked him his reasons for telling me to get out of that carriage. He then told me to keep my seat. I took hold of his arm and asked him his reasons and what right he had in turning me out, and talking to me in the way that he did. He replied that he had some reasons, but requested me to keep my seat. And I followed him out, but he took care to be out of my way after that. I found he was the conductor, and probably took me for somebody's servant just because I had a darker skin than he had. Confounded fool. The first time that I ever received such treatment—not in England or France or anywhere else—but in this country, I must be treated like a dog, to go and come at an American's bidding. Here I must state that I am disappointed at the Americans . . ."

Relations with the United States

Although Prince Alexander might be having his own personal troubles in the United States, relations between the two countries were improved by the visit of Dr. Judd. The American commissioner Ten Eyck had been instructed earlier to work out a treaty similar to the one between Hawaii and Great Britain. However, the terms he offered in 1847 were not acceptable. The following year James J. Jarves, who was now in Boston, had been given the authority to negotiate a treaty with Secretary of State John M. Clayton. Dr. Judd, on his way through San Francisco, had made a similar treaty with the new commissioner to Hawaii, Charles Eames. The two treaties were combined and signed by Jarves and Clayton on December 20, 1849. On the whole, it was a good treaty. It regulated relations between the two countries until Hawaii was annexed to the United States.

After California was admitted to the Union in 1850, many Americans moved to Hawaii. The spirit of annexation was in the air, and there were rumors that some filibusterers from California planned to seize the Islands. A renewal of French claims brought new problems for the Hawaiian government. Some Americans in Hawaii thought that the time was ripe to act to prevent any new French moves. The subject of annexation was introduced in the American Congress.

144

In the face of these difficulties, the King was persuaded that the best course would be to enter into a treaty whereby the Islands would enter the American union as a state. Such a treaty was drafted by Wyllie and David Gregg, the new American commissioner, in the summer of 1854. For some months the matter dragged on. Finally it came to a halt with the death of the King on December 15.

But during all this period of trouble and uncertainty one constructive action was taken. A new constitution for the Hawaiian kingdom was written.

Constitution of 1852

In 1851 the legislature adopted a resolution to appoint three commissioners to draw up a new constitution. The King appointed Dr. Judd, the Nobles appointed Judge John Ii, and the Representatives appointed Judge William L. Lee.

The new document, mainly the work of Judge Lee, was published in the *Polynesian* in November, 1851. It was adopted by the legislature and sent to the King for his signature on June 14, 1852. The constitution provided for a two-house legislature. A House of Nobles, not to exceed thirty members, was to be appointed by the king for life. A House of Representatives, numbering not less than twenty-four nor more than forty members, was to be elected annually. The privy council was now separated from the House of Nobles. The office of *kuhina nui* was continued.

The new constitution was a very liberal one. Its adoption by the King was one of the most statesmanlike gestures in his long reign. The life of the land had been preserved. At least for the moment the dangers from foreign entanglements had decreased.

Summing Up the Chapter

A new influence came to the Islands with the arrival of the French Catholic Mission. For a time Governor Boki favored the mission, but Kaahumanu opposed the Catholics. The first two priests were expelled from the Islands. New trouble broke out later when they returned and other priests arrived. After the death of Kinau in 1839, the climate was better for religious toleration. That same year the French Captain Laplace used force to make the Hawaiian government accept a treaty which contained outrageous demands. In 1843 Lord George

145

Paulet, commander of a British frigate, forced the Hawaiian King to turn over his government to British control. The British government in London did not back up his move, and the Islands were again declared independent. By mid-century, efforts were being made in the Islands and in Washington to annex Hawaii to the United States, but they met with no success. The new Constitution of 1852 gave more liberal government to the Hawaiian kingdom.

13

Sugar and the Land

We have followed the activities of the missionaries, the whalers and traders, and the politicians and lawyers during the reign of Kamehameha III. Now let us look at another revolution which was taking place: a revolution in agriculture. The two most significant phases of it were the growth of the sugar industry and the end of the feudal system of landholding.

Captain Cook, who had a sharp eye for the land and its fruits, noticed "spots of sugar cane on the higher ground" in the islands he had discovered. Apparently the Hawaiians made little attempt to make sugar from this cane but merely chewed the soft stalks for the sweet sap inside. It would be many years before men would have the energy and mechanical skill to produce the crop that would completely change the economy of the land.

It is not clear who made the first efforts to produce sugar commercially in the Islands. There is a story that an enterprising Chinese tried to make sugar on the island of Lanai as early as 1802. He brought with him from China a crude mill of granite rollers and some pans for trying out the syrup, but his project ended in failure. Marín, the Spanish jack-of-all-trades who had settled on Oahu, experimented with sugar-making in 1819. Eight years later an Englishman, John Wilkinson, tried to grow cane in Manoa Valley.

147

At an early sugar mill a carabao turns stone grinding wheels to extract the juice from the sugar cane. The juice is then boiled down to molasses.

The Founding of Koloa Plantation

The first successful venture in the sugar industry began in 1835. In that year three young New Englanders—Peter Brinsmade and William Ladd from Hallowell, Maine, and William Hooper from Boston—leased from Kamehameha III a 980-acre tract of land at Koloa, Kauai. The lease was for fifty years at an annual rental of $300. It provided for a mill-site at Maulili pool, with the use of the waterfall for power, and gave them the privilege of building a road to the nearby landing, which they were free to use. They later leased a warehouse site at the landing from Kaikioewa, the governor of Kauai.

The young partners had come to Honolulu in 1833. Brinsmade and Ladd brought their wives, who were sisters. The men operated a successful business under the name of Ladd & Company. They wished to expand their business and decided to look into the possibilities in sugar. William Hooper agreed to manage the plantation, even though he had little experience in agriculture and could not speak Hawaiian.

Despite all obstacles—the shortage of laborers, the need for improving mill rollers, the lack of money for paying the workers, and the thousand and one difficulties that lie in the path of farmers in a new field—the partners stubbornly developed their holdings. At the end of the first year Hooper could write in his diary that he had built over twenty thatched and adobe houses for his workers, put water power to his mill, planted 25 acres of cane and thousands of coffee and other trees, and put 48 taro patches in order.

For twelve years Ladd & Company had their ups and downs under a series of managers. At the end of that time Dr. Robert W. Wood came into the possession of the plantation and it entered a new period of new problems and achievements.

Sugar Becomes King

Soon after Koloa plantation began operating, stone mills appeared on Maui, Hawaii, and Oahu. Some were run by Chinese. Some were simple ones operated by the mission stations for their own use. In the ten-year period following 1837, sugar production increased noticeably although sales abroad were small. The California Gold Rush of 1849 caused a temporary boom, not only for sugar but for other Island crops. Another boom occurred at the beginning of the Civil War when the Union blockade kept Louisiana sugar from reaching northern markets.

As the market grew, new improved mills appeared. Sugar acreage expanded, and the plantation became "Big Business." The various owners began to join together to employ certain Honolulu commercial agencies, or factors, to buy their milling equipment, find markets, and handle financing.

The founder of the first factoring agency was James Hunnewell, who in 1826 started a store that later became C. Brewer & Company. Another agency was begun by a German sea captain named Hackfeld. His drygoods and general merchandise store, founded in 1849, later became American Factors. An English merchant founded a business house in Honolulu in 1840. Operating under the name of Theo. H. Davies & Company, it also entered the sugar business. S. T. Alexander and H. P. Baldwin, sons of American missionaries, gave their names to still another successful sugar agency.

In 1837 Samuel Northrup Castle and Amos Starr Cooke, members of the eighth company of missionaries sent to Hawaii by the American Board, reached Honolulu. Neither was an ordained minister but both took an active part in the work of the mission. In June, 1851, they published a notice in the weekly *Polynesian* announcing that they were going into business under the name of Castle and Cooke. This firm was the fifth of the "Big Five" factoring agencies, which still occupy an important place in Hawaii's business community.

By 1867 Castle and Cooke were servicing four sugar plantations on Maui, Oahu, and Hawaii. The one on Hawaii was the Kohala Sugar Company, founded in 1863 by the Reverend Elias Bond. It is interesting to note his influence in some of the quaint regulations drawn up for the guidance of plantation employees:

"Said company shall not distill nor manufacture any spirituous liquors from the products of the Plantation.

"The laborers and all belonging to the Plantation are requested to attend church once at least every Sunday.

"There is to be no card playing.

"No fighting is allowed under penalty of one dollar for each offense; the money is to be laid out on Books and Papers.

"No quarreling with or whipping wives is allowed under penalty of one dollar for each offense.

"No tittle tattling is allowed, or gossiping."[1]

Other companies sprang up to service the young sugar industry. For repairing milling machinery, Theophilus H. Davies helped to finance the Honolulu Iron Works Company in 1875. A cabinetmaker named Christopher Lewers opened a shop which supplied construction material. Out of it has come Lewers and Cooke, Ltd., one of Hawaii's most important construction firms. A handsome sailor named Benjamin Dillingham married a missionary's daughter, went into the railroad business and built a warehouse to handle sugar. Captain William Matson started a steamship line to take sugar and other island products to the United States. James Campbell tried his fortunes on Maui and later founded the Pioneer Mill plantation. Waldemar Knudsen, son of a noted Norwegian, came to Hawaii by way of California after a series of misfortunes and won success as a sugar planter. Paul Isenberg, a German immigrant, became a noted sugar proprietor on Kauai.

[1] Castle and Cooke, *The First 100 Years* (Honolulu, 1951), p. 18.

150

The growing and processing of sugar cane developed from a shaky experiment in the 1820s to become the basis of the economy of Hawaii by the 1870s.

Those were exciting, bustling days in Hawaii! Vigorous, inventive men were seeking their fortunes, and in so doing they were building a new community in the Pacific.

Solving the Labor Shortage

By mid-century new sources of labor were needed. The native Hawaiians were not suited to the monotony and regularity of field work. Then too their number had been tragically reduced by epidemics, which swept away thousands. On the one hand, the planters were rapidly increasing acreage and sugar output through irrigation and improved methods. At the same time, field hands were not available to take care of the crops.

In 1850 the newly organized Royal Hawaiian Agricultural Society, a group of residents interested in improving marketing and crop control, discussed ways of importing workers from abroad. China seemed to offer the best source, so a contract was made with the captain of a British ship to bring laborers from South China ports. In January, 1852, about 200 of them arrived, followed by 100 more in August.

They were brought in under a contract labor system, which allowed them three dollars a month for a period of five years. Transportation, food, clothing, and housing were also provided. The Masters' and Servants' Act of 1850 established penalties for workers who broke their contracts, and for planters who treated the workers cruelly or unjustly.

A steady stream of Chinese entered the Islands until the end of the century. Many of them paid their own way, and many who had served their term under contract went back to China. On the whole they were good plantation workers. As time went on, many began to leave the canefields and flock to the towns, especially Honolulu, where they got into the retail trade and truck gardening.

During the second half of the nineteenth century the lack of field workers continued to be a problem. The government tried to solve the problem by encouraging the immigration of contract laborers from countries other than China. However, the difficulties arising from this policy caused even more problems, which are discussed in later chapters.

Reforms in Landholding—The Great Mahele

To succeed in such a large-scale enterprise as sugar planting, capital, labor, and land are needed. The land was there, but how were the planters to gain title to it?

Before the coming of the foreigners, as we have seen, landholding was managed under a feudal system. One defect in the system was that no landholder could be sure of keeping his property. When he died, the land went back to the king, who would reassign it at will. Any tenant could be put off the land by his landowner. His only protection was that of custom, not that of written law.

The early years of the whaling trade brought a greater demand for products of the soil. Foreign traders tried to get land on which to build stores and houses. As early as 1825, Lord Byron, who had brought the body of Liholiho (Kamehameha II) back from London, advised a council of chiefs to pass laws allowing legitimate children of chiefs to inherit land. This law was adopted, and it made the position of the chiefs more secure. It did not, however, help the commoners or the foreigners, who could still lose their rights as tenants.

By the time Kamehameha III came to the throne, an increasing number of foreigners were demanding ownership of land with a clear title. This led to the passage of the famous Bill of Rights of 1839. It stated that land could not be taken from the people except by due process of law. The Constitution of 1840 went on to say that the land was not the private property of the king, but was owned in common with the chiefs and people under the management of the king. Thereafter the common people, although they could not obtain absolute ownership, were not forced off their land without the use of legal means.

The Constitution of 1840 defined a number of rights and privileges of landowners and tenants. However, it did little to assure foreigners that they could get legal title to the property in which they had invested money. The problem became so pressing that an act was passed in December, 1845, creating a board with the pleasant title "Commissioners to Quiet Land Titles." These commissioners were to decide the rights and interests of all people, including foreigners, who had claims on land before the passage of the act. They had full power to decide these claims. Their decision could be appealed to the Supreme Court of Hawaii any time within a ninety-day period. They could not give new titles to land, but only gave land to those who had an interest in it. A law passed in 1850 gave to aliens the right to obtain a clear title to land.

The job of the commissioners was a very difficult one. To judge fairly, the commission had to consider overlapping interests among people who did not understand the principle of individual ownership. Many people did not apply for title to their land. Others quickly sold their holdings without realizing their value. The actual surveying of the land was a problem because there were few qualified surveyors in the kingdom. Some of the missionaries offered to help with the surveying and to persuade people to apply for titles to their land.

After the appointment of the land commission, the next step in land reform was to decide the rights of the King, the chiefs, and *konohikis* in the various undivided portions of the land. A committee was chosen to set up guidelines for the division of lands within the kingdom. Their proposals were as follows:

1. The King was to retain all his private lands, subject only to the rights of tenants. The tenants could take fee simple title to one-third of the land cultivated by them. The King's titles were to be recorded in the same book with all other titles.

153

2. One-third of the remaining lands were to be owned by the Hawaiian government; one-third would go to the chiefs and *konohikis* in proportion to their holdings; one-third would go to the commoners who actually tilled the soil. This division would take place whenever any of the parties desired it.
3. The division would not affect any lands that the King or one of the earlier kings had already granted to any Hawaiian subject or foreigner.
4. To cover the costs of the transfer, the chiefs and *konohikis* could either give one-third of their lands to the government or pay a sum equal to one-third of the unimproved value of their lands.

Each *mahele* (division) was a signed quitclaim agreement between the King and a chief or *konohiki*. The first was signed in January, 1848, and the job was completed about six weeks later. The individual divisions were written down in a large "Mahele Book." After a partition was agreed upon, a chief presented his claim before the land commission and received an award for the lands. After he paid the commission fee, he received a Royal Patent.

Important to the native tenants were the *kuleana* lands on which they depended for their living. These lots may have resembled the highly cultivated taro plots in the Waipio Valley on Hawaii.

Werner Stoy, Camera Hawaii

Now a further division of land was made between the King and the government. The King signed two instruments, both contained in the "Mahele Book," by which he set aside the larger portion of his lands for the benefit of the government and kept other lands for himself and his heirs. The part that he kept became known as crown lands. Kamehameha III and his successors sold, leased, and mortgaged these lands at will until 1865. In that year a law was passed declaring that crown lands should not pass out of the hands of the king and his heirs. When the monarchy toppled in 1893, the remaining crown lands were seized and made a part of the public domain.

The last step in the Great Mahele had to do with the rights of the native tenants, wherever they lived. An act passed in August, 1850, provided for titles for native tenants. To get these titles they had to prove that they actually improved the land they lived on and depended on it for their living. These lands were known as *kuleana* lands.

The *kuleana* lands were mostly highly cultivated taro lots, much more valuable than the waste or forest land which made up a large part of the area assigned to the King and the chiefs. Many native tenants did not file their claims. Others filed but did not defend their claims before the land commission. Still others gave up their claims to the chiefs. Many natives sold their *kuleanas* and moved to the more exciting atmosphere of the town. Often small holdings became part of large plantations. Thus one of the purposes of Kamehameha III in his support of the Great Mahele—to settle commoners on their own land—was in part defeated.

Summing Up the Chapter

Little was done to develop the sugar industry until 1835 when Koloa plantation was founded. Sugar mills appeared all over the Islands. Factoring agencies were formed to handle the buying, marketing, and financing of groups of sugar plantation owners. Because of a labor shortage in the Islands, workers had to be imported from abroad. The old feudal system of landholding was no longer satisfactory. Under Kamehameha III and later rulers, laws were passed that divided the land and gave clear legal titles to the owners. For various reasons many of the natives did not keep the lands assigned to them.

14

Shifting Influences and a New King

In the issue of January 1, 1855, *The Friend* published a black-bordered lead story with the headline "Kamehameha III Is Dead."

"It is with unfeigned sorrow that we announce the death of the King of the Hawaiian Islands. He expired at his palace in Honolulu, December 15th, at 15 minutes before 12 M. The melancholy event was immediately made known to the public, by the royal and national standards being lowered to half-mast, and firing of minute guns, according to his age.

"The most respectful allusions to the event were made in the several Churches of Honolulu on the following Sabbath. Great preparations are making for the most imposing celebration of the funeral obsequies. The remains of His Majesty are now lying in state at the Palace."

Worn out physically and wearied by the many dangers that threatened his country, the King died after an illness of five or six days, in the forty-second year of his life. His memory has remained dear to the Hawaiian people because of the liberal constitution that he granted in 1852, the Great Mahele or land division which he authorized, and the many pioneering efforts in education and general welfare during his reign.

The Smallpox Plague

One event that darkened the last years of the reign of Kamehameha III was the outbreak of smallpox in the Islands. In February, 1853, the ship *Charles Mallory* arrived from San Francisco, where the disease was common. She was flying a yellow flag on her foremast, a sign that she had smallpox aboard.

Upon arrival, the crew were quarantined in a house near Kapiolani Park and watched closely. The sick man was put in a separate house provided for the Board of Health by Prince Lot Kamehameha. The vessel was quarantined for twenty-one days, and all bedding was burned. Eventually the man recovered and the vessel departed.

In May two women on Maunakea Street in Honolulu came down with the disease and were moved to a building on Queen Street which was made into a hospital. It is thought that they became infected as a result of laundering the clothing of seamen who had been exposed to smallpox in San Francisco.

Desperate attempts to prevent the spread of the pox failed, and panic swept over the Hawaiian community, especially in Honolulu and the Ewa district where the disease was most severe. Three commissioners of public health—Mr. Parke, Dr. Rooke, and Dr. Judd— were given full power to make any necessary regulations.

They set up temporary hospitals and limited travel between the islands. Frantic efforts were made to vaccinate the people. After August the plague was not so severe. The whaling ships arrived in September, with crews of two or three thousand, most of whom had not been vaccinated. They were kept on board until Honolulu doctors were able to vaccinate them. According to Mr. Parke, only one foreigner died of the plague. The deaths among the local population, however, were very high. The commissioners of public health estimated the number of cases at 6405 of whom 2485 died.

Some members of the foreign community charged Dr. Judd and Richard Armstrong with being responsible for the spread of the plague. The King was asked to dismiss the two men. The King finally asked the advice of the privy council. By a vote of five to four, the council recommended that the two ministers be dismissed. All the ministers then resigned, but were reappointed with the exception of Dr. Judd. He was replaced by E. H. Allen, who had been serving as the American consul at Honolulu.

Moves Toward Annexation

Another problem that faced the King came from among the growing number of Americans living in the Islands. Americans by mid-century were seized by the fever of expansion. They had come into possession of rich new lands in Oregon and Washington, and the war with Mexico had given them most of the remaining lands of the West. The Gold Rush had brought thousands of Americans to the West Coast, and now there were exciting prospects of trade with the Far East. The location of Hawaii made it a very desirable steppingstone on the long journey to Japan and China. Americans living in the Islands argued that the Hawaiians were a dying race. They claimed that foreign nations, especially France, threatened the monarchy. The only solution to these problems would be to annex Hawaii to the United States.

Early in 1854 the King was asked to try to arrange an annexation treaty with the United States. The King instructed Minister Wyllie to discuss the matter with David L. Gregg, a new American commissioner. While the talks were going on, there was much activity for and against annexation. It was opposed by the British and French representatives, while a local "Committee of Thirteen" was in favor of it. In Washington the British and French ministers spoke to Secretary of State William L. Marcy about the matter. In Congress there were speeches in favor of making the Islands a part of the Union. American newspapers also supported the movement.

The talks between Gregg and Wyllie proceeded slowly, probably because Prince Alexander Liholiho, the King's heir, believed that annexation was not necessary nor desirable. Then in November came the report that a band of filibusterers was coming from California to overthrow the government by force. It happened that at this moment a number of British, French, and American warships were in Honolulu harbor. Wyllie received promises from the commanders of the ships that they would protect the Hawaiian government from any such attempt. The Prince and Wyllie were now sure that annexation would not become necessary. When the King died a few weeks later, all talks were broken off. It is very probable that the proposed treaty would not have been approved by the U.S. Senate for the reason that the United States had already agreed to respect Hawaii's independence. The threat of annexation had passed, but it would arise again!

The New King

Alexander Liholiho, who came to the throne as Kamehameha IV, was born in 1834, the son of Governor Kekuanaoa of Oahu and Kinau. Since Kamehameha III did not have any children, he adopted Liholiho, his nephew, as his heir. Liholiho's rank as High Chief came from Kinau, who was the daughter of Kamehameha I and thus the half-sister of both Kamehameha II and Kamehameha III.

In the same edition of *The Friend* that described the death of Kamehameha III, the editor wrote about Alexander:

"He was educated at the Royal School, when under the charge of Mr. A. S. Cooke. As a scholar he exhibited many good qualities. At the examinations of that school, he always appeared well versed in the ordinary branches of a good English education. In bookkeeping, surveying, and arithmetic, he exhibited a more than ordinary acquaintance, as we are able to testify from our own personal recollection . . . During the last three or four years, he has been, more or less, actively engaged in the affairs of the government. He has been at the head of the military department of the kingdom, and an active member of the House of Nobles. As a member of that body, he has often exhibited an ability, as a parliamentary debator, which would have done credit to a person of more years and greater experience."

After two years on the throne, the handsome young King gladdened the hearts of his subjects by announcing that he was to be married. His bride was the lovely and talented Emma Rooke, a granddaughter of John Young, the trusted lieutenant of Kamehameha I. In childhood she had been adopted by Dr. T. C. B. Rooke, an English physician who had married Emma's aunt.

The wedding took place in June, 1856, at Kawaiahao Church, with the Reverend Richard Armstrong officiating. The King, as nervous as any other bridegroom, forgot the ring. The situation was saved, however, when a prominent government official, Elisha Allen, pulled a ring from his finger and offered it to the King. It was a brilliant wedding, and thousands of Hawaiians gathered on the church grounds to honor the young couple. One of the bridesmaids was Victoria Lydia Paki, who was later to become Queen Liliuokalani.

159

1853 Smallpox epidemic

1854 Death of Kamehameha III
Alexander Liholiho is proclaimed Kamehameha IV

1854 Republican Party formed
Crimean War begins

1855 Liholiho ascends the throne as Kamehameha IV

1856 Peak of the whaling industry

Marriage of Kamehameha IV to Emma Rooke

First irrigation project completed on Kauai

1857 Dred Scott Decision

James Buchanan inaugurated 15th U.S. president

1858 Birth of Prince Albert. the official heir

1858 England takes control of India

1859 John Brown takes the arsenal at Harper's Ferry

1860 Queen's Hospital built. Hawaii's first hospital

1861 Abraham Lincoln inaugurated 16th U.S. president

U.S. Civil War begins

1862 Death of Prince Albert

Dr. Thomas Staley. first Anglican bishop. arrives

1862 Homestead Act

Bismarck becomes prime minister of Prussia

1863 Death of Liholiho. Kamehameha IV. age 29

1863 Emancipation Proclamation

Lot ascends the throne

King Kamehameha IV, (1834-1863) Alexander Liholiho,
reigned from 1854 - 1863.

King Kamehameha IV and his Queen leave Kawaiahao Church after their wedding. Bearers carry feather *kahilis*, an important symbol of royalty.

Two years later the Queen gave birth to a son. There was great joy among the Hawaiians, since it seemed to ensure the continuance of the Kamehameha line. The privy council gave the child the title of "His Royal Highness the Prince of Hawaii" (*Ka Haku o Hawaii*) and in 1859 he was officially named the heir of Kamehameha IV.

Decline of the Hawaiian Population

In his first message to the legislature in 1855, the King called attention to the disastrous decrease of the native population. He recommended that public hospitals be established and that something be done to prevent the spread of foreigners' diseases among the Hawaiian people. Money was voted for this purpose, but it was not used.

The King and Queen continued to press for hospitals for sick and penniless Hawaiians. Finally, in 1859, the legislature gave its approval to the collection of funds for a medical center. Immediately the royal couple went through the community asking personally for subscriptions to the hospital fund. A board of trustees managed the association

162

and opened a temporary dispensary. By the spring of 1860, they were able to buy a tract of land at the corner of Beretania and Punchbowl Streets. By the end of the next year a permanent two-story building had been put up and named Queen's Hospital. Dr. William Hillebrand was put in charge of the hospital, and money was voted by the legislature to maintain it.

At first the superstitious natives were afraid to use the new hospital. They were accustomed to the services of their old *kahunas* and had little faith in the scientific methods of the *haole* doctors. As time passed, they began to come in great numbers for treatment and prescriptions. The new Queen's Hospital located on the same site as the old building is a lasting monument to Kamehameha IV and his gentle Queen.

Up-to-date medical care is available at Queen's Hospital and Medical Center in Honolulu. The cornerstone of the original building was laid on July 17, 1860. Photo courtesy of Queen's Medical Center.

Foreign Relations

One of the most important aims of Kamehameha IV was that of making a trade treaty with the United States whereby Hawaiian and American goods would be exchanged without the payment of duty. He thought that such a treaty might remove the threat of annexation and do away with the fears of the American sugar planters. Such a treaty would furnish a much larger market for Hawaiian sugar, and the whole economy of the Islands would benefit.

Chief Justice William L. Lee went to Washington in the spring of 1855 to confer with President Franklin Pierce and Secretary of State William L. Marcy. The talks were carried out in a friendly atmosphere, and finally a satisfactory treaty was signed by Marcy and Lee. It was quickly ratified by the Hawaiian government but ran into difficulties in the American Senate. The Hawaiian cabinet sent Elisha H. Allen, finance minister, to Washington to try to help the treaty along. All efforts failed. Southern sugar planters and western wool producers were strong enough to keep the treaty from being ratified.

Another problem in foreign relations had to do with the unsatisfactory treaty that had been made with France in 1846. The Hawaiians wanted a more liberal treaty, more like those they had signed with the United States and Great Britain. They objected to the low import tax on French brandy and to the right of Frenchmen to be tried by a jury picked by the French consul. The French, on the other hand, complained that Catholics were being oppressed in Hawaii and that official documents could be written only in the English and Hawaiian languages.

Finally, the French consul, Emile Perrin, was given the power to make a new treaty with ministers Wyllie and Allen. After long and sometimes bad-tempered discussion, a treaty was ironed out. The King was not completely satisfied with it, but he wished to stay on cordial terms with the French and agreed to its ratification in September, 1858.

Religious Movements

In that same year an interesting debate took place in Honolulu over the possibility of establishing an Episcopal chapel in Hawaii. A number of people had been members of the Church of England or of the Protestant Episcopal Church in America and naturally wished to have their children brought up in that faith. The King and the Queen

Most of the stone to build St. Andrew's Episcopal Cathedral in Honolulu came from England. King Kamehameha IV and Queen Emma were sponsors of the Anglican Episcopal Church in Hawaii and founded the church in 1862.

Camera Hawaii

warmly supported the project. Minister Wyllie also favored the establishment of an Episcopal Church in the Islands. The American missionaries were very much against the move. They charged that the way was being prepared for a union of church and state, that the British influence would become too powerful, and that their own work would be forgotten or valued less.

Nevertheless, the King went ahead with the project, partly because of remorse and sincere repentance arising from an unfortunate action that occurred in September, 1859. While on an excursion of a royal party to Maui, the King became jealous of his friend and private secretary, Henry Neilson. It was whispered that Neilson, an American of a good family, was guilty of improper conduct involving the Queen. The enraged King, after a period of heavy drinking and brooding, took a pistol and shot Neilson. The young man died as a result of the wounds. It was later proved that Neilson was innocent of the charges. The King was overcome with grief. He even thought of giving up the throne but was kept from this drastic action by his advisers and by public opinion. He tried to find peace in religion and determined to encourage the Episcopalians to come to Hawaii.

165

Church authorities in London and prominent Episcopalians in America learned of his wishes. Committees were formed to raise money for the mission, and the King offered land for a church site. He also personally asked Queen Victoria of England for support. In 1861 Dr. Thomas N. Staley of Queen's College, Cambridge in England, was chosen by the Archbishop of Canterbury to become the bishop of a diocese in the Hawaiian Islands. The church was to be called the Hawaiian Reformed Catholic Church. Later, the name was changed to the Anglican Church in Hawaii.

Queen Victoria had agreed to be godmother to the little Prince of Hawaii. Mrs. Synge, the wife of the new British consul-general in Hawaii, was to represent her at the baptismal service, which Bishop Staley was to conduct. Before the bishop reached Honolulu, on October 11, 1862, a grievous blow struck the royal family and, indeed, the whole kingdom. The little prince died of brain fever after a short illness.

A week after the bishop's arrival, the inaugural sermon was preached. A few weeks later the royal couple and several high ranking officials were confirmed as members of the church. At first the services were held in a building on Nuuanu Street. Later a church was built on the site of the present St. Andrew's Cathedral.

In 1863 the American Protestant mission in Hawaii was cut loose from its parent organization, the American Board of Commissioners for Foreign Missions. The time had come for the American missionaries to handle their own affairs, to train Hawaiian pastors, and to reorganize parishes. The Hawaiian Evangelical Association, formed in 1854, was now reorganized and its "Board" took over the duties of the American Board.

Another important religious development was the Mormon movement in Hawaii, which had begun in 1850. After some successes, especially on the island of Lanai, the Mormon missionaries were ordered by Brigham Young, the leader of Mormons in America, to return to Salt Lake City, partly because of the "Mormon War" in Utah. The untrained native elders, who were left in charge of the mission, were not able to give it the necessary life. Into this situation stepped the colorful and much-disputed figure of Walter Murray Gibson, who arrived in Honolulu in the summer of 1861.

Gibson was the son of English emigrants who had gone to the United States. After varied experiences in New York, Central Amer-

166

In 1919 the followers of Mormonism built at Laie, Oahu, a beautiful temple, which is often referred to as "Hawaii's Taj Mahal."

ica, California, and the East Indies, he visited Salt Lake City. Here he met Brigham Young, became interested in Mormonism and was baptized in that faith. After being made a missionary, he found his way to Hawaii, accompanied by his daughter Talula. He quickly became the leader of the Mormons in Hawaii. Gibson raised money to buy the lands on Lanai that had been leased by the Mormon community on that island. Here he made his home.

By 1864, some of Gibson's activities caused Brigham Young to send an investigating group to Hawaii. The group found that Gibson himself had the title to the lands on Lanai, which had been bought with church funds. For this and for other questionable activities, he was excommunicated, and most of his followers left the island. Gibson kept the land, which he turned into a sheep ranch. Later on, this most unusual man was to hold a key position in the political affairs of the Islands.

In 1865 the Mormon mission, which now included elders sent from Salt Lake City, bought lands for a gathering place at Laie on the island of Oahu. The mission grew steadily until today the Mormons occupy a strong and respected position in business, church, and educational circles in Hawaii.

The Civil War and Hawaii

On May 9, 1861, the *Pacific Commercial Advertiser* told the people of Honolulu that a great civil war had broken out in the United States. Its startling headlines read, "War! Attack on Fort Sumter by the Confederate Army! Unconditional Surrender by Major Anderson!"

In the September 2 issue of *The Friend,* Editor Samuel Damon penned an editorial that probably reflected the prevailing feeling of most of the Americans living in Hawaii. Referring to the bombardment of Sumter, he wrote:

"In all honesty, we can say, that never before were we more proud of our country, as 'the land of the free and the home of the brave.' Whatever shall be the issue, whether the South is reunited to the North, or an independent nation is established, of this we are sure, that blows will be struck for freedom, and battles fought for constitutional liberty, which will benefit the down-trodden and enslaved, not of one but many lands—We have no fears regarding the final result."

Even though the American residents sympathized with the North, there seemed to be only one sensible course for the Hawaiian government to follow. Following the example of Great Britain and France, the government declared itself neutral in the struggle between North and South.

The effects of the war in Hawaii were mainly economic. The whaling industry, as we have noted, was already showing signs of decline. Now whaling ships were pressed into wartime service or laid up for the rest of the war. Many whalers were sunk by Confederate privateers. A few Island residents joined the Union forces, including an ex-naval officer from Kauai named William Reynolds. The sugar industry boomed because of heavy demands and higher prices. A number of new plantations were started.

Finally the war ended, and, on May 13, 1865, the *Advertiser* came out with the sad news of Abraham Lincoln's assassination. The June 1 issue of *The Friend* appeared with heavy black columns containing a long and eloquent sermon by the editor on the death of the President.

Summing Up the Chapter

The last years of the reign of Kamehameha III were darkened by a smallpox plague, which caused much loss of life among the natives. The King sent commissioners to the United States to try to have the Islands annexed to the United States. They were not successful. The new King, Kamehameha IV, was married soon after he ascended the throne. Their only son and heir died while still a small boy. The King and Queen took the lead in setting up a hospital that would serve the poor. A new treaty was made with France, but Hawaii failed to get a free-trade treaty with the United States. During this time, the Episcopal Church came to Hawaii, the American missions separated from their home board, and the Mormon missionaries brought a new influence. The American Civil War hurt the whaling industry but helped the sugar planters.

15

The End of the Kamehameha Dynasty

Midway during the course of the Civil War, an official notice was printed by *The Friend* in its issue of December 1, 1863. The notice, dated November 30 and addressed to foreign diplomats and consuls in Honolulu, stated:

> Sir:
> It is with a sorrow that I cannot express, that I make known to you that it has pleased Almighty God to call hence to a better world, at a quarter past 9 o'clock this morning, my Sovereign, King Kamehameha IV.
> R. C. Wyllie
Minister of Foreign Affairs

Then followed a proclamation issued by Her Royal Highness, the Princess Victoria:

> It having pleased Almighty God to close the earthly career of King Kamehameha IV, at a quarter past 9 o'clock this morning, I, as Kuhina Nui, by and with the advice of the Privy Council of State, hereby Proclaim, Prince Lot Kamehameha, King of the Hawaiian Islands, under the style and title of Kamehameha V. God Preserve the King!

> Given at the Palace, this thirtieth day of November, 1863.
> (Signed) Kaahumanu

(It was not unusual for the Kuhina Nui to take the title of Kaahumanu)

The new king was the older brother of Kamehameha IV. Like his younger brother he had been well educated at the Chief's Children's School or Kula Keiki Alii and had travelled widely. In 1860 he had visited California and British Columbia. During his career he had held many positions of trust in the government. He was well qualified to assume the leadership of Hawaii, having energy, strength of character, and an even disposition. His ability had been proven when, during Alexander's reign, he had served as commander of the army and as Minister of the Interior. While Kamehameha V did not possess the brilliancy of his predecessor, he had a better grasp of practical affairs. During the last six years of his brother's reign he had served as interior minister and for over a year had headed the department of finance. During his reign he entered personally into all discussions of importance and selected ministers who supported his ideas. Some of his acts were strongly attacked, but he believed that his policies were for the good of Hawaii.

Kamehameha V, "the last great chief of the olden type," and true grandson of Kamehameha the Great, believed that the king's right, going back to Kamehameha I, was to lead the people firmly. He could be called a benevolent dictator as he refused, upon his inauguration, to take the oath to maintain the liberal Constitution of 1852. He wanted his subjects to be thrifty and hardworking, and felt that they needed to be protected from waste and idleness. Thus, he refused to repeal the law against selling liquor to the native population and required people to both be educated and own property before they could vote. He feared that universal suffrage would lead to a republic in Hawaii that would be annexed by the United States. Therefore, his first major act as king was directed towards the revision of the constitution.

While Lot may have been tough with his people, he was equally hard with the *haoles.* Lot meant to be a ruling monarch and did not care much what *haoles* thought of him. The white men, especially the Americans, did not care for Lot either. This caused a problem in race relations and made the national legislature a strange place to be in where white members refused to learn Hawaiian and Hawaiian representatives refused to speak English. The fact that anything at all got accomplished there was due largely to the parliamentary interpreter, William Ragsdale, who was half-Hawaiian and half-white. Mark Twain, who visited Hawaii during Lot's reign,

171

1863 Lot ascends throne

1864 New constitution replaces that of 1852
Bureau of Immigration established

1865 Lee surrenders at Appomattox; Civil War ends
President Lincoln assassinated and Andrew Johnson becomes president
13th amendment ending slavery

1866 Kalaupapa leper colony founded on Molokai

1866 Civil Rights Act of 1866

1868 First Japanese laborers brought to Hawaii

1868 14th amendment granting citizenship rights

1869 Ulysses S. Grant becomes 18th U.S. president
Transcontinental railroad completed

1870 Alexander and Baldwin founded
Defeat of reciprocal trade treaty with U.S.

1870 15th amendment. black suffrage
Italy unites

1871-72 Hawaiian Hotel built

1871 Germany unifies

1872 Iolani School established
Legislature passes several acts to protect the rights of laborers
Death of Lot Kamehameha

1873 William Lunalilo is elected king
Father Damien arrives at Kalaupapa
Mutiny of household troops

1874 Lunalilo dies of tuberculosis

King Kamehameha V, (1830-1872) Lot Kamehameha,
reigned from 1863 - 1872.

173

upon the occasion of his visit to the legislature said of Ragsdale:

Bill Ragsdale stands up in front of the Speaker's pulpit, with his back against it, and fastens his quick black eye upon any member who rises, lets him say half a dozen sentences and then interrupts him, and repeats his speech in a loud, rapid voice, turning every Kanaka speech into English and every English speech into Kanaka, with a readiness and felicity of language that are remarkable— waits for another installment of talk from the member's lips and goes on with his translation as before. His tongue is in constant motion from eleven in the forenoon till four in the afternoon, and why it does not wear out is the affair of Providence, not mine.

Lot disliked Americans because he feared that Hawaii would become a republic after the model of the United States, and thus come under American domination. With this in mind, he engineered a bloodless coup d'etat at the beginning of his reign to force upon his people a new, conservative constitution limiting the democratic tendencies of his kingdom.

The Constitution of 1864

As an *ali'i*, Kamehameha V believed that he should be firmly in control of the government. He was a strong-minded and plain-spoken man who, like his brother, was often irritated by the controls put upon him by the Constitution of 1852. He did not believe that all Hawaiians should have the vote, since they were not ready to use it intelligently. This privilege, he thought, should be given to those who had a certain amount of property and education. He did not take an oath to support the existing constitution. Instead he issued a proclamation calling for delegates to be elected to a convention to draw up a new constitution.

The King's plan called forth much heated discussion among all classes and in the newspapers. In order to explain the proposed changes to his people, the King left Oahu and journeyed to the outside islands. Upon his return in June, 1864, he conferred with his advisors, especially Wyllie and Attorney General Charles Harris. Carefully he wrote the draft of a new constitution, which he presented to the convention on July 7 at a meeting held in Kawaiahao Church.

The members of the convention were not able to agree, especially on the question of the vote. Impatient at the delay, the King dissolved the meeting and announced that his constitution would be the law of the land.

The Constitution of 1864 was somewhat shorter and far less liberal than that of 1852. Providing for a number of changes, it abolished the old office of *kuhina nui,* increased the power of the king and his cabinet, and set up a one-house legislature. While it did not deny the common people their voting rights, it stated that voters born after 1840 must pass a literacy test, and it set up a property qualification for both voters and representatives. Despite the way in which it was presented, the constitution lasted for the next twenty-three years. Thus, while critics said Lot's reign would be despotic, the king actually enjoyed his rule with few significant problems.

Problems of Immigration

Very soon after Kamehameha V came to the throne, he began to study the problem of the scarcity of field hands to work the sugar plantations. Early in 1864 some leading agriculturists had founded a "Planters' Society" to deal with the problem. One of the leaders was Minister Wyllie, who, as owner of the Princeville Plantation on Kauai, had a personal interest in the matter. The King asked some of his ministers to confer with the society to find ways to obtain a fresh labor supply.

As a result of the recommendations of this conference, a Bureau of Immigration was formed in December, 1864 to regulate and encourage the flow of immigrants to the Islands. Commissioners were sent abroad to hunt for capable workers. In 1868 the first group of Japanese was brought to Hawaii under a three-year contract with pay at four dollars per month. No more Japanese came in until 1885 when 200 entered. After that there was a steady influx of Japanese until 1908. Large numbers of Portuguese, mostly from the island of Madeira, began to arrive in 1878. Added to this racial mixture were a few Norwegians and Germans. Beginning in 1906, under an agreement with the Philippine government, many Filipinos entered Hawaii.

The importing of contract workers from China, Japan, and other sources partly satisfied the needs of the planters. However, it met with much disapproval not only in Hawaii but also in the United States and Great Britain. The "coolie trade," as it was called, was compared by many to the slave system in the United States. In 1872 the legislature passed several acts to protect the rights of the laborers. The general problem of labor supply and immigration, however, remained to plague the successors of Kamehameha V.

Leprosy in Hawaii

A new and alarming threat to the health of Hawaii's people came in the 1860s—the dreaded disease of leprosy. In Hawaii it was known as the *Mai Pake* (Chinese disease) because it was mistakenly believed to have been brought from China. There had been some cases of it before the reign of Kamehameha IV, but by 1865 it had become such a threat that the legislature took steps to handle it. The board of health was to segregate those who suffered from the disease and to establish an isolated community for those who were incurable.

The board chose a site on the island of Molokai for an isolation settlement. Here, on a peninsula separated from the rest of the island by rugged cliffs, a leper colony was started in 1866. At first the patients were sent to Kalawao on the eastern section of the peninsula but later they were moved to Kalaupapa in the west.

The story of leprosy and the Kalapapa settlement is too long to tell here. It is a story of neglect and mismanagement, of sorrow, of self-sacrifice and high idealism. A leading character in the story is, of course, Father Damien, who first began to work with the lepers in 1873. Today leprosy is quite rare in Hawaii. "Hansen's Disease," as it is now called, has been conquered by medical science. People suffering from the disease are no longer forced to go to Kalaupapa unless they wish to go.

Foreign Relations

The outbreak of the Civil War in the United States caused a flurry in foreign relations. The Hawaiian government had negotiated a policy of neutrality during the Crimean War in 1853 fought between European powers. Minister Wyllie thought that the Con-

One of the most tragic diseases brought to Hawaii by foreigners in the 1800s was leprosy or Hansen's disease. Hawaiians suffering from this disease were sent to the isolated settlement of Kalaupapa on Molokai. Many of those treated, whose cases are fully arrested or cured, choose to remain on this lovely peninsula which juts out from the cliffs of Molokai's north shore.

federacy should have belligerent rights, but the king did not want to displease Washington. Hawaii officially proclaimed neutrality in 1861 and the U.S. accepted this. However, several factors, including the pro-British monarchy, the introduction of the Anglican church by Kamehameha IV, and the repeal of the liberal constitution of 1852 by Kamehameha V cooled the relations between Hawaii and the United States. Nevertheless, in 1863 the United States raised the status of its representative in Hawaii to minister resident, the highest diplomatic rank of all countries having representatives in Honolulu at that time. This action was recognized as a high compliment by the Hawaiian kingdom.

Economics

Kamehameha V's time saw radical changes in the economic life of Hawaii. Whaling declined and lost its place to sugar as the prime industry in the islands. A severe economic depression occurred as a result of the whaling disaster of 1871, when thirty-three vessels that

177

had been regularly expected in the islands were trapped in ice elsewhere. Left by their crews, cargoes were abandoned and lost. As whaling died, sugar rose, and with this steam machinery was introduced on sugar plantations. Production increased with King Lot's and his government's negotiations to promote a reciprocity treaty, the nature of which would allow sugar into American ports on a duty-free basis.

The Civil War in the United States caused sugar prices to rise and stimulated sugar planting in Hawaii. Many new plantations were established and in 1865 the exportation of sugar was ten times what it had been in 1860. Expansion during these years was too rapid and based largely on borrowed money. When the war ended, prices dropped. Business failures forced a number of plantation bankruptcies. 1867 was marked by a drop in production, but this decline was recovered in 1868. By 1871 sugar exportation reached a new peak of ten thousand tons. Yet the sudden expansion of the sugar industry slowed down after 1869, and the period from 1872 to 1873 was a time of depression.

At this time sugar was not the only important crop in Hawaii's economy. Early attempts at cultivating rice succeeded by 1861 and a craze for rice planting swept the islands, coinciding with the arrival of some Asian immigrants. Coffee raising, begun during the reign of Kamehameha III, was seriously set back by an insect blight, but continued. Livestock, however, did very well during the third quarter of the nineteenth century. Ranches were successful. Lot, as a prince, had been the first president of a Grazier's Association organized in 1856 on Oahu. A final product cultivated at this time was *pulu,* a silky or woolly fiber which grows at the base of tree fern fronds and was used as a filling for mattresses and pillows. *Pulu* was exported to California between 1851 and 1884. Thus sugar, rice, coffee, *pulu,* and products of the livestock industry made up the bulk of Hawaii's domestic exports during the reign of Kamehameha V. All of these important changes in the economy increased the need for better means of transportation among the islands and between Hawaii and her foreign markets.

Transportation and Commerce

During the reign of Kamehameha V (1863-1872) several important advances in transportation were made. Steamer transportation between Honolulu and San Francisco and between Honolulu and Australia became a reality due to American interest in the Pacific and the Far East. Completion of the Pacific railroad across the United States in 1869 also aroused interest in Hawaii. With steamers bringing more travelers to the islands than ever before, the people of Honolulu realized the need for more and better hotels. The government assumed responsibility for this project and during 1871-72 built the Hawaiian Hotel at the corner of Richards and Hotel Streets for over $110,000. Unfortunately, this construction doubled the national debt and led to the political downfall of two cabinet ministers, John Mott Smith and C. C. Harris, who had promoted the project. Thus, under Kamehameha V, tourism expanded as did the sugar industry and other forms of diversified agriculture. These developments occurred as new transportation forms and routes were established.

The End of the Kamehameha Dynasty

King Lot, the last Kamehameha, had been in ill health for a few years. As Lot was a bachelor, his sister, the Princess Victoria Kamamalu, was named his successor by the Constitution of 1864 which he had established. Unfortunately, she died in 1866 and the king was pressured to marry and provide an heir. He declined to marry; neither did he have children. He died on December 11, 1872 on his fortieth birthday. Of the two brothers, Lot had been the most Hawaiian by nature. There were rumors, at his death, that a female *kahuna*, Kamaipuupaa, influenced him and that he waited until the last moment to name his successor to the throne because of his superstition that such an appointment would bring about his own death. Thus, when King Lot died in 1872 there was still no named successor. The seventy-seven year reign of the Kamehamehas ended leaving Hawaii without a ruler.

Summing Up the Chapter

With the death of Kamehameha IV, his elder brother became Kamehameha V. Lot proclaimed the Constitution of 1864, which gave more power to the king and to the educated and propertied classes. The Bureau of Immigration was formed in the same year to regulate and encourage people to come to work in the Islands. By the 1860s leprosy had become a threat in the Islands, and a leper colony was founded in an isolated spot on Molokai in 1866. Father Damien de Veuster began to work with the lepers of Kalaupapa in 1873. The policies of Lot Kamehameha were similar to those of Alexander. The foremost problems involved foreign relations, particularly with the United States. The danger of annexation had been barely averted earlier under Kamehameha III and a substitute policy was still needed. American born sugar planters hoped Hawaii would be annexed to the United States so that they could avoid heavy import duties in the markets of California and Oregon. The government sought, instead, a reciprocity treaty which would allow Hawaiian and American products to be exchanged duty free. With the advance of sugar and other forms of agriculture came the advance in transportation methods and the opening of new trade routes.

16

Lunalilo, the People's Choice

As Kamehameha V lay dying on December 11, 1872, he called the High Chiefess Bernice Pauahi (Mrs. Charles R. Bishop) to his bedside and asked her to be his successor. Although she was the last living descendant of Kamehameha the Great (Kamehameha I), she refused to accept the offer. The subject was dropped and the King died an hour later.

With the death of Kamehameha V, the throne of Hawaii was vacant. Under the Constitution of 1864 the king had the right to appoint his successor, provided that this appointment was approved by the Nobles. Inasmuch as Kamehameha V had passed away without naming a successor, the decision of who would be king was left to the legislature.

The cabinet promptly ordered the legislature to meet to elect a new king. The American minister to Hawaii, Henry A. Peirce, and the British representative, Theo. H. Davies, feared rioting and bloodshed. Each, therefore, asked his government to send a warship to Hawaii to help to keep the peace. The United States sent the *U.S.S. Benecia,* which arrived before the legislature met.

Candidates for the Throne

Although there were several possible candidates for the throne, the contest centered around two—William C. Lunalilo and David

Kalakaua. Lunalilo was the highest ranking *ali'i* and was descended from the half-brother of Kamehameha the Great. He was well-educated and was popular with all classes of people. According to Minister Peirce, David Kalakaua ". . . [is] well educated, speaks English well, [is] of polished manners and bearing." Davies described Kalakaua also as "intelligent and well-educated, and mingling freely in general society." Kalakaua held a commission as a colonel in the Hawaiian army.

Following the death of the King, a mass meeting was held, supposedly to pass resolutions of sympathy. After the resolutions were passed, the real purpose of the meeting became evident—to pass a resolution nominating Lunalilo to be king. This resolution was greeted with enthusiastic applause. On the Neighbor Islands informal meetings were held with the same results.

No immediate action was taken by the candidates. Many people were anxious during these days since this was the first time in Hawaiian history that the country had been left without a ruler. Large numbers of people gathered in Honolulu. Some people feared that with so many people in the capital lawlessness might break out. In the old days the death of a ruling chief had been a signal for riotous sprees. The only remnants of the old customs were the nightly mourning sessions at the palace grounds. Apparently business went on as usual. The courts of justice remained open, and criminals were still prosecuted in the name of the King, as if he were living. Still, though life went on, the shadow of a great crisis rested on the land. Men were gripped by an unknown fear.

Six days after the death of the King, Lunalilo published a message to the people. Even though he claimed that he was the King's successor, he wanted the people to make the decision. In his message he stated his claim as follows:

> *"Whereas,* It is desirable that the wishes of the Hawaiian people be consulted as to a successor to the Throne, Therefore,
> "Notwithstanding that according to the law of inheritance, I am the rightful heir to the Throne, in order to preserve peace, harmony and good order, I desire to submit the decision of my claim to the voice of the people . . ."

William C. Lunalilo was elected to the empty throne by an overwhelming popular majority. Called "The People's Prince," he reigned from 1873 - 1874.

Lunalilo wanted every man in the kingdom to take part in the election. He also promised to amend many of the provisions of the constitution and to give the people a greater voice in the government.

Lunalilo's message was received with great enthusiasm by all groups in the community. Because everyone wanted to settle the question of a new ruler, Lunalilo's words increased his already great popularity. The election, of course, had to be unofficial since only the legislature had the right to decide who would be king. Nevertheless, everyone felt that the legislature would be guided by the wishes of the people. So great was Lunalilo's popularity that he was called "The People's Prince."

Shortly after the publication of Lunalilo's message, a group calling itself the "Skillful Genealogists" secretly published a circular in which Lunalilo's claim to be descended from Kamehameha's half-brother was attacked. This attack backfired, for it only served to anger Lunalilo's supporters and to cause them to work harder. To this day no one knows positively who wrote the attack on Lunalilo. Then, as now, many suspected it was Kalakaua.

A few days later Kalakaua published his own proclamation. It was written in the poetic style of old Hawaii and reads, in part, as follows:

"O my people! My countrymen of old! Arise! This is the voice!

"Ho! all ye tribes! Ho! my own ancient people! The people who took hold and built up the Kingdom of Kamehameha.

"Arise! This is the voice!

"Let me direct you, my people! Do nothing contrary to the law or against the peace of the Kingdom. Do not go and vote.

"Do not be led by the foreigners; they had no part in our hardships, in gaining the country. Do not be led by their false teachings."

Kalakaua further promised to bring back the "Law of the Splintered Paddle," repeal all personal taxes, put native Hawaiians into the national government, and amend the Constitution of 1864. He warned the people against the liberal Constitution of 1852. What Kalakaua objected to was the supposed influence of the foreigners over Luna-

184

lilo. The struggle for the crown brought into sharp focus the attitudes of the two men. Kalakaua's words proved to be an accurate blueprint to much of his behavior when he later became king.

The Election of Lunalilo

If Kalakaua's message was designed to influence the voters, it must have been a disappointment to him. On New Year's Day, 1873, Lunalilo won a popular election by a landslide. The next question was whether the legislature would be guided by the wishes of the people. The people feared that Kalakaua had great strength in the legislature. A great crowd of Lunalilo's supporters filled the building and the streets surrounding it. Before the balloting began, Lunalilo's supporters succeeded in having a motion passed in the legislature that required each member to sign his name on the back of his ballot. Such extreme action was not necessary, for all votes were for Lunalilo. The people had won. Later, Queen Emma wrote in a letter that hundreds of Hawaiians were ready to tear to pieces any member who was suspected of opposing Lunalilo.

Lunalilo's coronation was held at Kawaiahao Church in a truly royal ceremony. The church was filled to capacity and an even larger crowd stood outside. Since he had no carriage of his own, Lunalilo walked to the church, refusing to borrow one. After the ceremonies he walked across the street to the palace amid the cheers of his devoted subjects to assume the heavy duties of being a king.

The new King changed the policies of Kamehameha V, who had tried to restore the absolute powers of the crown. Here was a king who believed in democratic government as shown by his wish to have every man in the kingdom help decide who should be king.

In many ways Lunalilo brought strength to the throne, although he had certain weaknesses. He had been left an orphan and was raised as a spoiled and petted prince at the royal court. Finally he was placed in the School for Young Chiefs, where he received a good education under Mr. and Mrs. Amos Cooke. He was a fine student, excelling in English literature. However, he had no training in practical matters and none in public administration. The new King was intelligent and witty, but generous to a fault. He had a good sense of humor but sometimes had difficulty in reaching a decision. His other great weakness was a fondness for alcoholic beverages. Nor did he enjoy good health.

Lunalilo in a simple black suit, walked to his coronation at Kawaiahao Church. A double line of soldiers stood along the route to the church.

Immediately upon becoming king, Lunalilo sent a message to the legislature recommending that the constitution be amended. The most important change that he suggested was the removal of property qualifications for voters. Some of the other changes he advocated were: (1) separation of the legislature into two houses, the House of Nobles and the House of Representatives; (2) a written explanation to accompany the king's veto; and (3) the right of cabinet ministers, who were automatically members of the House of Nobles, to be heard in the House of Representatives.

Problems of the Government

When Lunalilo became king, there was an economic depression in Hawaii. The great days of the whaling fleets were gone. Exports of sugar had dropped seriously because of the United States' tariff. The price of sugar in San Francisco was low, and labor costs were high. These unfavorable conditions in the sugar industry affected the entire nation since the prosperity of Hawaii depended on sugar.

The Honolulu Chamber of Commerce asked the King to make another effort to secure a treaty whereby Hawaiian sugar could enter the United States tax-free. In view of past attempts to make such a treaty, many people felt that the United States would not be interested unless some incentive were offered. There was talk of offering the United States the Pearl River Lagoon in exchange for the tax-free admission of Hawaiian sugar into the United States. The King discussed this suggestion with his cabinet, and it was agreed that this might be done. The idea of giving Pearl Harbor to a foreign government aroused a great deal of opposition among the Hawaiian people as well as others. When it became clear that the legislature would not approve giving territory to a foreign power, the offer was withdrawn.

So pressing was the problem of landing Hawaiian sugar in San Francisco tax-free that once more there was some talk of annexation to the United States if a trade treaty could not be secured. However, at no time was there widespread support for annexation among the native Hawaiians. In the United States there was little interest in Hawaii. High American tariffs caused sugar planters to look toward Australian and New Zealand markets. There was talk of obtaining a reciprocity treaty with those two countries. However, the entire question of a trade treaty was set aside for the remainder of Lunalilo's short reign.

HAWAIIAN MONEY

Before the Europeans and Americans arrived, the Hawaiians had no need for money, since barter was the method of exchange. Certain articles such as feathers and adzes were highly prized but apparently were not used for money in the usual sense. Early in the nineteenth century sandalwood was used to pay the debts of the chiefs to foreign traders. Soon the sandalwood was paid for in a variety of foreign coins which became exchange mediums. When Kamehameha I died in 1819 he left a sizable sum in foreign gold and silver coins that had been brought in by various ships.

In 1847 Kamehameha III issued an official copper cent. Because more small denominations were needed, a number of individuals and firms were permitted to make their own token money, which served for payments until it could be redeemed in gold or silver. As

early as 1836 the Koloa plantation on Kauai was pay
ing its workers in pasteboard script in denominatio˒ ₃
of 12½ cents, 25 cents, and 50 cents, which could ᴐe
exchanged in the company store. The earliest issues
of this "money," according to one authority, were made
by overprinting French theater tickets.

The presence of American missionaries and traders
led the Hawaiians to think in terms of dollars and cents
rather than in the monetary units of other countries.
Thus we hear of Hawaiian terms for the cent (*keneka*),
the dollar (*dala*), the half dollar (*hapalua*), the quarter dollar (*hapaha*).

During the 1870's and 1880's a number of plantations struck tokens accepted only at company stores.
The Kahalui Railroad in Maui issued a copper token
worth 75 cents.

In 1883 the Hawaiian coinage was brought into
conformity with that of the United States. Claus
Spreckels, a banker and planter, persuaded the King
to request the coinage at the San Francisco mint of one
million dollars in silver denomination, with specifica-
tions like those of U.S. coins. The U.S. Secretary of
Treasury approved, and the coins were struck off—
$500,000 in dollars, $350,000 in half dollars, $125,-
000 in quarters, and $25,000 in dimes. The five-cent
piece and the one-eighth (12½ cents) piece were patterns only, and not minted. The engraver at the Philadelphia mint made handsome designs for the Hawaiian
silver coins, and they are of considerable interest to
coin collectors today.

During Lunalilo's reign the government began to enforce laws im-
partially, even unpopular laws. The liquor business was controlled.
The land office received more attention. But it was the strict enforce-
ment of the leprosy laws that caused the most unhappiness among the
Hawaiians. The people did not understand the seriousness of the disease nor the importance of isolating lepers. To them, being sent to the
leper settlement on Molokai was the same as a death sentence.

On the advice of Dr. Trousseau, medical member of the Board of
Health, the laws for segregating the lepers were vigorously carried out.
In 1873, 560 persons were sent to the leper settlement, doubling its
population. It was difficult for the small settlement to handle that
number, but every effort was made to meet the emergency with the

188

small amount of money the legislature had set aside. A pipeline was installed to bring fresh water to the lepers. The year 1873 also marked the arrival of Father Damien, who devoted his life to helping the lepers on Molokai.

During the reign of Lunalilo there was a mutiny of the household troops. The men revolted against the strict discipline of the drill master and some acts of the adjutant general. Neither of these was Hawaiian. Although the number of mutineers was not large, since there were only sixty men in the army of the small kingdom, the uprising showed the anti-foreign temper of the Hawaiians. Any attempt to put down the mutiny by force might have led to civil war and violence toward most of the foreigners in the kingdom. Some felt that the mutiny was being used to advance the personal fortunes of some of the chiefs. The person whose name was mentioned most frequently in this connection was Kalakaua. Other people felt that it provided a good excuse to disband the troops and save money. There was also a stronger insistence on changing the cabinet. After the King had interviewed the mutineers and had persuaded them to lay down their arms and go home, he disbanded the household guard.

The Death of Lunalilo

While the mutiny was taking place, the King was quite ill. He had developed a lung infection that within a few months would lead to his death from tuberculosis. The King went to Kailua on the island of Hawaii to try to win back his health. Many people were concerned that he might die without choosing an heir, but he steadfastly refused to do so. Queen Liliuokalani described the situation in her book, *Hawaii's Story:*

> ". . . During our stay we were often visited by emissaries from Honolulu, urging upon the king the appointment of a successor, or praying him to return to the capital for the consideration of a subject, to all of which suggestions he appeared to be at least indifferent, if not absolutely opposed. In fact, he said openly enough that he himself owed his sceptre to the people and he saw no reason why the people should not elect his successor. I suppose it is no secret, but a matter of history, that the person most ambitious to succeed him in the rule of the Hawaiian nation was Emma, the widow of Liholiho, Kamehameha IV . . ."

189

Queen Liliuokalani might have been more fair to Queen Emma and mentioned her (Liliuokalani's) brother, David Kalakaua, and his hopes for the throne.

The talk of annexation and cession of Pearl Harbor solidified the Hawaiians' feeling against foreigners. A definite anti-American sentiment developed, encouraged by the writings of Walter M. Gibson. The anti-missionary attitude was further shown by the bitterness of Queen Emma, who was pro-British and favored the Church of England. All of this strong anti-foreigner feeling influenced the legislative elections. Practically all of the men elected were Hawaiians and were favorable to Kalakaua.

The day after the legislative election the guns on Punchbowl, an ancient volcanic crater overlooking Honolulu, began firing every minute, announcing Lunalilo's death. Lunalilo's will provided for the establishment of a home for the old and the poor among the Hawaiians. Today, the monument to the King's love of his people is known as Lunalilo Home.

Because he felt that his mother had been slighted when her remains were not moved to the Royal Mausoleum in Nuuanu Valley along with those of other chiefs, Lunalilo preferred to be buried next to her on the grounds of Kawaiahao Church.

The Royal Mausoleum in the Nuuanu Valley on Oahu is the burial place of five ruling kings and one queen of the Kamehameha and Kalakaua dynasties.

Summing Up the Chapter

Since Kamehameha V had not named an heir to the throne, the choice was left to the legislature. William C. Lunalilo and David Kalakaua were the chief candidates. Lunalilo, who was the choice of the people, won all the votes. The new King tried to make the government more democratic. There was talk of giving Pearl Harbor to the United States in exchange for a treaty by which Hawaiian sugar would enter the United States tax-free. There was even talk of annexation, although it was not favored by the native Hawaiians. During the reign of Lunalilo, the leprosy laws were strictly enforced. It was during a short mutiny of the household troops that the King became ill. Lunalilo would not name an heir to the throne, and his death from tuberculosis left the kingdom without a king once more.

17

His Oceanic Majesty, King Kalakaua

The death of Lunalilo threw the tiny kingdom into a state of confusion. Twice within fourteen months a king of Hawaii had died without naming a successor. It was, therefore, again necessary for the legislature to elect a king.

The day following Lunalilo's death, Colonel David Kalakaua announced his candidacy for the throne. Kalakaua had much support among the *ali'i* and the common people, particularly those from the Neighbor Islands. Most of the foreigners, including the Americans, were also pro-Kalakaua.

The next day Dowager Queen Emma, the widow of Kamehameha IV, said that she too was a candidate for the throne. Queen Emma was closely attached to the British community and while on a trip abroad had become a good friend of England's Queen Victoria. Queen Emma and her husband had helped to establish the Protestant Episcopal Church in Hawaii. This was the church of most Englishmen and of many Americans. Naturally, the English element was favorable to her cause.

Thus, it was felt that Kalakaua's election would mean that the American influence would continue to predominate. The election of Queen Emma would mean closer ties with Great Britain.

King David Kalakaua, whose reign saw the building of the present Iolani Palace, the growth of a broad spectrum of cultural and economic activities, and the revival of the hula, was known as the "Merry Monarch." He ruled from 1874 - 1891.

1874 February 12, Legislature elects new king, David Kalakaua

1875 Reciprocity treaty with U.S.

1877 Princess Liliuokalani named heiress to the throne

1878 Hawaiian Bell Telephone started
Portuguese begin to arrive

1881 Kalakaua begins trip around the world

1883 Coronation of King Kalakaua and Queen Kapiolani

1887 Bayonet Constitution adopted
Kamehameha Schools founded

1889 Wilcox Revolt

1891 Death of Kalakaua

1874 England takes control of Suez Canal

1876 General Custer's defeat at Little Big Horn

1877 Rutherford B. Hayes is inaugurated as 19th president
Queen Victoria becomes Empress of India

1882 Chinese Exclusion Act
Britain occupies Egupt

1885 Grover Cleveland becomes 22nd U.S. president

1886 American Federation of Labor formed

1887 Diamond Jubilee of Queen Victoria
Germany attempts to annex Samoa

1888 William II becomes Kaiser of Germany

1889 Benjamin Harrison becomes 23rd U.S. president
Brazil becomes a republic

1890 Sherman Anti-Trust Act

The Election of Kalakaua as King

The legislature met in the courthouse on February 12, 1874, to elect a new king. While the election was taking place, a great crowd made up mostly of Queen Emma's supporters, who centered mainly on Oahu, gathered outside. When the voting had been completed, thirty-nine of the members had voted for Kalakaua and six for Queen Emma.

A committee of the legislature, headed by dignified Major Moehonua, tried to leave the courthouse to tell Kalakaua of his election as king. When the committee stepped into the Major's carriage, the mob seized the carriage and tore it to pieces. The committee members were barely able to escape with their lives and sought safety in the courthouse as the mob forced its way into the building. The non-Hawaiian members of the legislature were not harmed by the mob. When Charles O. Carter tried to reason with the mob, he was picked up bodily, set down at the edge of the crowd, and warned to keep out of the way. Native legislators who could not escape were savagely beaten, and the entire building became a scene of great destruction. One of the legislators was thrown out of a window and another died of injuries a few days later.

In order to prevent further rioting and loss of life, the newly-elected King Kalakaua, together with Minister of Foreign Affairs, Charles R. Bishop, and Oahu's Governor, John O. Dominis, appealed to the American and British representatives to land marines from three warships anchored in the harbor. Sailors and marines were sent promptly from their ships and restored order by evening. They remained on shore for a week, giving the new government an opportunity to become firmly established.

Kalakaua had hoped for an elaborate coronation to be held in Kawaiahao Church. In view of the recent disturbance, his councilors advised him to have a simple coronation ceremony performed as quickly and quietly as possible. On February 13, 1874, at noon, Kalakaua took the oath of office. On that same day, Queen Emma recognized him as king and advised her supporters to do the same.

One of the first acts of the King was to name a successor to the throne, thus settling the problem that had caused so much difficulty. He named his younger brother, William Pitt Leleiohoku, his heir. This appointment met with general approval as the prince was a popu-

195

Throne Room, Iolani Palace—Feather *kahilis*, ancient standards of Hawaiian royalty, flank the twin (replica) thrones under a red velvet canopy at Iolani Palace, Honolulu. The room is open to the public.

lar member of the royal family. Such action proved to be unnecessary as Kalakaua outlived his younger brother.

What sort of man was Kalakaua? As stated in the previous chapter, he came from a line of high chiefs of the island of Hawaii. His queen, Kapiolani, was descended from the ruling family of Kauai. Kalakaua was well educated and could speak fluently in either English or Hawaiian. He possessed such charming manners that he could take his place in the highest society either at home or abroad. He loved music and the arts. Robert Louis Stevenson, the famous English author, while on a visit to Hawaii, stated that Kalakaua's conversations "revealed a cultivated mind steeped in Hawaiian history and legend." This interest in Hawaii's past continued throughout Kalakaua's reign, as he tried to revive the ancient customs.

Unlike earlier kings, Kalakaua enjoyed the gay festive elements of life to the extent that he was nicknamed the "Merry Monarch." To look upon Kalakaua only as a playboy king would do him an injustice, for he also took his royal duties seriously and considered himself the father of the Hawaiian people.

Some writers have referred to Kalakaua as "Kalakaua Rex." He believed in the hereditary right of the great chiefs to rule; therefore, the king should be the real ruler of the country. Before becoming king he had gained much experience as an administrator as well as a legislator and held a commission as a colonel. The Constitution of 1864 gave the king broad powers and he used them to achieve his purposes. Since Kalakaua is such a controversial figure it is difficult to judge some of his activities. His enemies accused him of being a tyrant, a demagogue, and a scoundrel. Whatever Kalakaua may have been, he loved the Hawaiian people and did everything in his power to build up the nation.

To strengthen his position, Kalakaua followed the old Hawaiian custom of touring the kingdom to meet as many people as possible. In a speech at Lahaina, Maui, he said, "The increase of the people, the advancement of agriculture and commerce, these are the objectives which my government will strive to accomplish." Kalakaua's trip to the various islands gave the people renewed confidence. To them he was *ali'i nui* (a great chief).

Reciprocity

Upon his return from the tour of the kingdom, Kalakaua was faced with the problem of improving business conditions. When he came to the throne there was a depression in Hawaii. The solution to the problem appeared to be to try again for a reciprocity treaty with the United States. The King commissioned Chief Justice E. H. Allen and H. A. P. Carter as representatives to the United States to negotiate a treaty of reciprocity, and they left for Washington on October 18, 1874.

To help the cause of reciprocity, Kalakaua himself sailed on the *U.S.S. Benecia* for San Francisco as a guest of the United States. His party included his brother-in-law, Governor John O. Dominis of Oahu, Governor John M. Kapena of Maui, and Henry A. Peirce, United States Minister to Hawaii. On November 29 the guns of the forts of San Francisco boomed their welcome to the first king to visit the United States. The leaders of the city arranged entertainment suitable for a king. A special train in which the King would travel from San

197

Francisco to Washington, D.C. was provided by the United States Government.

Kalakaua was received in state by President Ulysses S. Grant and invited to appear before both houses of Congress. He made a great impression on Washington, both diplomatically and socially. The King visited New York and Boston. After a triumphal journey lasting three months, he returned to Honolulu aboard the *U.S.S. Pensacola.*

In the meantime negotiations for the treaty were taking place between the Hawaiian representatives, Allen and Carter, and the American Secretary of State, Hamilton Fish. Louisiana sugar interests and New Englanders trading in West Indian sugar opposed the treaty, but it was finally signed on January 30, 1875. It went into effect the following year after the necessary legislation had been passed in both countries over stiff opposition. The Hawaiians who objected to the treaty felt that it made their country more dependent than ever on the United States and would some day cause Hawaii to be taken over by the United States.

The treaty provided that many Hawaiian goods, particularly unrefined sugar and rice, would be admitted into the United States tax-free. In exchange it provided for a number of American products to be admitted duty-free to Hawaii. An important provision of the treaty was that Hawaii would not make a similar agreement with any other nation. This clause assured the supremacy of American economic interests over the British. It was added because of the shipment of sugar to Australia, New Zealand, and British Columbia in 1873. The Americans had been told that the entire sugar crop of 1875-1876 would be sent to these British colonies. The treaty was to run for at least seven years. When it was renewed in 1887, it carried the added provision that the United States should have exclusive use of Pearl Harbor. Other outcomes of the reciprocity treaty influenced much that happened in Hawaii during Kalakaua's reign and, in many ways, led to the overthrow of the monarchy.

Kalakaua's Cabinets

Kalakaua also came into conflict with the *haole* element in Hawaii by making full use of the king's right to appoint and dismiss cabinet members. The struggle between the King and the constitutional reformers became so bitter that it is difficult to read the newspapers or

198

The one-time capital of Hawaii and whaling village of Lahaina, Maui, is one of the places where King Kalakaua spoke on his tour of the kingdom in 1874. Today this rustic seaport is a year-round haven for seekers of sun and the tranquil atmosphere of Old Hawaii.

biographies of prominent people of that time and get an unbiased picture of most of Kalakaua's reign. The lines were sharply drawn between the King's party and the so-called Missionary party. Both sides made much use of newspapers to gain support for their views.

The first cabinet Kalakaua appointed consisted of competent men and was generally acceptable to all elements of the population. But in 1876 Kalakaua dismissed this cabinet and appointed a new one. The men in the new cabinet were perhaps more able than the ones they replaced. His dismissal of cabinets aroused great opposition within the Missionary party.

The Missionary party believed that the government of Hawaii should be a constitutional monarchy like that of England. The king should have a position of great dignity and be the social head of the government, but he should have very little real power over the government. This party believed that the legislature, as representatives of the people, should control the cabinet ministers and the cabinet should be responsible to it rather than to the king. The attempt to limit the

199

king's power through a constitutional monarchy was the basis of the political struggle during Kalakaua's reign. The struggle became more and more bitter and finally resulted in the adoption of the Constitution of 1887 by which the king was stripped of much of his political power.

In 1878 Claus Spreckels, a prominent California financier, had entered the Hawaiian political scene. Spreckels acquired land on Maui for a sugar plantation. Since this land was located in the dry area of Maui, Spreckels had to get water for irrigation purposes before he could grow sugar on his land. He applied to the cabinet for water rights and was turned down. By means of a loan he persuaded Kalakaua to dismiss the cabinet and appoint a new cabinet. The new cabinet gave Spreckels the water rights.

Much of Kalakaua's difficulty came from the presence of Celso Caesar Moreno, an Italian soldier of fortune. Moreno had been authorized by the United States Government to promote telegraphic communication between America and Asia. During this period an alleged scandal involving a member of the cabinet came to light the day the legislature closed. Kalakaua immediately dismissed the cabinet and appointed a new one with Moreno at the head as Minister of Foreign Affairs. From the confused accounts of the time it seems that the Hawaiians supported Moreno' and looked upon him as a friend and savior of the Hawaiian race.

The non-Hawaiians in the kingdom were enraged at Moreno's appointment. Five days later, Moreno resigned. Kalakaua then made this elegant and stormy figure Ambassador Extraordinary and placed in his charge three Anglo-Hawaiian boys who were to be educated abroad.

In the meantime the Planter party (also known as the Missionary party) followed up its victory by insisting on an all-foreign cabinet of their choosing. The King yielded and appointed Green, Carter, Armstrong, and Walker as the new cabinet members. Kalakaua also appointed four new members to the Privy Council: Walter Murray Gibson, an ardent supporter of the King and champion of the Hawaiian people, and three Hawaiians. The Planter party was most unhappy at having been outwitted.

The Trip Around the World

The reciprocity treaty by promoting the growth and sale of sugar brought a greater demand than ever for laborers. Kalakaua decided

200

to make a trip around the world to study the matter of immigration. This would give him an opportunity to meet other rulers, and perhaps secure more laborers for Hawaii. We might say that he also had a political motive for the trip. By learning the ways of other rulers he hoped he could better protect his own people.

Preparations were quickly made for the journey. In 1877 Prince Leleiohoku, the King's brother and heir, died, and Kalakaua named his sister, Princess Liliuokalani, heiress to the throne. She was, therefore, named regent during the King's absence. The opposition insisted that Kalakaua pay for the trip from his private income; consequently, he could not take a large staff. The journey started in January, 1881. Other members of the party were Charles H. Judd, Court Chamberlain; and William Armstrong, Attorney General; along with Robert, the King's valet, who was said to be a German baron.

The royal party sailed to San Francisco with the King traveling incognito since he was limited in funds. Despite this, San Francisco gave him a royal welcome and outdid itself in making Kalakaua welcome. Public officials and private citizens competed with each other to honor him.

From San Francisco Kalakaua sailed to Japan. As his ship steamed into the Bay of Yedo, the King was greeted by salutes from the warships of several nations. A representative of the Emperor of Japan bade Kalakaua welcome and invited him to become the guest of the Emperor. Kalakaua was the first king of a western nation to visit Japan and was treated with as much honor as the mightiest sovereign on earth. During the series of elaborate entertainments, the Emperor of Japan presented Kalakaua with the Star and Broad Scarlet Cordon of the Rising Sun. In turn Kalakaua presented the Emperor with the Grand Cross of the Order of Kamehameha. Kalakaua's visit to Japan set the tone of the trip and he was delighted with the ceremonious manner in which he was received by other crowned heads of his host countries.

Kalakaua continued his triumphal tour through China, Siam, Burma, India, and Egypt. In Italy he had an audience with the Pope and was received by King Umberto. He also visited Belgium, Germany, Austria, France, Spain, and Portugal. In England he was driven to Buckingham Palace in Queen Victoria's own coach. While in Europe, he ordered furnishings for his new palace (Iolani Palace) and also two jeweled crowns and a scepter for the coronation he had planned on his return to Hawaii. Again he crossed the United States, once more winning the hearts of the American people. Upon his return to Honolulu most of his subjects were overcome with joy.

The Coronation

The morning of February 12, 1883, the ninth year of Kalakaua's reign, began with the sun breaking forth after three days of torrential rains. The morning star was seen in the heavens along with the sun. The Hawaiians regarded this as a happy omen.

Honolulu streets were filled with joyful, chattering people and strolling musicians. Homes and public buildings and even foreign battleships in the harbor were decorated for the occasion. The new palace was adorned with ropes of greenery, flowers, and bunting. A pavilion decorated with the coats-of-arms of foreign nations provided the stage for the coronation.

The coronation ceremony consisted of a mixture of ancient Hawaiian ritual and customs Kalakaua had noted in European courts. The ceremony began with a recitation of the King's genealogy by the Marshal of the Household, John Kapena. Then other symbols of royalty were presented to the King: the Sword of State; the golden feather cloak of Kamehameha; the *pulo'ulo'u* (taboo stick) and the Kahili of Pili, both symbols of chieftainship; the scepter, the ancestral noonday torch; and last of all, the crowns. The King placed his crown on his own head and then placed one upon the Queen's head. The royal couple then knelt while the Reverend Alexander Macintosh, rector of Saint Andrew's church, pronounced the benediction. The coronation was followed by a reception in the throne room. That evening, a brilliant ball was held with singing and *hulas* especially composed for the occasion.

The members of the opposition were upset by the cost of the coronation, but they were even more disturbed by the return of the *hula,* which they considered immoral and heathenish.

Walter Murray Gibson

Probably Kalakaua's strongest supporter and, in turn, the greatest enemy of the Missionary party was Walter Murray Gibson. It is almost impossible to get an accurate account of Gibson's life since he was such a controversial figure. As we noted in Chapter 16, he came to Hawaii as a Mormon missionary and established a Mormon settle-

202

King Kalakaua's coronation took place on this specially built stand. Here the King crowns Queen Kapiolani, after having first crowned himself.

ment on Lanai.

Leaving his Lanai ranch, which he developed from the former Morman lands, in the capable hands of his son-in-law, Gibson moved to Honolulu. Here he established an English-Hawaiian newspaper in 1873 to fight the annexation movement. Through his newspaper he supported the election of Kalakaua. After Kalakaua was elected, Gibson stopped publishing his paper and returned to Lanai. Because his sympathies were with the Hawaiian people and he felt they were being exploited, he ran for the legislature in 1878. Following his election he became a leading figure in the King's party. While serving in the legislature he supported several bills to improve the health of the Hawaiians. He secured passage of a bill to publish a pamphlet in Hawaiian on health so that the declining Hawaiian race could be rebuilt. It was Gibson who introduced the bills in the legislature for the construction of Iolani Palace and for the erection of the statue of Kamehameha so that the Hawaiians would take pride in their heritage. Gibson supported the building of Iolani Palace from his personal funds and even went into debt for the project.

Although there is little record of Gibson's having received more than an eighth grade education, he spoke several foreign languages and was held to be a man of intellect and culture even by his enemies. He possessed courtly manners and rarely appeared to become upset even when mistreated by his enemies. In debate Gibson met attack with courtesy and wit and infuriated his enemies because he could not be provoked to anger. He was unswerving in his loyalty to the Hawaiian people and their King. Gibson advised the Hawaiians not to hate foreigners but to remember the good things they had brought and be appreciative of those foreigners who had helped them. He also encouraged the Hawaiians to be optimistic about the future. At his coronation, Kalakaua whispered to Gibson, "I owe this day to you. I will remember that always." In the meantime a plot to assassinate Gibson and to promote trouble during the coronation had been foiled.

In 1882 Gibson was appointed head of the cabinet and remained in office until 1887. During this period the government was having money difficulties. Word was received that Claus Spreckels wanted to open a bank in Honolulu. Spreckels himself soon arrived and offered to lend the kingdom $1,000,000 in exchange for a bank charter and the taking away of the planters' bank charter. It was finally agreed that Spreckels would send $1,000,000 in coins, which bore the head of Kalakaua on them, in exchange for six per cent government bonds. It is claimed that Spreckels made an additional $150,000 in minting the coins.

The opposition condemned Gibson for the extravagance of the coronation and for bringing a group of the Sisters of Charity to work among the lepers. Every appropriation for the Board of Genealogy brought cries of extravagance. On the other hand they accused the government of sales of exemptions, which enabled the lepers to avoid being sent to the settlement at Kalaupapa.

In later legislatures, a bill to subsidize Spreckels' son's Oceanic Steamship was introduced. Spreckels' bill for a national bank was defeated; however, he and William G. Irwin did open a small savings bank. The opposition saw their own control of the economic life of the Islands being challenged and charged Spreckels with attempted monopoly.

The law that aroused the greatest furor was the one licensing the sale of opium. Gibson voted against this bill, but it passed by a small majority. The bill provided for the license to be sold at public auction.

However, there seems to have been some attempt made to secure the license by bribery. Many historians feel that it was the opium scandal that caused Gibson's downfall and gave the opposition control of the cabinet.

Attempts at Empire Building

During 1887-1888, when Germany tried to annex the Samoan Islands, Gibson sent a proclamation to the world powers asking them to guarantee Samoan independence. H. A. P. Carter was commissioned as Envoy Extraordinary, but his mission was doomed to failure. The United States did not want to become involved. Also, by the time Carter reached Europe, much of the remaining real estate in the Pacific was in the process of being gobbled up by the Great Powers. Such actions conflicted with Kalakaua's dreams of heading a great Polynesian confederation. Gibson encouraged this ambition, for all of his life his sympathies were with the downtrodden people.

In the legislature of 1886, the government obtained an appropriation of $30,000 for the formation of the Polynesian confederation. As a first step John E. Bush was commissioned as Envoy Extraordinary and Ambassador Plenipotentiary. Henry Poor, an Anglo-Hawaiian, accompanied Bush as Secretary of the Legation. Henry Strong was commissioned to make sketches and collect specimens for the Hawaiian National Museum.

When Bush and his companions arrived in Samoa in January, 1887, they were welcomed by King Malietoa. Bush presented the Samoan with a grand uniform and the Grand Cross of the Royal Order of the Star of Polynesia. Soon after Bush's arrival, Malietoa agreed to a political confederation of Hawaii and Samoa. Minister Carter was to represent both kingdoms in Washington.

Kalakaua signed the treaty on March 20. To further his dreams of a Pacific empire he refitted the old *Explorer* and translated its name into Hawaiian, *Kaimiloa*. Kalakaua had earlier tried to bring the Gilbert Islands and the New Hebrides under Hawaii's protection; perhaps, with a navy he would now succeed. The *Kaimiloa* carried a crew of Hawaiian youths from the Reform School. But, it was an ill-fated venture from the beginning, for later the crew mutinied and the stores were sold.

The German government was thoroughly annoyed with Kalakaua's dream of a Pacific empire. Count Otto von Bismarck, the German

Chancellor, threatened to shoot Kalakaua's legs in two, despite his American protection. Bismarck further threatened to cause trouble in Hawaii for the Americans if the Americans made trouble for the Germans in Samoa. The Reform party obtained control of the government and the Samoan alliance was ended, thus also ending Kalakaua's dream of empire.

The Bayonet Constitution of 1887

The spendthrift policies of Kalakaua enraged the Missionary party. Since Kalakaua's coming to the throne, the cost of running the government and the public debt had risen markedly. The Hawaiians, or the King's party, felt that the Missionary party should not object to their enjoying some of the prosperity resulting from the reciprocity treaty.

The more extreme among the Hawaiians wanted to drive the *haoles* from the land and restore the ancient Hawaiian culture. The extremists among the foreigners formed a secret political organization called the Hawaiian League, which had a group within it that favored overthrowing the monarchy and securing annexation to the United States. The opium bribe mentioned earlier was the spark that caused the League to flare into action. It should be pointed out here that the majority of the League members were in favor of establishing a constitutional monarchy. If this did not come about, it would go along with the minority, which proposed immediate overthrow of the monarchy. A mass meeting was called by the Hawaiian League. At the time of the meeting, the military force of the League, The Hawaiian Rifles, was assembled outside of the meeting hall. The King was frightened and offered in turn to transfer his powers to the representative of the United States, Great Britain, or Portugal. Each refused, but they advised him to sign a new constitution.

The King gave in and dismissed Gibson from office. Gibson was arrested by Col. V. V. Ashford, Commander of the Hawaiian Rifles. Col. Ashford proposed to hang Gibson, but the executive committee of the League refused to go along with him and gave Gibson his choice of leaving the Islands or standing trial for embezzlement. Gibson chose exile and died six months later in San Francisco.

Yielding to pressure from the Hawaiian League, the King appointed W. L. Green to form a cabinet. Green was to be Premier and Minister of Finance; Godfrey Brown, Minister of Foreign Affairs; Lorrin A. Thurston, Minister of the Interior; and Clarence W. Ashford, Attor-

206

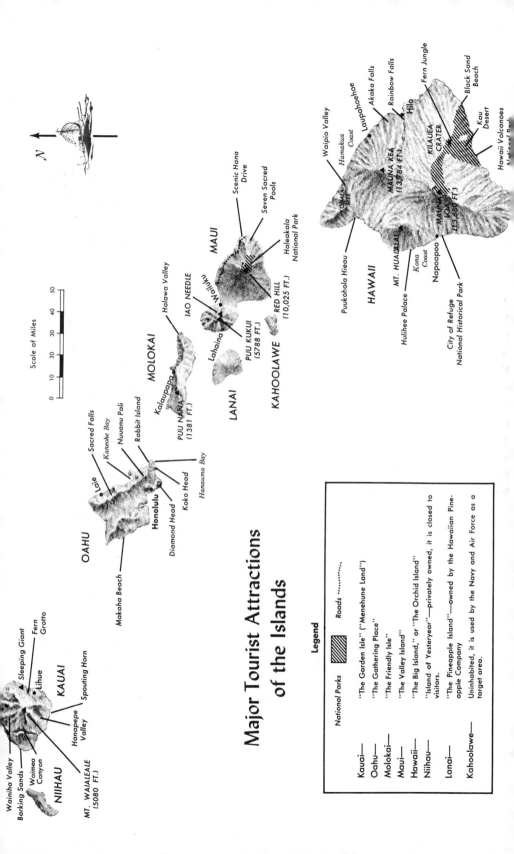

Major Tourist Attractions
of the Islands

Scale of Miles
0 10 20 30 40 50

N

NIIHAU

KAUAI
Wainiha Valley
Barking Sands
Waimea Canyon
Hanapepe Valley
MT. WAIALEALE (5080 FT.)
Sleeping Giant
Lihue
Fern Grotto
Spouting Horn

OAHU
Makaha Beach
Sacred Falls
Laie
Kaneohe Bay
Nuuanu Pali
Rabbit Island
Koko Head
Hanauma Bay
Diamond Head
Honolulu

MOLOKAI
Kalaupapa
Halawa Valley
PUU NANA (1381 FT.)

LANAI

KAHOOLAWE

MAUI
Scenic Hana Drive
Seven Sacred Pools
Haleakala National Park
RED HILL (10,025 FT.)
Wailuku
IAO NEEDLE
Lahaina
PUU KUKUI (5788 FT.)

HAWAII
Waipio Valley
Hamakua Coast
Laupahoehoe
Akaka Falls
Rainbow Falls
Fern Jungle
Hilo
Black Sand Beach
KILAUEA CRATER
Kau Desert
Hawaii Volcanoes National Park
MAUNA KEA (13,784 FT.)
MAUNA LOA (13,680 FT.)
KOHALA Mts.
MT. HUALALAI
Kona Coast
Napoopoo
City of Refuge National Historical Park
Hulihee Palace
Puukohola Heiau

Legend

National Parks

Roads ··········

Kauai— "The Garden Isle" ("Menehune Land")

Oahu— "The Gathering Place"

Molokai— "The Friendly Isle"

Maui— "The Valley Island"

Hawaii— "The Big Island," or "The Orchid Island"

Niihau— "Island of Yesteryear"—privately owned, it is closed to visitors.

Lanai— "The Pineapple Island"—owned by the Hawaiian Pineapple Company.

Kahoolawe— Uninhabited, it is used by the Navy and Air Force as a target area.

ney General. Kalakaua objected to the appointment of Thurston, but at Green's insistence, gave in.

Five days after the new cabinet was formed, the members presented the King with a new constitution to sign. This Bayonet Constitution of 1887 was really a revision of Kamehameha V's Constitution of 1864. After several hours of argument, Kalakaua signed this document, which stripped him of most of the executive powers he had exercised since he began his reign in 1874. One of the important changes was that the king could take no official action without the approval of the cabinet. Thus the king was forced to share the executive power. The new constitution also provided that the cabinet would still be appointed by the king but could not be dismissed without the approval of the legislature. The king's veto could be overridden by a two-thirds vote of the legislature. It also provided that the king could not organize any military or naval forces without approval from the legislature.

The new constitution provided for important changes in the legislature. Most important of all, the nobles were to be elected instead of appointed by the king. Because of the financial requirements for both candidates and voters, the election of the nobles was, in effect, in the hands of the non-Hawaiians.

The constitution also contained a curious provision that any man over twenty who could read and write English, Hawaiian, or some European language, and who had lived in Hawaii for one year could vote for a representative as long as he took an oath to uphold the constitution and had paid his taxes. This provision allowed foreigners to vote for representatives without becoming citizens of Hawaii.

Wilcox's Revolt

The Reform party's Committee of Thirteen had selected the new cabinet for the King. They and their lieutenants had drawn up the Constitution of 1887. Following the publication of this constitution a Hawaiian Committee of Thirteen called upon the King to sign a constitution that they had drawn up. This Hawaiian constitution restored the king's rights. Kalakaua refused to sign this second constitution.

The cabinet decided that the Hawaiian youths who had been sent abroad to be educated at government expense should return to Hawaii. Among these was Robert Wilcox, who was one of the three youths who had accompanied Moreno abroad. Wilcox was now a graduate in engineering and military science of the Royal Military Academy of Turin, Italy. While in Italy, he had been inspired by the deeds of the Italian patriot Garibaldi and had dreamed of leading Hawaii to the heights of glory. When he returned home he could not find employment suitable to his education.

Soon after his return, Wilcox began plotting to overthrow the despised rule of the Reform party and to restore the land to the Hawaiians and their King. Here again the history of the period is clouded, for some say he merely wanted to back Kalakaua and drive the hated reformers from political power. Others say that he also wanted to depose Kalakaua and have Liliuokalani, the King's sister and heir, take the throne. Nevertheless, at dawn on July 30, 1889, Wilcox led a group of 150 men into the palace grounds and took possession. He took two field pieces from the armory and set them up at either side of the palace.

Wilcox's scheme of taking charge of the government buildings and then inviting the King back to proclaim a constitution did not work as planned. Kalakaua refused to come. The cabinet acted quickly to put down the revolt. They called out the Honolulu Rifles in full force and armed the government officials with rifles. From buildings surrounding the palace, the *haoles* sniped at Wilcox's men. The next morning Wilcox surrendered. Seven men had been killed and twelve wounded. Wilcox was charged with conspiracy and, according to the law, tried before an all-Hawaiian jury. The results of the trial were a foregone conclusion: Wilcox was acquitted.

Although military action proved ineffective, political action did prove to be helpful to the King and his party. The King won the support of many people who might be able to help him. The Chinese merchants gave employment to large numbers of Hawaiians at a high enough salary to enable them to vote. The King was aided by the formation of a society called the Hui Kalaiaina (Political Economy party). This society, whose members were native Hawaiians, had as its objective the restoration of the Constitution of 1864. The King's party grew stronger as the elections for the legislature of 1889 approached, while the Reform party was weakened by severe quarreling among its members. Needless to say, the Reform party did not win a majority in the legislature, and the cabinet was voted out. A compromise cabinet was formed.

The Death of the King

When King Kalakaua came to close the session of the legislature of 1890 the members were shocked by his sickly appearance. His voice broke as he concluded, "I pray the Almighty that He continues to protect our beloved country." On the advice of his physicians the King left for San Francisco aboard the cruiser *Charleston*. As before, the King was given a noisy welcome, but he did not enjoy his stay as his health became worse. He died there on January 20, 1891, and his body was returned to Hawaii aboard the *Charleston*.

The *Charleston* was sighted off Diamond Head in the dim dawn light. As the ship came closer the official lookout was horrified to see the flag at half-mast and other signs of mourning. He immediately telephoned to Prime Minister Cummins. The news spread rapidly. Soon all of the flags were flying at half-mast. The arches and buildings gaily decorated to celebrate the King's homecoming were hastily draped in black. Kalakaua was buried with great ceremony that would have pleased even him.

According to Kalakaua's will, his sister Liliuokalani, who had been acting as regent during his absence, was heir to the throne. Before her brother was buried, the cabinet insisted she take the oath of office as Queen, thus bringing to an end the period of the elected kings.

Summing Up the Chapter

The election of King Kalakaua rather than Queen Emma to the throne meant that American influence would be stronger than English influence in Hawaii. Because of a mob uprising after his election, Kalakaua had only a simple coronation. Although he was known as the "Merry Monarch," Kalakaua was a strong ruler who tried to build up his nation. He himself paid a visit to the United States to help in the making of a trade treaty between the two countries. Under the new treaty unrefined sugar and rice, as well as some other Hawaiian goods, could enter the United States tax-free. Kalakaua made a trip around the world to study the matter of immigration. Nine years after he became king, Kalakaua was honored at elaborate coronation ceremonies.

There was a long and bitter struggle between Kalakaua and the constitutional reformers. Probably the strongest supporter of the King was Walter Murray Gibson, who was head of the cabinet from 1882 to 1887.

Kalakaua dreamed of heading a great Polynesian confederation. A political confederation of Hawaii and Samoa was formed, but it ended when the Reform party came into power in Hawaii. Kalakaua's enemies accused him of spending too much money. A Hawaiian League was formed that wanted to overthrow the monarchy and join the Islands to the United States. When force was threatened, the King agreed to a new constitution, which took away much of his political power, and dismissed Gibson from office. This so-called Bayonet Constitution of 1887 was really a revision of Kamehameha's Constitution of 1864.

Robert Wilcox, a Hawaiian youth who had studied abroad at government expense, tried without success to restore the land to the Hawaiians and their King by means of force. Two years later the Reform party was so weakened that a compromise cabinet was formed. However, the struggle had been too much for Kalakaua, who was so ill that his doctors suggested a voyage to San Francisco. He died there in 1891 and his body was returned to Hawaii. By his will, his sister, Liliuokalani, who had been acting as regent, was to be the Queen.

18

Changes Under the Elected Kings

When the reciprocity treaty went into effect, it gave Hawaii a firm base for its growing sugar industry. Sugar could be sent to the United States without being taxed as a foreign product. In 1875, twenty-five million pounds of sugar were exported. Just fifteen years later exports had risen to ten times that amount. How was it possible to expand sugar production so rapidly?

How Sugar Production Expanded

Having a sure profitable market meant that more money could be spent to expand the plantations already in existence and to start new ones. Mainland capital flowed more rapidly into Hawaii for investment in sugar plantations, irrigation projects, and sugar mills. Most of the boom resulted from the hard work and faith of men already in Hawaii. One exception was Claus Spreckels. He had not favored the reciprocity treaty, because he had made a fortune from beet sugar in California. But soon after the treaty went into effect, he lost no time in coming to Hawaii. He acquired land on Maui, as we have seen, to establish a large sugar plantation.

Sugar needs a great deal of water—both to grow the cane and to process the cane at the mill. One pound of sugar in the sugar bowl must have 2000 pounds of water to grow the cane from which the sugar is made. By comparing a rainfall map with one showing the location of sugar plantations we can see that half of the sugar is grown on land that receives less than an average rainfall of 75 inches needed to grow sugar cane without irrigation. In order to have more land for sugar production, the growers developed large irrigation projects. The first irrigation project had been completed on Kauai in 1856.

The first of the big irrigation projects was the 17-mile Hamakua Ditch on Maui. It was built by S. T. Alexander and H. P. Baldwin to bring forty million gallons of water a day from the wet side of Haleakala to their plantation located on the dry plain of Central Maui at Paia. Claus Spreckels followed the example of Alexander and Baldwin and built a ditch 30 miles long that delivered fifty million gallons of water a day to his lands in Central Maui. A third ditch was dug a few years later and the dry, dusty plain of Central Maui began to yield rich crops of sugar. Other islands copied the Maui irrigation system. Benjamin Dillingham and James Campbell solved the problem of getting water for the semi-desert region on Oahu by drilling artesian wells at Ewa.

> During the construction of the Hamakua ditch, a grave crisis arose. The workers refused to lower themselves by rope, hand over hand, into the deep gorge of Maliko, which was about 200 feet deep at that point. H. P. Baldwin, who had lost one arm, met this crisis by sliding down the rope himself, using his legs and his one arm. The workmen, shamed by this daring act, did not hesitate to follow. To maintain the men's morale and to keep track of the progress of the work, Mr. Baldwin performed this dangerous feat day after day.

The technology for the production of sugar also was improving. Samuel Burbank had invented a deep plow at Koloa plantation some years earlier. Fertilizer was used more effectively to aid the growth of sugar cane. David Weston had introduced a centrifugal machine for separating sugar from molasses; this machine made it possible to make high grade sugar at lower costs. Other new and more efficient methods of production were introduced at the sugar mills, such as the diffusion process plant by Colonel Z. S. Spalding for the Makee Sugar Company on Kauai in 1888.

New sugar mills were built. Expensive milling and harvesting machinery had to be imported from the United States. The Honolulu Iron Works was called upon to expand its facilities to manufacture equipment for the plantations.

The expansion of the agency or factoring system also aided the growth of the sugar industry. The factors acted as business agents for the plantations: taking care of the sale and shipping of the sugar crops, buying the supplies needed by the plantations, insuring crops, and financing many of the plantations. As the sugar industry expanded the owners of poorly managed plantations had to turn over stock to the factors. In some instances these factors had to take over the management and even the ownership to keep the plantations producing sugar.

By 1882 the planters and their agents realized that because of the problems of labor supply and other matters of common interest, they should form an organization. It came to be known as the Planter's Labor and Supply Company. Information was shared throughout the sugar industry by the publication of the *Planters' Monthly,* which was edited by three lawyers, S. B. Dole, W. R. Castle, and W. O. Smith.

In order to achieve rapid expansion of sugar production, the plantations needed an adequate supply of cheap labor. As we have seen in Chapter 16, a Bureau of Immigration was created to find workers in other countries. Practically all labor imported during the monarchy was brought in under an agreement that provided for free food, shelter and medical care, as well as for wages. At the end of the contract period, the laborer was given free passage back to his native land if he did not choose to remain in Hawaii. Many of the plantation workers chose to return to their native countries or to go to the United States mainland, where they felt there was greater opportunity. Finding labor for the plantations thus proved to be a continuous problem.

In addition to the descendants of the missionaries such as the Baldwins, Rices, Cookes, and Wilcoxes, many other young *haole* men began to establish firms that are well-known today in Hawaiian business circles.

A Welshman named Theophilus Davies took over a bankrupt merchandising house and built it into the well-known firm of Theo. H. Davies. Davies also helped finance and establish the Honolulu Iron Works. The manager of the Honolulu Iron Works, Alexander Young, soon branched into business for himself.

Hawaii's most important banker, Charles Reed Bishop, stopped in Hawaii on his way to Oregon. He was captivated by the Islands and remained. He married one of the last living descendants of Kamehameha I, Bernice Pauahi, who was one of the largest landholders in the kingdom. Bishop started out working for the government and then went into the banking business. At first he financed the whale oil business. After the reciprocity treaty, Bishop's banking business grew rapidly while he was helping finance the growth of the sugar industry.

Development of Transportation Under the Elected Kings

Before the signing of the reciprocity treaty, most of the interisland traffic was carried on by sailing vessels. Various attempts at providing steamer service among the islands were not successful because of the competition from the large fleet of sailing vessels.

The most famous of the interisland steamers of the 1860's and 1870's was the *Kilauea*. It got a great deal of the passenger business, but not enough of the freight business to keep its operation profitable. For a while the government took over the *Kilauea's* operation. In 1877 the government ordered the wooden steamer *Likelike* built in San Francisco. This ship and the old *Kilauea* were sold to Samuel G. Wilder, who organized the Wilder Steamship Company and put several other steamers into service. In 1882 competition in the interisland steamer trade began when the Inter-Island Steam Navigation Company was founded. In 1905 the two companies were consolidated to form the Inter-Island Steam Navigation Company. This company became the parent of the present Hawaiian Airlines.

Practically continuous steamship service between Honolulu and the West Coast began in 1867 when the Postmaster General of the United States made a contract for monthly mail service with the California, Oregon and Mexico Steamship Company. The United States Government agreed to pay $75,000 a year for this service. There were many ups and downs in the fortunes of this company and others that tried to supply transpacific steamer service to Hawaii. For many years after 1875 the Pacific Mail Steamship Company maintained a service between San Francisco and Australia, stopping at Honolulu. Spreckels' son organized the Oceanic Steamship Company in 1882, which offered

215

The *Akamai,* a typical interisland steamer in use during the late nineteenth century, approaches Lahaina, Maui, on its regular run between Honolulu and Lahaina. On the hillside above the town is Lahainaluna School.

regular service between San Francisco and Honolulu. Oceanic extended its services to the British possessions "down under." In 1882 Captain William Matson sailed the *Emma Claudina* into Hilo Bay, marking the modest beginning of a shipping line that later controlled water traffic between Hawaii and the Mainland. Favoring steam over sail, Matson added one steamship after another, as his line expanded to carry cargo to and from the Islands.

Railroad and Land Transportation

The story of railroading on Oahu centers chiefly around one man, Benjamin F. Dillingham. His was one of the many Horatio Alger stories of foreign businessmen in Hawaii during this period. He was a sailor, and while stopping in Hawaii in 1865, he was thrown from a horse and broke his leg. His ship sailed on. After he recovered he decided to stay in Hawaii, and with the help of Alfred Castle went into business. He was also closely associated with James Campbell and some other men and began to acquire farm lands. Realizing that the development of the land depended on cheap and efficient transportation, Dillingham and his associates obtained a franchise from

216

King Kalakaua for the Oahu Steam Railway as part of the Oahu Railway and Land Company. Soon Dillingham expanded the railroad to most of the island; however, he never achieved his goal of circling the entire island with his railroad. He encouraged the establishment of sugar plantations on the new land opened by the railroad, filled in swamps, and built wharves and warehouses for shipping sugar and handling general cargo. By the end of Kalakaua's reign railroads were in operation on the islands of Maui and Hawaii, as well as on Oahu.

With the growth of the sugar and rice industries, railroads alone were not adequate for land transportation. The government was called upon to spend large sums of money building roads and bridges on the various islands to help meet the needs of the growing economy. By 1888 Honolulu boasted of its first mule-drawn streetcar. Soon afterwards this line was extended to the suburb of Waikiki, which was then considered to be quite a distance from downtown Honolulu.

In 1888 the Hawaiian Tramways Company began operation in Honolulu. This first mule car was part of the first Rapid Transit Street Railway System which connected Honolulu with the suburban resorts.

Electricity and Telephones

King Kalakaua had a surprise for his guests at his inaugural ball, for he had the throne room illuminated with electric lights. This was the first use of electricity in the kingdom. It was not until 1891 when the Hawaiian Electric Company was started that others could have electricity.

Less than two years after Alexander G. Bell obtained his patent on the telephone, Charles Dickey had installed a telephone line between his home and the store he managed. King Kalakaua, intrigued with the telephone, had a line strung between Iolani Palace and the royal boat house. Dickey might be called the father of the telephone in Hawaii, for he came to Honolulu in 1878 to establish the Hawaiian Bell Telephone Company, which would serve the capital city.

Soon a second telephone company, the Mutual Telephone Company, was started by Judge Widemann and other prominent citizens of Honolulu. For a while there was a telephone war in Honolulu. Mutual finally bought out Hawaiian Bell, and William Brown was chosen to head the new Mutual Telephone Company. Gradually the Mutual Telephone Company bought other companies on the Neighbor Islands, so that the country was served by a single telephone company.

Cultural Life of the Kingdom

One of the outstanding aspects of Kalakaua's reign was the attempt to revive and record many of the ancient traditions of the Hawaiians. This interest led to the establishment of a society, *Ka Hale Nau-a* (The Temple of Wisdom), which was dedicated to research in the origins of mankind.

Kalakaua tried to preserve the ancient history of the Hawaiian people as found in old chants, which had been forbidden by the missionaries. At one point in his reign he assembled a group of the *kahuna kuahau* (historians) and each brought his ball of knotted *olona* cord. At this gathering the ancient Hawaiian chant of creation, the *Kumulipo,* was recorded and preserved. Later monthly meetings of the "Ball of Twine" society were held at the palace. The missionary group was angered by this attempt to restore *kahunaism.* What made matters worse was the revival by the King of the *hula,* which had been outlawed when the missionaries were powerful in the government.

218

Kalakaua loved music. At the beginning of his reign, he and his sister and brother each had a musical group. They frequently composed original music, which they sang. Kalakaua wrote the words for the national anthem of the kingdom, "Hawaii Pono'i," which was set to music by Captain Henry Berger. Captain Berger had been brought to Hawaii to organize the Royal Hawaiian Band.

Robert Louis Stevenson in Hawaii

One of the important visitors to Hawaii during Kalakaua's reign was Robert Louis Stevenson. He came to Hawaii after spending six months in the South Sea Islands, where he came to love the Polynesian people and their way of life. He became fast friends with Kalakaua. Frequently he was the King's guest at breakfast. Often they spent the morning discussing Hawaiian history, archaeology, and legends.

Henry Poor gave a *luau* in honor of the Stevensons, at which the King and Princess Liliuokalani were special guests. The menu consisted of delicacies usually prepared for such a feast—baked dog, chicken, pig, *poi,* raw fish, cooked fish, crabs, *limu,* and roast *kukui* nuts. What made this *luau* doubly memorable was that Mrs. Stevenson

Robert Louis Stevenson (at left), while on a trip through the Pacific to aid his health, stayed in Hawaii for six months, leaving in June, 1889. During this time, he and King Kalakaua (at right) became good friends.

Hawaii State Archives

presented the King with a rare pearl, and Mr. Stevenson read a sonnet he had prepared for the occasion:

The Silver Ship, my King—that was her name
In the bright islands whence your fathers came—
The Silver Ship, at rest from winds and tides,
Below your palace in your harbour rides:
and the seafarers, sitting safe on shore,
Like eager merchants count their treasures o'er.
One gift they find, one strange and lovely thing
Now doubly precious since it pleased a king.

The right, my liege, is ancient as the lyre
for bards to give to kings what kings admire.
'Tis mine to offer for Apollo's sake;
and since the gift is fitting, yours to take.
To golden hands the golden pearl I bring:
The ocean jewel to the island king.

Stevenson rented the Brown residence in Waikiki to escape the hubbub of downtown Honolulu and to have the peace he needed to complete his book, *The Master of Ballantrae*. His Waikiki residence was next door to Ainahau, the home of the little Princess Kaiulani. He and Kaiulani became fast friends and spent many pleasant hours under the banyan tree at Ainahau, where he wove many fascinating tales for her delight.

When Stevenson learned that Kaiulani was to be sent to England to complete her education and discovered now unhappy she was at leaving the Islands, he wrote a poem to comfort her. In their meeting place under the banyan tree he told her of the beauty of England and composed the tribute to her.

To Kaiulani
Forth from her land to mine she goes,
the island maiden, the island rose,
Light of heart and bright of face,
the daughter of a double race.
Her islands here, in Southern sun,
shall mourn their Kaiulani gone,

220

And I, in her dear banyan shade,
look vainly for my little maid.
But our Scots island far away
shall glitter with unwonted day,
And cast for once their tempests by
to smile in Kaiulani's eye.

Written in April to Kaiulani in the April of her age; and at Waikiki within easy walk of Kaiulani's banyan. When she comes to my land and her father's and the wind beats upon the window (as I fear it will), let her look at this page; it will be like a weed gathered and pressed at home; and she will remember her own islands and the shadow of the mighty tree. And she will hear the peacocks screaming in the dusk and the wind blowing in the palms, and she will think of her father sitting there alone. RLS

Having heard a great deal about the work of Father Damien among the lepers at Kalaupapa, Stevenson was eager to visit the settlement. Before he could get there, the good father had died of the disease. Stevenson decided to go to the settlement anyway to see it for himself. In August, 1889, a private letter criticizing Father Damien was published in a Sydney, Australia newspaper. The Reverend Charles M. Hyde was the author of the letter, which was directed to the Reverend H. B. Gage. Stevenson wrote a blistering reply to the writer. He refused to accept any money for the publication of material he had written in defense of Father Damien, and turned over all receipts to the leper fund.

Education

During this period an increasing number of American patterns in education were adopted in Hawaii. Although English had been the language of business, diplomacy, and the government itself since 1850, most children enrolled in the common schools were taught in the Hawaiian language. The remainder of the school population attended government English schools or private schools. However, the number of schools in which English was taught had been continually rising since the time when Richard Armstrong headed the public school system.

Changes were also made during this period in the control and administration of the schools. Many of these changes, too, were in keeping with American public school practices. A school board of five lay persons was appointed and given authority to hire a superintendent and formulate policy. The men who became superintendents, in the following years, had been trained in America, and the policies they recommended derived from American patterns. Local school committees had the authority to hire teachers.

Toward the end of the monarchy, American textbooks were adopted, bought by the board, and sold to the students at cost. School buildings were improved and better equipment was bought for them.

Teachers were required to take an examination for certification. Much attention was given to improving the quality of instruction through the training of teachers at Lahainaluna and in-service training institutes. English classes for persons above school age were started. These classes formed the basis of the present extensive adult education program.

By the end of the monarchy, there were only 10,700 children attending the public schools. However, during the period of the elected kings, the curriculum for these children had been extended and improved.

Summing Up the Chapter

Because of a favorable reciprocity treaty with the United States, Hawaiian planters wanted to produce as much sugar as possible. In order to increase the amount of land that could be used for sugar, water had to be brought in through long irrigation ditches. Methods of producing sugar were improved. Workers were brought from other countries under a contract system. Interisland and transpacific steamship service was started. By the end of Kalakaua's reign, railroads were operating on three of the main islands. Electricity and telephones came to the Islands before the end of the century. Kalakaua tried to keep alive early Hawaiian culture. He also encouraged the development of music. Robert Louis Stevenson visited the Islands at that time and was a friend of Kalakaua and the royal family. Also important during this period was the adaptation of American patterns of school administration and teaching methods to the Hawaiian public school system.

19

Queen Liliuokalani and Annexation

So important was it to maintain the royal line that the cabinet was determined that Liliuokalani be named queen immediately upon her brother's death, although she preferred to wait until after his funeral. The cabinet insisted that she take the oath of office, which included a promise to uphold and defend the Constitution of 1887.

The new ruler, Hawaii's first and only reigning queen, came to the throne with the title of Liliuokalani. Everyone agreed that she had none of the weaknesses of her brother, Kalakaua. Like her brother, however, she was devoted to the welfare of the Hawaiian people. To help her people, the Queen leased 10-acre plots of land on the island of Hawaii at reasonable rents to Hawaiians. The income from these rents was placed in a trust fund for Hawaiians. She intended to donate all income from the crown lands as an endowment for the Liliuokalani Education Fund. Liliuokalani even recommended a cut in her income as queen so that there would be more money for teachers' salaries.

Background of a Queen

She was born on September 2, 1838, and was named Liliu (Lydia) Kamakaeha Kaolanialii Newewelii. At the age of four she was enrolled in the Royal School. There she received her education along with four other rulers of Hawaii. She had an easy and dignified man-

223

ner combined with the superior attitude of one accustomed to rule. Her voice was pleasant with a musical ring to it. She spoke English fluently. Like Kalakaua, she had a great deal of musical talent. Although she had composed many other songs, she is best remembered for her beautiful, "Aloha 'Oe."

She spent much of her life at the royal court. During Kalakaua's two trips abroad, Liliuokalani had remained in Hawaii and acted as regent so that she had first-hand experience in guiding the affairs of Hawaii. In 1887 Liliuokalani accompanied Queen Kapiolani, her sister-in-law, to the Diamond Jubilee of Queen Victoria. While she was abroad on this trip, the news of the terms of the constitution that Kalakaua had signed shocked her so greatly that she canceled a tour of the rest of Europe and returned to Hawaii at once. Upon her return, Liliuokalani found the Hawaiian people greatly aroused and fearing for their independence.

Trouble Begins

Unfortunately, the Queen seemed fated to have trouble from the very beginning of her short reign. Soon after she came to the throne, her husband, Governor John Owen Dominis, died. With his passing, the Queen lost a badly needed and level-headed adviser.

One of the first acts of Queen Liliuokalani was to name her niece, Princess Kaiulani, as her heir to the throne. Princess Kaiulani was the daughter of the Queen's sister, Princess Likelike, and the Honorable A. S. Cleghorn. The nomination was well received by the House of Nobles, and Kaiulani was honored by the American warship, *Mohican,* with a twenty-one gun salute.

Queen Liliuokalani came to the throne during a difficult period in Hawaii's history. A period of economic depression had affected the sugar industry. Changes in the tariff policy of the United States did away with the advantages Hawaii had enjoyed under the reciprocity treaty. This depression strengthened the desire among many businessmen for annexation to the United States.

The struggle for political power, which began under Kalakaua, broke out again during the legislative session of 1892. The legislature was composed of men representing three political parties. The National Reform party, which supported the Queen, won a small majority in both houses. The Reform party, headed by Lorrin A. Thurston,

224

Queen Liliuokalani was the last ruler of Hawaii before the islands became a republic in 1893, a territory of the United States in 1898, and the 50th State in 1959. She reigned from 1891 - 1893.

1887 Bayonet Constitution adopted
Kamehameha Schools founded

1889 Wilcox Revolt

1891 Queen Liliuokalani ascends the throne
Hawaiian Electric Company started

1892 Struggle for political power in legislature

1893 Overthrow of the monarchy; provisional government established

1893 Grover Cleveland becomes 24th U.S. president

1894 Republic of Hawaii; new constitution established July 4, naming Sanford Dole president

Counterrevolution

1894 Sino-Japanese War begins
Wilson-Gorman Act passed

1896 Plessy v. Ferguson

1897 William McKinley becomes 25th U.S. president

1898 Annexation of Hawaii to the United States. July 7

1898 Spanish-American war begins

1899 Boer War begins

1900 Organic Act established Territory of Hawaii, June 14

1900 Boxer Rebellion in China

1901 President McKinley assissinated

consisted mostly of men opposed to strengthening the powers of the crown. A third party, the Liberal party, was headed by a group of malcontents—Robert W. Wilcox, John E. Bush, D. L. Huntsman, and others. In May, 1892, some of the Liberal party leaders were arrested for plotting treason, but they were acquitted by the Supreme Court.

The major issues of the 1892 session of the legislature were the control of the cabinet and the attempt to change the constitution. This led directly to the overthrow of the monarchy. When Liliuokalani became Queen, she appointed her cabinet from members of the National Reform party, which supported her views. This cabinet was voted out of office as soon as the legislature met. The Queen then appointed two more cabinets from among her followers. These also were voted out of office. After this she named a cabinet made up entirely of members of the Reform party in order to avoid delay in carrying on state business. The Liberal party leaders were unhappy because they had not been named to the cabinet. Some of them joined with the National Reform party to overthrow the Reform party ministry, then in office; a move which succeeded. The Queen again appointed members of her party, the National Reform party, to the cabinet two days before the legislature adjourned.

While in session, the legislature passed lottery and opium bills. The feeling was that the lottery would provide additional income. If the importation of opium were lawful, its sale would be easier to control since large amounts of it had been smuggled into Hawaii.

The matter of a new constitution had been discussed since 1887 when the "Bayonet Constitution" was adopted. During the legislative sessions of 1890 and 1892 proposals to amend or rewrite the constitution were made with the strong backing of Kalakaua and Liliuokaalani. Both times these measures were voted down. The Queen's opponents, many of whom claimed that they believed in a democratic form of government, voted down a bill to hold a constitutional convention to do away with property qualifications for voting!

Overthrow of the Monarchy

When the bill to hold a constitutional convention to give back the right to vote to the common people was defeated, a cry of protest was raised across the kingdom. Petitions bearing thousands of signatures poured into Iolani Palace asking the Queen to issue a new constitution

In Honolulu harbor in 1901 sailing vessels could be seen alongside steamships. Probably the harbor looked much like this when Queen Liliuokalani

in the same way as Kamehameha V did. Queen Liliuokalani states in her book, *Hawaii's Story by Hawaii's Queen,* that she was spied upon and betrayed by people close to her. The proposed new constitution contained provisions to do away with property qualifications for voting, to restore the appointment of Nobles by the Crown, and to deny the right to vote to foreigners who were not Hawaiian citizens.

After the legislature had adjourned on January 14, 1893, the Queen returned to her palace to discuss the proclamation of a new constitution with her ministers. Two of them had agreed to sign the new constitution, and the Queen tried to persuade the others to do the same. The ministers feared that proclaiming the new constitution might have fatal results. After two hours of discussion the Queen gave in to her ministers. Hawaiians had filled the palace grounds, eagerly awaiting the moment when their Queen would restore their rights. Late that afternoon she announced to the expectant crowd that the proclamation of a new constitution would have to be delayed. She asked the people to return peacefully to their homes. Reluctantly her subjects departed.

hurried back from Europe to protest the Constitution of 1887, and when the *Charleston* returned with the body of Kalakaua in January, 1891.

On Monday she issued a statement that the constitution would not be changed except by means provided in the constitution itself. The Queen's statement came too late. On the Saturday before, the Annexation Club, which had been formed in the spring of 1892, called a meeting in the armory and formed a Committee of Public Safety. Sugar-planter Henry Baldwin urged moderation, but he was shouted down by inflammatory speakers such as Lorrin A. Thurston. A secret plan of action to do away with the monarchy, set up a provisional government and apply to the United States for annexation was agreed upon.

When the meeting of the annexationists became known, the Hawaiians called a mass meeting for the same hour in Palace Square for all those who were against annexation. The chairman, Antone Rosa, presented a resolution pledging loyalty to the Queen and promising to support her plan to seek constitutional changes only by legal means.

At the annexationists' meeting, the fate of Hawaii as an independent kingdom was sealed. Resolutions were passed denouncing the Queen and giving the Committee of Safety the power to take whatever steps were necessary to secure the protection of liberty, life, and property in Hawaii. The Committee of Public Safety had asked United States Minister John L. Stevens, to land troops because of the unrest in the community. At five o'clock on Monday a force of sailors and marines was sent ashore from the *U.S.S. Boston.*

When the cabinet members saw the armed forces of the United States marching up the street, they immediately met with Oahu's Governor A. S. Cleghorn. Governor Cleghorn protested to Stevens that the landing of troops was a violation of international law and that he would enter a formal protest to the American Government.

In the meantime, the annexationists had been busy. They had previously asked former Marshal of the Kingdom, Mr. Soper, to be commander-in-chief of their armed forces. He had refused to go along with the overthrow of the monarchy, agreeing with Sanford B. Dole and Judge Hartwell that such a move would be unwise in view of the treaty that pledged the United States and Great Britain to protect Hawaii's independence. Dole proposed that Queen Liliuokalani give up the throne in favor of Princess Kaiulani and that a regency be set up. At a second meeting, Soper agreed to take command of the armed forces if Dole would head the new government. Dole was hastily summoned and, after thinking over the matter for some time, agreed to take on the leadership of the new government.

The actual overthrow of the monarchy proved to be a rather unexciting affair except for a single incident that might have momentarily turned the tide of events. Mr. W. O. Smith's office, where the final arrangements for setting up the provisional government were made, was being watched by a half dozen policemen. These policemen had orders to arrest any of the members of the Committee of Public Safety if they headed toward the palace. As Sanford Dole stood at the door of the building with his pockets full of treasonable papers, a shot was heard. The policemen who had been on guard hurried to investigate the shooting, leaving the committee members free to go to the government building and to take possession of it. With practically no audience, except the government clerks, Henry A. Cooper read the document putting an end to the monarchy and declaring the establishment of a provisional government until terms of union with the United States could be agreed upon. As the reading of the proclamation neared its end, a letter announcing the overthrow of the monarchy was sent to United States Minister Stevens. He replied promptly with a letter recognizing the provisional government.

The pistol shot that had enabled the committee to carry out its plan had been fired by John Good, the driver of a wagon load of ammunition being transported to the revolutionists. The shot hit the policeman who had tried to stop the wagon. The wounded policeman was carried to the hospital by some of his fellow policemen who should have been watching Smith's office.

The provisional government was in control. The Queen, wishing to avoid bloodshed, had refused to allow Marshal Wilson to take action against the revolutionists. Believing that the American Government would refuse to support these actions, just as England had done in the case of Lord Paulet, the Queen abdicated under protest "to the superior force of the United States Government . . . (and) to avoid collision of armed forces and perhaps loss of life."

Colonel Soper discharging the Royal Household Guard after the revolution.

The Provisional Government

The provisional government immediately ordered that all arms be turned in and that the country be ruled by martial law. *Habeas corpus* was suspended. The provisional government asked that, in view of the situation, the American minister assume a quasi-protectorate over the Islands. Two weeks after the revolution the American flag was raised over the government building to the resounding boom of a salute from the *U.S.S. Boston*. Queen Liliuokalani withdrew to her private home, Washington Place.

One of the first acts of the provisional government was to require everyone to take an oath of allegiance to the new government. Some people took the oath to protect their jobs with the government. Rather than swear allegiance, the Royal Hawaiian bandsmen resigned in a body. Many Hawaiians took to wearing hat bands with the inscription *Aloha'aina* (Love of Country). Many patriotic songs were composed and widely sung. The most famous of these songs was "Mele 'Ai Pohaku" (Stone Eating Song) in which the Hawaiians declared they would eat stones rather than sign the "loathsome oath" to the provisional government and be disloyal to their Queen.

The new government, popularly known as PG (Provisional Government), consisted of an executive council of four men who handled the administrative departments of the government. Judge Sanford B. Dole was president of the executive council and, for a time, took charge of foreign affairs. Legislative authority was given to an advisory council of fourteen men.

The new administration promptly sent a commission, headed by Lorrin A. Thurston, to Washington to make a treaty of annexation with the United States. The Queen also prepared to send a commission to plead her case. The Queen's representatives were refused passage aboard the planter-owned vessel taking the provisional government's representatives to the United States. The delay gave the provisional government the advantage inasmuch as its representatives arrived in Washington first.

The time factor was particularly important because President Benjamin Harrison had been defeated for re-election. President Harrison had ordered a treaty of annexation drawn up and presented to the Senate. The opposition of some Senators delayed the treaty and it had not been passed by the end of Harrison's term of office. When President Grover Cleveland came into office, one of his first acts was to

The Executive Council of the Provisional Government from left to right: James A. King, minister of interior, Sanford B. Dole, president, W.O. Smith, attorney general, P.C. Jones, minister of finance.

withdraw the treaty of annexation from the Senate. President Cleveland's action in the matter may have been partly influenced by Princess Kaiulani, who came to Washington with her guardians, Mr. and Mrs. Theophilus Davies, to plead the cause of the monarchy. There was a great deal of debate in the public press of the United States about the revolution in Hawaii and annexation.

President Cleveland appointed James Blount, a former chairman of the House Foreign Affairs Committee, to go to Hawaii to look into the conditions under which the monarchy had been overthrown. Since Blount's commission gave him full power over all American officials and naval officers in Hawaii, he was nicknamed "Paramount Blount." Blount tried to carry out his investigation with complete fairness to both sides.

Shortly after his arrival, Blount ordered that the American flag be removed from Hawaiian government buildings, the American troops be returned to their vessel, and the American protectorate be withdrawn. As Blount left Hawaii, the Royal Hawaiian Band played "Marching Through Georgia," an insult to Blount, who had been a colonel in the Confederate army.

In his report to Secretary of State Walter Gresham, Blount charged that the revolution was the result of a conspiracy between Minister Stevens and the revolutionary leaders. He went on to say that if all of

Ex-Queen Liliuokalani mounting the steps to the government house after her arrest. Hawaii State Archives photo.

the citizens of the Islands were allowed to vote on the question of annexation to the United States, the proposition would be overwhelmingly defeated. On the basis of Blount's report, President Cleveland decided that the United States ought to undo the wrong done to Hawaii and restore Queen Liliuokalani to her throne.

America was divided on the question of the restoration of the Queen to her throne. Part of the division was political in nature, with the Republican party in favor of annexation and the Democrats against it. The agents of the provisional government worked hard at stirring up American sympathy toward annexation.

President Cleveland appointed Albert S. Willis as Minister to Hawaii. Willis' instructions were to present himself to the provisional government. After that, he was to tell Queen Liliuokalani that President Cleveland wanted to restore her to the throne if she would show complete forgiveness to those who had overthrown her government. During her first interview with Willis, Queen Liliuokalani said that she could not grant amnesty as it was beyond her powers as a constitutional ruler.

She went on to say that she could not act on the matter without the advice of her ministers. There was a second interview during which Willis read his notes from the previous interview and then asked the Queen if the notes were correct. She said they were. Later, the Queen was quoted as saying that the revolutionists would be beheaded. This statement made lurid reading in the American papers. Just before Christmas the Queen sent Willis a note stating that she would grant amnesty to all. She promised to forget past misdeeds and work in peace and friendship for the good of the country.

Willis met with President Dole and the cabinet and read them the Queen's message of amnesty and called upon them to surrender the power of the provisional government to the Queen. President Dole asked for time to think over the matter. He sent Willis a long letter refusing to restore the monarchy, and saying that the United States had no right to interfere in the internal affairs of Hawaii. President Cleveland realized that the monarch could not be restored without armed intervention. He was forced to let the matter drop.

The leaders of the provisional government realized that as long as President Cleveland remained in office, annexation would be impossible. They would have to wait patiently for annexation until some future date. Consequently, the Hawaiian legislature, on March 15, 1894, passed an act calling for a constitutional convention to establish a republic and to give the Islands a more permanent form of government.

The Organization of the Republic

The constitutional convention was organized in such a way as to insure that the supporters of the revolution would be in control of it and any later government. The original draft of the proposed constitution was mostly the work of President Sanford Dole and Lorrin Thurston. After much discussion and amendment of details, it went into effect on July 4, 1894.

The constitution named Dole as president. The president's term of office was to be for six years and he could not succeed himself. The election of the president was to be by the legislature after the term of the first president had expired. The men who had headed the four departments under the provisional government were reappointed by Dole to serve in the cabinet under the republic.

The legislature consisted of two houses—the Senate and the House of Representatives. Each house consisted of fifteen members. Membership in either branch of the legislature was open only to men of property. A certain degree of wealth was also required in order to be able to vote for candidates for both houses of the legislature. Voters as well as members of the legislature had to take an oath to support the republic and promise not to assist in the re-establishment of the monarchy. They also had to be able to speak, read, and write either Hawaiian or English. Some additional provisions of the constitution were designed to keep Orientals and other newly arrived immigrants from becoming citizens.

Although the government of the republic was patterned after that of the United States, it had several unique features. It provided for a fifteen-member Council of State, which had the power to appropriate money when the legislature was not in session. Members of the cabinet were *ex officio* members of the legislature without the right to vote. Under the republic the government was highly centralized and did not contain any units of local government. It was a republic more in name than in actual fact since so few people could take part in the government.

In vain Queen Liliuokalani protested the establishment of the republic to both the United States and Great Britain. The new government was soon recognized by all countries with which it had diplomatic relations. On July 14, 1894, Chief Justice Albert F. Judd administered the oath of office to President Dole in an impressive ceremony. The band played "Hawaii Pono'i," a new 36-foot flag flew from the central flagstaff of the executive building, and the cannons boomed a national salute. Thus, the new republic was launched.

Counterrevolution

During the summer and fall of 1894 the supporters of the Queen under the leadership of men such as Samuel Nowlein, Robert Wilcox, Lot Kamehameha Lane, Charles T. Gulick, and William G. Rickard, conspired to overthrow the republic. Weapons were ordered and shipped from San Francisco and were to be distributed at various points along the shoreline of Oahu with the remainder being discharged in Honolulu. The first part of the plan was carried out successfully. However, when the vessel carrying the weapons arrived at Honolulu harbor, the great enthusiasm of the Hawaiians caused them to violate orders that only a small group should gather at the dock. Although the large crowds were orderly, many Hawaiians were beaten by the police and several were arrested.

Robert Wilcox mounted his horse and rode swiftly to Diamond Head where the ship lay off-shore. Working feverishly through the night, the crew brought the arms and ammunition ashore and buried them in the sands at the foot of Diamond Head. Rumors had put the republic's government on guard. An advance unit of rebels was intercepted. In a brief skirmish, a prominent supporter of the republic, Charles L. Carter, was fatally wounded. There were a few more skirmishes and the side of Diamond Head was shelled, but the revolt was completely put down within two weeks.

Although Queen Liliuokalani knew of the plot, she did not actively take part in it. Nevertheless, she and her two nephews, Princes David Kawananakoa and Jonah Kuhio Kalanianaole, along with 200 others were arrested on suspicion. During her imprisonment in the palace, Liliuokalani signed a document in which she gave up all claim to the throne and took an oath of allegiance to the Republic of Hawaii.

The prisoners were tried by a military court. In thirty-five days, 190 cases were tried and nearly all were found guilty. The Queen's sentence was five years imprisonment at hard labor and a fine of $5000. Other heavy sentences—including death in a few cases—were imposed. However, at the insistence of President Dole and strong public opinion, including pressure from the United States, sentences were lightened. The death sentences were changed to imprisonment. By the end of 1895, under pressure from home and abroad, the republic released all remaining prisoners on parole. The victory of the government over the revolutionists and its leniency in dealing with them put the Republic of Hawaii in a strong position at home and before the rest of the world.

Life Under the Republic

Business in Hawaii was given a big boost by the passage in the United States Congress of the Wilson-Gorman Act in 1894. This act discontinued the bounty of two cents a pound to American sugar producers and restored the tariff on sugar imported into the United States.

The Hawaiian sugar industry once more profited from the preferential treatment given it by the reciprocity treaty.

Under the republic, industry doubled or trebled and many great fortunes were made. The planters built fine houses, which were luxuriously furnished and supplied with all of the accessories to be found in a mansion in New York or Chicago—baths, electric lights, and telephones.

Some Hawaiians felt the republic was a police state. Because of their fear of informers, many large gatherings were broken up and people arrested on suspicion of treason. At one point, large gatherings were prohibited. Many of the puritanical laws were revived. Dancing of the *hula* was forbidden and Sunday concerts were stopped. Finally, when Sunday concerts were resumed, only European classical musical numbers could be played. Despite all this, many balls were given by wealthy Caucasians, particularly when a naval vessel was in port.

With the expansion of the plantations, there was need for more laborers. In the 1880's the government imported contract laborers from Japan in order to counterbalance the great number of Chinese workers in the country. By the middle of the decade, the Japanese made up about one-fourth of the population. Some people feared that Hawaii might become a Japanese colony. Various measures were adopted to reduce the number of Japanese immigrants and increase the number of Chinese. The planters tried to bring in more Caucasian workers, but this proved to be too expensive.

After 1894 the importation of laborers was conducted by Japanese companies. In 1896 officials of the Hawaiian government became convinced that these Japanese emigration companies were engaged in fraudulent practices, and admission to Hawaii was refused to 1200 Japanese immigrants. The Japanese government protested and sent a warship to Honolulu. One young member of President William McKinley's administration, Assistant Secretary of the Navy Theodore Roosevelt, reacted violently. The commanding officer of the naval force at Honolulu was given secret instructions to try to promote a friendly settlement of the dispute, but if the Japanese used force, he was to take possession of the Islands and declare them an American protectorate. The Department of State assured the Japanese government that all of its rights in the Pacific would be respected if the United States were to annex Hawaii. Fortunately, the disagreement with Japan was finally settled in a peaceful manner and the Hawaiian government agreed to pay the Japanese $75,000 for any losses suffered.

Annexation

With the election of a Republican administration in the United States in 1896, the country was more sympathetic to annexation. However, it was not the incident with Japan that finally caused the balance in Congress to swing in favor of annexation, but the outbreak of the Spanish-American War on April 25, 1898. The sinking of the battleship *Maine* in the harbor at Havana, Cuba, greatly increased sentiment in favor of annexation. Dewey's victory in Manila emphasized Hawaii's strategic importance to the United States, for no battleship afloat at that time could steam from San Francisco to Manila without stopping midway.

In the meantime, the Hawaiians cast neutrality aside and welcomed the American troops on their way to the Philippines. The first Hawaiian Red Cross unit was formed at this time. The "boys in blue" rode free on the street cars and were feted at picnics and *luaus*.

To help the cause of annexation, President and Mrs. Dole made a trip to Washington early in 1898. However, there were many powerful interests in the United States working against annexation. The sugar interests, represented by such men as Claus Spreckels, fought it. The Democratic party was also opposed to it.

Although a majority of the American senators were in favor of annexation, the necessary two-thirds majority for ratification of the annexation treaty was not available. Therefore, those in favor of annexation decided to try to achieve their goal by a joint resolution, which required only a simple majority of both houses of Congress for passage. This method had been used in the annexation of Texas. Two resolutions were introduced, one in the Senate on March 16, 1898, and the other in the House of Representatives on May 4. By July 6, 1898, both houses of Congress approved annexation and the next day President McKinley signed the bill.

The news of annexation reached Honolulu on July 13, 1898. Fire bells rang, factory whistles blew, firecrackers exploded, and the artillery in front of the executive building boomed out a 100-gun salute. The crowd that had gathered at the waterfront to hear President Dole

The festivities celebrating Hawaii's annexation to the United States included a huge bonfire at the foot of Punchbowl Crater. Here people rush down Fort Street toward the fire, which lighted up the whole city.

read the news marched uptown with the band. At one point Captain Berger handed the baton to Dr. McGrew, who had worked so hard for annexation, and he directed the playing of the "Star-Spangled Banner." That evening a group of citizens lit a huge bonfire at the foot of Punchbowl.

The formal transfer of sovereignty did not take place until August 12, 1898, in a simple and restrained ceremony. The same flag that Minister Blount had ordered lowered in 1893 was once more raised over the Hawaiian Islands. There were Americans, Portuguese, Chinese, and Japanese attending the annexation ceremonies—but no native Hawaiians.

The Islands were officially a part of the United States but, until the passage of the Organic Act, they continued under the laws of the republic. The same officials remained in office for another two years.

240

Summing Up the Chapter

Trouble faced Liliuokalani, Hawaii's only reigning queen, almost as soon as she came to the throne. The country was in the middle of an economic depression. The struggle for political power continued. The two main issues—control of the cabinet and the question of changing the constitution—finally led to the overthrow of the monarchy. Although the Queen wished to proclaim a new constitution, she could not command the support of her ministers. The Annexation Club wanted to do away with the monarchy, set up a provisional government and ask to be annexed to the United States. Those who were against annexation pledged loyalty to the Queen and supported her plan to change the constitution only by legal means. The annexationists formed a Committee of Public Safety and asked the United States minister to land sailors and marines to help keep order.

A provisional government was formed, headed by Sanford Dole. The overthrow of the government was accomplished peacefully. Liliuokalani gave up her throne under protest, believing that the actions of the American minister would not be supported by the United States Government. Representatives of the Queen and those of the new provisional government went to the United States to plead their cause. Opinion in America was divided on the question of restoring the Queen to her throne or of annexing the Islands to the United States. President Cleveland studied the matter for some time and decided against any action. On July 4, 1894, a new constitution for the Republic of Hawaii went into effect. Attempts by supporters of the Queen to overthrow the republic failed.

A change in the United States tariff brought prosperity again to the sugar planters and a need to import workers from abroad. With the coming to office of President McKinley and the outbreak of the Spanish-American War, the question of annexation again arose. By joint resolution of the Senate and the House of Representatives annexation of Hawaii was approved. The annexation ceremonies on August 12, 1898, were attended by peoples of many nationalities but not by native Hawaiians.

Appendix

The Hawaiian Language

Inasmuch as this is a book about Hawaii, many Hawaiian words have been used in it. We shall attempt here to give the reader a little understanding of the language and of the problems that were involved in putting it into writing.

The credit for giving the Hawaiian language a written form goes to the early missionaries. They realized that to succeed in Christianizing the Hawaiians, they must learn to speak Hawaiian and translate the Bible into that language.

In trying to reduce the Hawaiian language to written form, the missionaries faced several problems. A basic one was that the pronunciation of words was not the same throughout the kingdom. Another confusing element was that the Hawaiians used consonant sounds that were between the sounds of English consonants with which the missionaries were familiar. Thus, the word for *room* was adapted by the Hawaiians as either *rumi* or *lumi*, depending on whether the Hawaiian speaker's pronunciation of *r* tended more toward the *r* or the *l* sound. The Hawaiians could hear no difference among the sounds commonly represented by the letters *l, r,* and *d.* In Hawaiian, the *w* sometimes has the sound of *w* in *well*, especially after *o* and *u;* but after *i* and *e*, it generally has a *v*-like sound. The Hawaiian word *iwi* (bone) is pronounced *ē vē.* The *k* sound is used in most parts of the state, but on Kauai the word *kapa* may become *tapa.*

Another problem that added confusion to the situation was that many foreigners who might have helped the missionaries with the work of putting the Hawaiian tongue into writing did not speak it correctly themselves.

The use of the glottal stop, written thus ' , sometimes confuses the foreigner. It is the sort of gulping sound one would make between the two words in the English phrase, "Oh—oh!" Omitting this sound frequently results in the speaker's saying a different word from the one intended. In Hawaiian, *pau*, pronounced *pow*, means *finished;* however *pa'u*, pronounced *pä ü*, means a Hawaiian *sarong.*

Besides the difficulties of inflection and rhythm, Hawaiian words are run together more than English words. When listening to a conversation in Hawaiian, one needs a keen ear to tell when one word ends and another begins.

243

The Hawaiian alphabet with only twelve letters is one of the shortest in the world.[1] It contains seven consonants and five vowels. The whole alphabet consists of the following letters: *a, e, h, i, k, l, m, n, o, p, u,* and *w*. Except for the *w*, which has already been discussed, the consonants are pronounced about the same as they are in English. The reader may wonder how the missionaries decided whether to use the *l* or the *r* and how they settled the *k* and *t* controversy. They simply took a vote on which letter to use!

Some of the vowels change their sound, depending upon whether they are in a stressed or an unstressed position. The unstressed sounds are more common, so they will be listed first:

Unstressed

a . . . . as *a* in about
e . . . . as *e* in get
i . . . . as *y* in pity
o . . . . as *o* in cold
u . . . . as *u* in June

Stressed

a . . . . as *a* in car
e . . . . as *e* in get
e . . . . as *e* in cafe
i . . . . as *i* in machine
o . . . . as *o* in cold
u . . . . as *u* in June

Vowels may be either long or short. Long vowels are always stressed, as in *holoku* (hōlō'kü).

In Hawaiian, the next to the last syllable is usually stressed. In longer words, alternating syllables are stressed, counting backward from the next-to-the-last syllable. Accented syllables do not receive as much stress as they do in English. All syllables in Hawaiian end with a vowel. The vowel is attached to the preceding consonant, if there is a consonant in the syllable.

Although each vowel is pronounced separately, the native speakers may pronounce two adjoining vowels so rapidly that they sound more like diphthongs in English. To the Hawaiian ear, the pronunciation of vowel combinations as diphthongs by the foreign speaker sounds more truly Hawaiian than would the speaker's attempt to pronounce each vowel separately as in the Hawaiian manner. For example, it would be advisable to pronounced *poi* to rhyme with *boy* and *pau* to rhyme with *now*.

One of the peculiarities of the Hawaiian language is that two consonants cannot follow each other. In making Hawaiian words from English not

[1] Scientifically speaking, the glottal stop might be considered the thirteenth letter in the Hawaiian alphabet. However, in most discussions of the Hawaiian language, it is not counted as a letter.

only must we have a consonant-vowel or vowel-consonant-vowel pattern, but also we are limited to the sounds in the Hawaiian language. Thus telephone becomes *kelepona* (kĕ lä′pō nə); bicycle is written *paikikala* (̗pī kē′kä lə); and automobile becomes *'okomopila* ('o ̗kō mō′pē lə).

Because Hawaiian is a living and growing language, twentieth century words have been adapted from English. We have already seen examples of this in the paragraph above. A word such as *'eleweka* ("ĕ lä vä kə) is borrowed from the English *elevator* and is simply clothed in Hawaiian garb.

Another way in which new terms have come into the Hawaiian language is through adaptation. When the Hawaiians first saw Captain Cook's ships, they thought of the large vessels as islands; hence they were called *moku* ('mō ̗kü). From this, steamers became *mokuahi* (fire ships); airplanes, *mokulele* (flying ships); and submarines, *mokulu'u* (diving boats). Some other interesting adaptations are camera, *pahu-pa'i-ki'i* (box for printing pictures); atom, *hunahuna* (fragments, particles, crumbs); movies, *ki'i'oni'oni* (moving pictures).

Many Hawaiian words now in common use in the Islands have been included in *Webster's Third New International Dictionary,* Unabridged. If you are a *malihini* (mälē′hēnē), a newcomer to the Islands, you will be able to learn a few Hawaiian words. If you are a *kama'aina* (̗kä ma-'ī nə), a long-time resident of Hawaii, you will be pleased to see so many words you use included in this dictionary.

Besides those Hawaiian words found in Webster's dictionary, we have listed some of the Hawaiian terms that are used in this book and in everyday speech in Hawaii. The pronunciations given are those of educated speakers, and many were supplied by Mrs. Mary K. Pukui, senior author of the *Hawaiian-English Dictionary.*

akamai	̗äkə′mī	Smart, intelligent.
aloha	ä′lo ̗hä	Greetings! Good-bye! Hello! Love, affection, kindness.
Diamond Head		Toward Diamond Head (used as a direction in Honolulu rather than north, east, south, or west).
Ewa	'ĕ və	Toward the village of Ewa (used as a direction in Honolulu rather than north, east, south, or west).
Haleakala	̗hälä ̗ä kä′lä	A dormant volcano 10,025 feet high on the island of Maui.
haole	'haù lä	Formerly, any foreigner, now a Caucasian.
haupia	haù′pēə	Hawaiian pudding made of cornstarch and coconut cream.

245

Hawaii	hə'wī ē	The largest island in the Hawaiian chain; called "The Big Island." One of the four counties in the state. Also, the State of.
heiau	'hā yaů	A pre-Christian place of worship.
holoku	ˌhō lō'kü	A woman's long one-piece gown usually made with some fitting and a train.
ho'omalimali	ˌhō'ōˌmälē'mälē	Soft soap, flattery.
hui	'hü ē	Club, association, syndicate.
Ka'ahumanu	ˌkä''ä hü'mänü	Favorite wife of Kamehameha I and, following his death, regent and *kuhina nui*.
kahuna	kä'hünä	A pre-Christian Hawaiian priest, an expert in a profession or in a craft.
Kalakaua	ˌkälä'kaůə	Elected king of Hawaii (1874-1891); known as the "Merry Monarch."
kalua	kä'lüə	Baked in an earth oven, an *imu*.
kama'aina	ˌkämä'īnä	Literally "child of the land," a person born in Hawaii or a long-time resident.
kamani	kə'mänē	Malabar almond tree; mastwood.
Kamehameha	kəˌmähə'mähə	Name of the first five kings of Hawaii. Usually used by itself to designate the first king by that name, Kamehameha the Great, who united all of the Hawaiian Islands under his rule.
Kanaloa	'kä nəˌlōə	One of the four great gods of old Hawaii. God of healing. Known both as a companion and an enemy of Kane, both were believed to be protectors of canoe builders, woodsmen, and fishermen.
kanalua	'känäˌlüə	Undecided members of the legislature refrain from voting by saying, "kanalua." Doubtful.

246

Kane	'kä nā	1. One of the four major gods of old Hawaii; god of life; various forms of Kane were associated with natural phenomena (heaven, earth, lightning, etc.). 2. With lower case "k", means male, husband, man.
kapa (tapa)	'kä pə	A coarse cloth commonly made from the bark of the paper mulberry plant and covered with geometric designs.
Kapiolani	kä pēō'länē	1. A high ranking chiefess who was one of the first converts to Christianity. 2. Queen of Hawaii and wife of King Kalakaua.
Kauai	'kaú͵i	The fourth largest island in 'the state; nicknamed "The Garden Isle" or "Menehune Land." One of the four counties in the state.
Kawaiahao	kä͵vīä'häō	A Congregational Church where several kings of Hawaii were crowned.
Kealakekua	kā'älä kā'küə	Village on the Island of Hawaii where Captain Cook met his death.
keiki	'kā kē	Child; immature plant.
kapu	'kä pü	Taboo, prohibited, consecrated.
kiawe (keawe)	kē'äwä	The algaroba tree.
Kilauea	͵kē͵laú'āə	An active volcano on the island of Hawaii.
kokua	kō'küə	Cooperation, help, assistance.
Kona	'kō͵nə	1. An area on the west side of the island of Hawaii, divided into two districts—North and South Kona. 2. Leeward sides of the Hawaiian Islands. 3. A hot, humid wind.
Ku	kü	One of the four major Hawaiian gods; Ku-kailimoku was the war god and special god of the kings on the island of Hawaii.
kuhina nui	kü'hēnə'nüē	Prime minister or associate ruler.

247

Kuhio	ˌkü hē′yō	Delegate to Congress (1902-1922). Full name was Prince Jonah Kuhio Kalanianaole.
Lanai	lä′näē	Called "The Pineapple Island"; this island forms part of Maui County.
lanai	lä′nī	Porch, veranda.
lauhala	ˌlaü′hälə	Dried pandanus leaves used for weaving.
laulau	ˌlaü′laü	Meat and fish (as pork and salmon) wrapped in leaves (as taro or *ti*) and baked or steamed.
lei	′lä	A wreath, garland, or necklace of flowers, leaves, shells, or other materials that is a symbol of affection in Polynesia.
Liholiho	ˌlē hō′lē hō	Kamehameha II, king of Hawaii (1819-1824), son of Kamehameha I.
Liliuokalani	lē′lēüō käˌlänē	Last ruler (queen) of Hawaii (1891-1893); sister of Kalakaua; author of song, "Ahoha 'Oe."
lomilomi	′lōmē′lōmē	A vigorous massage used by the Hawaiians to relieve pain and fatigue.
lomi salmon	′lō mē	A Hawaiian dish consisting of salmon worked with the fingers, mixed with onion, and seasoned.
Lono	′lō nō	One of the four major Hawaiian gods, worshipped as the god of fertility and agriculture. God of the makahiki.
luau	lü′aü	A feast at which Hawaiian food is served.
Lunalilo	′lünə′lē lō	First elected king of Hawaii (1873-1874).
mahalo	mä′hä lō	Thanks, gratitude.
mahimahi	′mähē′mähē	Dolphin.
Maika'i no.	′mīˌkä'ē ′nō	Fine, thank you.

248

maile	'mī lā	A native twining shrub (*Alyxia olivaeformis*) with shiny fragrant leaves, used for decoration and leis.
makahiki	ˌmäkə'hēkē	Ancient Hawaiian harvest feast.
makai	ˌmä'kī	Toward the sea; (used as a direction rather than north, east, south, or west).
malihini	mä lē'hē nē	A newcomer to Hawaii.
Maui	'maů ē	One of the four counties in the state. Also the name of the second largest island nicknamed "The Valley Isle."
mauka	'maůˌkə	Toward the mountains (used as a direction rather than north, east, south, or west).
Mauna Kea	'maůnäˌkāä	A dormant volcano and tallest peak in Hawaii, 13,784 feet tall.
Mauna Loa	'maůnäˌlōä	The largest single mountain mass in the world; 13,680 feet high; located on the island of Hawaii; still an active volcano.
menehune	ˌmene'hünä	A small mythical Polynesian being, usually pictured as a dwarf, who built fish ponds, roads, temples. If the work was not completed in one night, it was left unfinished.
mo'i	mō''ē	A Hawaiian ruling chief, king, sovereign, or queen.
Molokai	ˌmōlō'käē	Called "The Friendly Island" and forms part of Maui County.
mu'umu'u	'mü'ü'mü'ü	A loose dress worn chiefly in Hawaii, having gay colors and patterns, and adapted from the dresses originally distributed by the missionaries.
Niihau	ˌnē ē'haů	Small, privately owned island, which is part of Kauai County. Called "The Island of Yesteryear."

249

Oahu	ō'ä hü	Called "The Gathering Place." Name of one of the Hawaiian Islands on which Honolulu, the state capital, is located. Also one of the counties in the state.
pali	'pä͵lē	Cliff; steep slope.
paniolo	͵pänē'ōlō	Cowboy.
papale	pä'pälā	Hat.
pau	paů	Finished, completed, consumed.
pa'u	pä''ü	A Hawaiian sarong.
Pehea 'oe?	pä'hāə ''oi	How are you?
Pele	'pe lä	The volcano goddess.
pili	'pē lē	A grass, formerly used for thatching houses; tanglehead.
pilikia	͵pēlē'kēə	Trouble.
poi	'pōē	A pastelike Hawaiian food made of pounded cooked taro root and traditionally eaten with the fingers.
puka	'pü kə	Hole, tunnel.
tutu	͵tü'tü	Granny, grandpa.
wahine	wä'hē nä	Female; woman; wife.
wikiwiki	͵wēkē'wēkē	Quickly; fast.

250

Facts About Hawaii

Rulers of Hawaii

Native Rulers

Name	Birth Date	Accession	Death
Kamehameha I	1758(?)	1795	May 8,
(Kamehameha the Great)			1819
Kamehameha II	1797	May 20,	July 14,
(Liholiho)		1819	1824
Kamehameha III	March 17,	June 6,	Dec. 15,
(Kauikeaouli)	1814	1825	1854
Kamehameha IV	Feb. 9,	Dec. 15,	Nov. 30,
(Alexander Liholiho)	1834	1854	1863
Kamehameha V	Dec. 11,	Nov. 30,	Dec. 11,
(Lot Kamehameha)	1830	1863	1872
William C. Lunalilo	Jan. 31,	Jan. 8,	Feb. 3,
	1835	1873	1874
(David) Kalakaua	Nov. 16,	Feb. 12,	Jan. 20,
	1836	1874	1891
Liliuokalani	Sept. 2	Jan. 29,	Nov. 11,
	1838	1891	1917

Liliuokalani was deposed on January 17, 1893, and the Hawaiian kingdom was ended.

President of the Provisional Government
Sanford B. Dole   January 17, 1893 to July 4, 1894

President of the Republic of Hawaii
Sanford B. Dole   July 4, 1894 to June 14, 1900

Hawaii was annexed to the United States of America on August 12, 1898; however, territorial government under the Organic Act was not established until June 14, 1900.

251

Appointed Governors

Name	Appointed By	Term
Sanford B. Dole	McKinley	1900—1903
George R. Carter	T. Roosevelt	1903—1907
Walter F. Frear	T. Roosevelt	1907—1913
Lucius E. Pinkham	Wilson	1913—1918
Charles J. McCarthy	Wilson	1918—1921
Wallace R. Farrington	Harding	1921—1925
(second term)	Coolidge	1925—1929
Lawrence M. Judd	Hoover	1929—1934
Joseph B. Poindexter	F. D. Roosevelt	1934—1938
(second term)	F. D. Roosevelt	1938—1942
Ingram M. Stainback	F. D. Roosevelt	1942—1946
(second term)	Truman	1946—1951
Oren E. Long	Truman	1951—1953
Samuel W. King	Eisenhower	1953—1957
William F. Quinn	Eisenhower	1957—1959

Hawaii became the fiftieth state on August 21, 1959.

Elected Governors

Name	Party	Term
William F. Quinn	Republican	1959—1962
John A. Burns	Democratic	1962—1974
George R. Ariyoshi	Democratic	1974—

Congressional Districts

The Hawaii State Senate is comprised of one senator from each of the following districts (as of 1983).

NO.	DISTRICT	NO.	DISTRICT
1	Hilo	14	Kalihi Valley/Moanalua
2	Keaukaha/Puna/Kailua/Kona	15	Salt Lake/Aliamanu
3	N.Kona/Hamakua/Kula/Hana	16	Foster Village/Halawa/Aiea
4	Kihei/Kahului/Makawao	17	Pearl City/Old Waipahu
5	Wailuku/Kahului/West Maui/	18	Waipahu/Ewa/Ewa Beach
	Molokai/Lanai	19	Makakilo/Leeward Coast
6	Makapuu/Aina Haina	20	Pac. Palisades/Waipio/Mililani
7	Waialae/Kahala/Upper Palolo	21	Wahiawa/Waimea Bay
8	Palolo/Manoa	22	Sunset Beach/Kahuku/Heeia
9	Kaimuki/Kapahulu/Waikiki	23	Kaneohe/Maunawili/Enchanted
10	Moiliili/Sheridan/McCully		Lake
11	Tantalus/Makiki/Downtown	24	Aikahi/Kailua/Waimanalo
12	Nuuanu/Liliha/Alewa Heights	25	Kauai/Niihau
13	Puunui/Kam Hts/Kalihi/Palama		

The Hawaii House of Representatives is made up of one representative from each of the following districts (as of 1983).

NO.	DISTRICT	NO.	DISTRICT
1	Hilo/Waiakea	27	Kalihi/Kalihi Valley
2	Keaukaha/Puna/S. Kona	28	Fort Shafter/Moanalua
3	Honaunau/N. Kona	29	Salt Lake
4	Kohala/Hamakua	30	Aliamanu/Foster Village
5	Papaikou/Kaumana/Hilo	31	Halawa/Aiea
6	Wailuku/Kahului	32	Pearl Ridge/Waimalu/Pearl City
7	Upcountry Maui/East Maui	33	Waiau/Newtown/Waimano
8	Kihei/Waikapu/Puamana/Paia	34	Pacific Palisades/Manana
9	W. Maui/Molokai/Lanai	35	Waipahu
10	Kalama/Hawaii Kai	36	Waipahu/Ewa Beach
11	Hahaione/Aina Haina/Wailupe	37	Ewa Beach/Ewa/Makakilo
12	Waialae Iki/Maunalani Hts.	38	Nanakuli/Maile
13	Kahala/Diamond Hd/Kaimuki	39	Mililani
14	Palolo/St. Louis	40	Crestview/Waipio/Whitmore Village
15	Kapahulu/Kaimuki	41	Wahiawa
16	Waikiki	42	North Shore/Kahuku
17	Moiliili/McCully	43	Laie/Kahaluu/Ahuimanu
18	Upper Manoa	44	Haiku/Heeia/Kaneohe
19	Moiliili/Lower Manoa/Makiki	45	Kaneohe/Keapuka/Puohala
20	McCully/Lower Makiki/Kapiolani	46	Kokokahi/Maunawili/Enchanted Lake
21	Tantalus/Makiki/Papakolea	47	Aikahi/Kailua
22	Kakaako/Downtown Honolulu	48	Keolu Hills/Waimanalo/Lanikai
23	Nuuanu/Pauoa	49	Waianae/Makaha/N. Kauai
24	Liliha/Alewa Hts.	50	Lihue/Kapaa
25	Kam Hts./Kalihi Palama	51	Koloa/Waimea/Niihau
26	Kalihi/Kalihi Kai/Iwilei		

A Breakdown of the Population

By County and County Seat

	1960 Census		1980 Census	
Hawaii County		61,332		92,053
Hilo	25,966		35,269	
Honolulu, City and County		500,409		762,843
Honolulu	294,179		365,000	
Kauai County		28,176		39,082
Lihue	3,908		4,000	
Maui County		42,855		70,991
Wailuku	6,969		10,260	
State		623,772		964,969

253

By Race

The U.S. census methods do not accurately describe Hawaii's unique and complex population. The full Hawaiians, part Hawaiians, Samoans, and others of mixed ancestry are not reported very well though these groups are recognized locally. More than one-fourth of Hawaii's people are of mixed ancestry, chiefly part Hawaiian. The figures below are those from the Hawaii State Department of Health, Hawaii Health Surveillance Program, special tabulation for 1980.

(Excludes persons in institutions or military barracks, on Niihau, or in Kalawao. Based on a sample survey of 14,407 persons.)

Ethnic stock	Total Number	Percent	Armed forces	Military dependents	Other civilians
All groups	930,271	100.0	35,098	63,309	831,864
Unmixed..................	676,344	72.7	33,494	54,272	588,576
Caucasian................	244,832	26.3	26,527	39,387	178,918
Japanese.................	218,176	23.5	442	1,804	215,930
Chinese..................	47,275	5.1	128	432	46,716
Filipino.................	104,547	11.2	1,720	3,939	98,889
Hawaiian	9,366	1.0	-	-	9,366
Korean	11,803	1.3	-	503	11,300
Negro	11,799	1.3	3,621	4,873	3,304
Puerto Rican	6,649	0.7	212	718	5,719
Samoan..................	11,173	1.2	594	1,484	9,095
Other unmixed or unknown ..	10,723	1.2	251	1,133	9,339
Mixed	253,927	27.3	1,604	9,037	243,288
Part Hawaiian............	166,087	17.9	659	1,343	164,086
Non Hawaiian............	87,840	9.4	945	7,694	79,202

The median age in 1960 was 24.3 years and in 1980 was 28.4 years.

Bibliography

Books

Alexander, Arthur C., *Koloa Plantation, 1835-1935.* Honolulu: Star-Bulletin Printing Company, 1937. A history of the oldest Hawaiian sugar plantation.

Alexander, Mary Charlotte, and Charlotte Peabody Dodge, *Punahou, 1841-1941.* Berkeley: University of California Press, 1941. A pleasant and authoritative account of events and personalities in the long history of this famous private school in Honolulu.

Alexander, William De Witt, *A Brief History of the Hawaiian People,* New York: American Book Company, 1899. A standard concise history for younger readers that carries the story of Hawaii down to the Annexation.

Ancient Hawaiian Civilization. Honolulu: Kamehameha Schools, 1933. Lectures by various authors delivered at the Kamehameha Schools, Honolulu.

Anderson, Bern, *Surveyors of the Sea: The Life and Voyages of Captain George Vancouver.* Seattle: University of Washington Press, 1960. Contains two interesting chapters dealing with Vancouver's relations with Kamehameha I.

Atlas of Hawaii. Honolulu: The University Press of Hawaii, 1973. Created by the Department of Geography at the University, this book provides a wide variety of demographic information ranging from plant and animal habitation to the racial make-up of the islands.

Bauer, Helen. Revised by Ann Rayson. *Hawaii: The Aloha State.* Honolulu: The Bess Press, 1982. A well illustrated single volume overview of Hawaii, its history, geography and people.

Beckwith, Martha, *Hawaiian Mythology.* New Haven: Yale University Press, 1940.

————, *The Kumulipo: A Hawaiian Sacred Chant.* Chicago: University of Chicago Press, 1951. An annotated text of a sacred chant that relates the history of the Kalakaua family. An important source of information about Hawaiian mythology and social customs.

Bingham, Hiram, *A Residence of Twenty-One Years in the Sandwich Islands* (2d edition). New York: Sherman Converse, 1848. A basic work in Hawaiian history.

Bryan, Edwin H., Jr., *Ancient Hawaiian Life.* Honolulu: Advertiser Publishing Company, 1938.

————, *The Hawaiian Chain.* Honolulu: Bishop Museum Press, 1954. A compact description of the geography and the geology of the Islands.

Buck, Sir Peter H., *Arts and Crafts of Hawaii.* Honolulu: Bishop Museum Press, 1957. A handsome, well-illustrated book, the last work of this scholar.

————, *Vikings of the Sunrise.* New York: Frederick A. Stokes, 1938. An account of the legends, traditions, and migrations of the ancient Polynesian seafarers.

Byron, Lord George, *Voyage of HMS Blonde to the Sandwich Islands in the*

Years 1824-1825 (1st edition). London: John Murray, 1826. A colorful description of the voyage compiled from various journals and notes of some of the officers who accompanied Lord Byron.

Campbell, Archibald, *A Voyage Around the World, 1806-1812.* Edinburgh: Constable, 1816. (4th edition printed by Allen Watts, Roxbury, Massachusetts, 1825.)

Castle and Cooke, *The First 100 Years.* Honolulu, 1951. A report on the operations of one of Hawaii's most powerful firms for the years 1851 to 1951.

Castle, William R., *Hawaii, Past and Present.* New York: Dodd Mead & Co., 1913. An early "travel guide" by a *kamaaina* resident.

Charlot, Jean, *Choris and Kamehameha.* Honolulu: Bishop Museum Press, 1958.

Chinen, Jon T., *The Great Mahele—Hawaii's Land Division of 1848.* Honolulu: University of Hawaii Press, 1958. A very short book with a useful bibliography.

Coan, Titus, *Life in Hawaii.* New York: D. F. Anson, 1882. A first-hand account of a hard-working missionary's activities, chiefly on the island of Hawaii, beginning in 1835.

Colum, Padriac, *Legends of Hawaii.* New Haven: Yale University Press, 1937. One of the best collections of Hawaiian legends.

Damon, Ethel M., *Father Bond of Kohala: A Chronicle of Pioneer Life in Hawaii.* Honolulu: The Friend, 1927. A well compiled and illustrated record of a life of service.

————, *The Stone Church at Kawaiahao, 1820-1944.* Honolulu: 1945. Published by the trustees of the church. A short readable history of the church.

Daniel, Hawthorne, *Islands of the Pacific.* New York: G.P. Putnam Sons, 1943.

Daws, Gavan. *Shoal of Time.* Honolulu: The University Press of Hawaii, 1968.

Day, A. Grove, *Hawaii and Its People.* New York: Duell, Sloan and Pearce, 1955. A social history of Hawaii, interestingly related.

————, *Hawaii: Fiftieth Star.* New York: Duell, Sloan and Pearce, 1960. A history of the new state designed for junior readers.

Day, A. Grove and Carl Stroven, editors, *A Hawaiian Reader.* New York: Appleton-Century-Crofts, Inc., 1959. A unique anthology by two professors of English at the University of Hawaii, with an introduction by James A. Michener.

Dibble, Sheldon, *A History of the Hawaiian Islands.* Honolulu: Thos. G. Thrum, 1919. Written between 1836 and 1843 by a missionary teacher at the Mission Seminary at Lahainaluna, Maui.

Edelman, Lilly. *Hawaii, U.S.A.* New York: Thomas Nelson & Sons, 1954. An interesting and informal account of young Americans in Hawaii. Contains good photographs.

Ellis, William, *Journal of William Ellis, A Narrative of a Tour through Hawaii in 1823.* Honolulu: Hawaiian Gazette Co., Inc., 1917. A reprint of the edition of 1827, a fascinating journal by an English missionary who lived in Hawaii for about two years.

Fornander, Abraham, *An Account of the Polynesian Race* (3 volumes). London: Trubner & Co., 1878-1885. Ancient history of the Hawaiian people to the time of Kamehameha I, by a circuit judge of the island of Maui. A fine reservoir of information on this period.

Fuchs, Lawrence H., *Hawaii Pono: A Social History*. New York: Harcourt, Brace and World, Inc., 1961. An interpretation of political and social changes in Hawaii, with emphasis on the years since 1900.

Gould, Maurice M. and Kenneth Bressett, *Hawaiian Coins, Tokens, and Paper Money*. Racine, Wisconsin: Whitman Publishing Co., 1960.

Gowen, Herbert H., *The Napoleon of the Pacific*. New York: Fleming H. Revell Co., 1919. A readable biography of Kamehameha I, based largely on the works of older historians like Fornander, Jarves, and Dibble.

Halford, Francis John, *Nine Doctors and God*. Honolulu: University of Hawaii Press, 1954. Lively account of nine missionary doctors, covering the period from 1820 to the close of the century, written by a Honolulu physician.

Hobbs, Jean, *Hawaii, A Pageant of the Soil*. Stanford: Stanford University Press, 1935. An excellent survey of the peculiarities of land tenure in Hawaii.

Hosaka, Edward Y., *Sport Fishing in Hawaii*. Honolulu: Bond's, 1944.

Hutchins, Wells A., *Hawaiian System of Water Rights*. U.S. Dept. of Agriculture and Board of Water Supply, City and County of Honolulu, 1946.

Ii, John Papa, *Fragments of Hawaiian History*. Honolulu: Bishop Museum Press, 1959.

Jarves, James Jackson, *Scenes and Scenery in the Sandwich Islands, 1837-1842*. Boston: James Munroe and Company, 1844. Another of the older guide books about the Islands, a companion to the author's *History*.

Johannessen, Edward, *The Hawaiian Labor Movement: A Brief History*. Boston: Bruce Humphries, 1956. A short summary devoted chiefly to the chronological development of the labor movement in Hawaii, descriptive rather than interpretative.

Judd, Gerrit P., *Hawaii—An Informal History*. New York: Crowell-Collier Publishing Company, 1961. A very useful, compressed history in paperback edition.

Judd, Laura Fish, *Honolulu: Sketches of Life in the Hawaiian Islands from 1828 to 1861*, reprinted by the *Honolulu Star-Bulletin*, 1928. A delightful and unpretentious compilation of personal recollections by a missionary wife, with a supplementary chapter by her son bringing the events down to 1880.

Kalakaua, David, *The Legends and Myths of Hawaii*. New York: Charles L. Webster & Co., 1888. This collection of fables and folklore by King

Kalakaua has a comprehensive introduction by R. M. Daggett, U. S. Minister to the Hawaiian Islands, who also edited the book.

Kamakau, Samuel M., *Ruling Chiefs of Hawaii.* Honolulu: Kamehameha Schools Press, 1961. Particularly interesting as an interpretation by a scholar of Hawaiian ancestry who lived close to some of the events he describes.

Keesing, Felix M., *The South Seas in the Modern World.* New York: The John Day Company, 1945. Issued under the auspices of the Secretariat, Institute of Pacific Relations, and the University of Hawaii, this book is based largely upon the first-hand observations of an outstanding anthropologist.

Krauss, Bob, *Here's Hawaii.* New York: Coward-McCann, Inc., 1960. A breezy, informal description of Hawaii today, with a foreword by James A. Michener.

Kuck, Loraine E., *Hawaiian Leis and How To Make Them.* Honolulu: Tongg Publishing Co., 1956. A paperback book on how to make *leis,* together with the history and customs associated with *leis.*

Kuykendall, Ralph S., *The Hawaiian Kingdom,* 3 Volumes. Honolulu: University of Hawaii Press, 1953. An indispensable work by the foremost historian of Hawaii.

Kuykendall, Ralph S. and A. Grove Day, *Hawaii: A History from Polynesian Kingdom to American Statehood,* revised edition. New York: Prentice-Hall, Inc., 1961. A skillfully compressed history designed for the general reader.

Lewis, Oscar, *Hawaii, Gem of the Pacific.* New York: Random House, 1954. An easy-to-read overview of Hawaii from ancient times to the present day.

Liliuokalani, *Hawaii's Story by Hawaii's Queen.* Boston: Lothrop, Lee, and Shepard Company, 1898. An affecting autobiography that presents the Queen's view of events leading to the loss of her throne.

Lind, Andrew William, *An Island Community.* Chicago: University of Chicago Press, 1938. A study of the economic and racial history of Hawaii with particular reference to land utilization.

————, *Hawaii's Japanese: An Experiment in Democracy.* Princeton: Princeton University Press, 1946. An analysis by a University of Hawaii sociologist of the Americanizing of Hawaii's Japanese, especially as influenced by World War II.

————, *Hawaii's People.* Honolulu: University of Hawaii Press, 1955. A brief, informative appraisal of the interaction and fusion of races in Hawaii.

MacKellar, Jean S., *Hawaii Goes Fishing: Techniques of Yesterday and Today.* New York: Graphic Books, 1956. Well illustrated with photographs.

Malo, David, *Hawaiian Antiquities.* Honolulu: Bishop Museum Press, 1951.

Written by one of the best authorities on Hawaiian practices and genealogy.

Mellen, Kathleen Dickenson. *The Gods Depart: A Saga of the Hawaiian Kingdom.* New York: Hastings House, 1956.

Morgan, Theodore, *Hawaii, A Century of Economic Change.* Cambridge: Harvard University Press, 1948. Particularly good on whaling, the fur and sandalwood trade, and the rise of the sugar industry.

Mrantz, Maxine. *Hawaiian Monarchy.* Honolulu: Tongg Publishing Company, 1974.

Porteus, Stanley D., *A Century of Social Thinking in Hawaii.* Palo Alto: Pacific Books, 1962. Copyright by Hawaiian Historical Society. Entertaining comments on papers presented at monthly meetings of the Honolulu Social Science Association.

Pukui, Mary K., *Waters of Kane and Other Legends of the Hawaiian Islands.* Honolulu: Kamehameha Schools, 1951. Contains stories from each island which are helpful in understanding ancient Hawaiian life and culture.

Pukui, Mary K., and Caroline Curtis, *Pikoi.* Honolulu: Kamehameha Schools, 1949. Authoritative legendary material which deals with the Polynesian migration.

Pukui, Mary K., and Samuel H. Elbert, *Hawaiian-English Dictionary.* Honolulu: University of Hawaii Press, 1957. The most comprehensive and definitive Hawaiian dictionary, compiled by two leading authorities on the Hawaiian language.

Smith, Bradford, *The Islands of Hawaii.* Philadelphia; J. B. Lippincott Company, 1957. A factual history of Hawaii and its people.

————, *Yankees in Paradise: The New England Impact on Hawaii.* Philadelphia: J.B. Lippincott Company, 1956. A very readable account of missionary problems and personalities.

State of Hawaii Data Book. Honolulu, Hawaii: Department of Planning Economic Development, 1981.

Stearns, H. T., *Geologic Map and Guide of Oahu, Hawaii.* U.S. Geologic Survey, 1939.

Stearns, Nora D., *An Island is Born.* Honolulu: Star-Bulletin Printing Company, 1935. A readable story of the geology of Oahu.

Steegmuller, Francis, *The Two Lives of James Jackson Jarves.* New Haven: Yale University Press, 1951. A biography of an early historian of Hawaii and editor of *The Polynesian.*

Stewart, C. S., *A Visit to the South Seas,* Vol. II. New York: John P. Haven, 1833. A U.S. Navy chaplain's narrative of a visit to the Sandwich Islands in 1829-1830.

Stone, Adrienne, *Hawaii's Queen Liliuokalani.* New York: Julian Messner, Inc., 1947. A sentimental, simply written account, suitable for younger readers.

Suggs, Robert C., *The Island Civilizations of Polynesia.* New York: New

American Library, 1960. A reconstruction of the prehistory of the Polynesians by a well known anthropologist who took a leading part in the first and second archeological excavations of the Marquesas. Available in paperback.

Thrum, Thomas G., *Hawaiian Annual and Standard Guide*. Honolulu: Star-Bulletin Printing Company. Published in various formats yearly since 1875, now appearing under the title *All about Hawaii*, in paperback. Extremely valuable statistics and informative articles.

Thurston, Lucy G., *Life and Times of Mrs. Lucy G. Thurston* (2d edition). Ann Arbor, Michigan: S. C. Andrews, c. 1875. Introduction by Lorrin A. Thurston. A sprightly and informative account of life in Hawaii over a time-span of 56 years, as written by the wife of a missionary.

Twain, Mark. *Letters from Hawaii.* Ed. A. Grove Day. Honolulu: The University Press of Hawaii, 1966.

Vandercook, John W., *King Cane, the Story of Sugar in Hawaii*. New York: Harper and Brothers, 1939.

Wist, Benjamin O., *A Century of Public Education in Hawaii, October 15, 1840, to October 15, 1940*. The Hawaii Educational Review, 1940. Provides a helpful background for an understanding of Hawaii's school system.

Yzendoorn, Reginald, *History of the Catholic Mission in the Hawaiian Islands*. Honolulu: Star-Bulletin Printing Company, 1927. Father Yzendoorn, SS.CC., tells the story of the Catholic missionaries in the Islands, with interesting comments about their relations with the Protestants.

Periodicals, Articles, and Newspapers

One of the most valuable sources of material concerning the history of Hawaii and the customs and manners of the Hawaiian people is the collection of Annual Reports and Papers of the Hawaiian Historical Society. Of particular interest are the following articles which have appeared in these publications. Numbers refer to Annual Reports unless otherwise noted.

Adler, Jacob, "Claus Spreckel's Rise and Fall in Hawaii," 67:1958

Alexander, W. D., "Early Improvements in Honolulu Harbor," 15:1907
————, "The Birth of Kamehameha I," 19:1912

Allen, Riley H., "Hawaii's Pioneers in Journalism," 37:1928

Billam-Walker, Donald, "Money of Hawaii," 48:1939

Blue, George V., "Early Relations Between Hawaii and the Northwest Coast," 33:1924

Bradley, Harold W., "Thomas ap Catesby Jones and the Hawaiian Islands, 1826-1827," 39:1930

Bryan, E. H., Jr., "The Contributions of Thomas G. Thrum to Hawaiian History and Ethnology," 41:1932

Cartwright, Bruce, "The First Discovery of Honolulu Harbor," 31:1922
————, "The Money of Hawaii," 38:1929

Castle, W. R., "Centennial Reminiscences," 28:1919

Clark, T. Blake, "Honolulu's Streets," 20:1938 (Papers)

Damon, Ethel, "From Manoa to Punahou," 49:1940

Davies, Theo. H., "The Last Hours of Liholiho and Kamamalu," 4:1896

Emerson, N. B., "The Honolulu Fort," 8:1901
————, "Mamala-Hoa," 10:1903
————, "The Poetry of Hawaii," 11:1904

Gould, James Warren, "The Filibuster of Walter Murray Gibson," 68:1959

Henriques, Edgar, "Hawaiian Canoes," 34:1925

Hobbs, Jean, "The Land Title in Hawaii," 40:1931

Howay, F. W., "Captain Henry Barber of Barber's Point," 47:1938

Hoyt, Helen P., "Hawaii's First English Newspaper and Its Editor," 63:1954
————, "Theater in Hawaii—1778-1840," 69:1960

Judd, A. Francis, "Lunalilo, the Sixth King of Hawaii," 44:1935

Judd, Bernice, "Koloa: A Sketch of Its Development," 44:1935

King, Samuel Wilder, "The Hawaiians as Navigators and Seamen," 34:1925

King, William H. D., "Arctic Whaling Fleet Disaster," 63:1954

Kuykendall, Ralph S., "American Interests and American Influence in Hawaii in 1842," 39:1930
————, "The Schooner *Missionary Packet*," 41:1932
————, "The Earliest Japanese Labor Immigration to Hawaii," 43:1934
————, "Constitutions of the Hawaiian Kingdom," 21:1940 (Papers)

Lyman, R. A., "Recollections of Kamehameha V," 3:1895

Morris, Penrose C., "How the Territory of Hawaii Grew and What Domain It Covers," 42:1933

Smith, Emerson C., "The History of Musical Development in Hawaii," 64:1955

Spaulding, Thomas M., "Early Years of the Hawaiian Legislature," 38:1929
————, "The Adoption of the Hawaiian Alphabet," 17:1930 (Papers)

Stokes, John F. G., "New Bases for Hawaiian Chronology," 41:1932
————, "Nationality of John Young, a Chief of Hawaii," 47:1938

————, "Hawaii's Discovery by Spaniards—Theories Traced and Refuted," 20:1938 (Papers)

Taylor, Albert Pierce, "Liholiho: A Revised Estimate of His Character," 15:1928 (Papers)

Westervelt, W. D., "Legendary Places in Honolulu," 18:1911

————, "The First Twenty Years of Education in the Hawaiian Islands," 19:1912

————, "Kamehameha's Method of Government," 30:1921

————, "The Passing of Kamehameha I," 31:1922

Among the available newspapers and periodicals are the following:

The Friend
The first issue of this monthly newspaper appeared in January, 1843, under the title of *The Temperance Advocate.* The second number added the words "And Seamen's Friend." In 1845 it appeared simply as *The Friend.* Published irregularly from 1847 to 1954.

The Hawaiian
Edited by Julien D. Hayne from May, 1895 to March, 1896. A short-lived anti-missionary, antiannexation publication, violent and crude in its views, but interesting.

The Hawaiian Spectator, conducted by "an Association of Gentlemen," Honolulu, 1838.
Essays by missionaries and writers including Richard Armstrong, John Diell, Artemas Bishop, Samuel Whitney, and James J. Jarves.

The Honolulu Advertiser
The oldest paper in Hawaii with an unbroken record down to the present. First issued in July, 1856, as a weekly under the name of *Pacific Commercial Advertiser,* edited by Henry M. Whitney. In 1882 the *Advertiser* became a daily.

The Honolulu Star-Bulletin
Hawaii's largest newspaper, now merged with the *Advertiser* in its printing and advertising operations. The first daily to live on to the present, this paper resulted from a merger of the *Evening Bulletin* and the *Hawaiian Star.* It appeared as a daily on April 24, 1882, one week ahead of the *Advertiser.*

The Polynesian
First issued as a weekly in Honolulu on June 6, 1840, edited by James Jackson Jarves. Within its scope, claimed the editor, were articles on "education, history, natural, civil, and political, biographies, discoveries, voyages, agricultural intelligence, statistics, languages, and commercial information."

Index

263